METAL MERMAID

KEZ WICKHAM ST GEORGE

Published by MMH Press, August 2020
Copyright © 2020 Kez Wickham St George

All rights reserved. No part of this book may be used or reproduced by any means, graphic, electronic, or mechanical, including photocopying, recording, taping or by any information storage retrieval system without the written permission of the copyright owner except in the case of brief quotations embodied in critical articles and reviews.

This is a work of fiction. Names, characters, businesses, places, events and incidents are either the products of the author/s' imagination or used in a fictitious manner. Any resemblance to actual persons, living or dead, or actual events is purely coincidental.

Because of the dynamic nature of the Internet, any web addresses or links contained in this book may have changed since publication and may no longer be valid. The views expressed in this work are solely those of the authors and do not necessarily reflect the views of the publisher and the publisher hereby disclaims any responsibility for them.

National Library of Australia
Cataloguing-in-Publication data:

Metal Mermaid/MMHPress

ISBN: (sc) 978-0-6488203-3-8

Dedications

To my husband, Lou,
who encourages me to be the storyteller
I have grown to become.

Chapter 1

A ripple of excitement travelled through the expectant crowd waiting for the sunset to deepen. Pink hues had started to creep thru the blue summer sky tingeing it with orange, yellow and pink.

Fifty or more people holidaying at the Happy Valley Camping ground in Albany, Western Australia. All now sitting, waiting in a natural amphitheatre of bush land, cocooned by large ghost gum trees.

The biggest tree–an old red gum–shed its bark like an unwanted overcoat shrugged off in great pieces; its insides displayed like toothless gums.

Any spare logs or ground below now covered in bodies of all descriptions, race, creed, religion who have no part of the spectacular show we were about to be part of.

A hum of settling down then quiet, dusk almost here, the children hushed, slight clearing of throats and a few coughs. *He* has arrived and by he, I mean a large, blue heron who has glided majestically onto a branch way up high. He makes his presence known, stately stepping from one long leg to the other, fluffing his wings, then settling down to show off his sleek lines. He preens himself, muttering into his chest his personal complaints of the day's annoying issues. Then in a mad squawking swoop, the pink and grey galahs land, the sunset highlighting the coral rose of their chests. Their greetings to each other a harsh screeching noise, pecking and sniping at each other to jostle for position.

The noise fades as the majestic heron taps his beak on a branch. With the experience of a professional, he holds us all enthralled; galahs now hushed in respect, as are the many other birds all now in their perches for the night, this one stately tree filled to overflowing with a mix of bird life. This is the moment we have gathered for. As the sky gives off one last orange flame the conductor points his long beak to the sky and lifts his wings, opening them in surrender, welcoming the dusk. The rose-tinted gum tree bursts with life as all the many mixes and breeds of Australian birdlife give one final salute to the day. It swells to a crescendo, each small chest puffed out with effort, each beak wide open, the sound thrilling, winding around us, under us, inside us.

As one or two smaller birds stop to gasp a breath of air the others carry on with the song of the night. Then slowly a hushed silence. Not one sound or peep from human or bird—this one moment in time is magical—not one noise for a microsecond and then it's gone, lost forever as the day changes to night.

As always, one grumpy galah fusses around, finding another more comfortable spot on his branch as the squawks of discomfort ease off to silence.

The night sky puts on the most dazzling display, a moody mauve turning to deep blue, small pinpricks of light flicker as the stars begin their show. The deep, dark blue creeps in. Brilliant stars like scattered sequins on black velvet now show off the Milky Way, too far away for the naked eye, its presence a splash of white in the night sky as the crescent moon shimmers a ghostly pale lemon. Our night-time show is over.

We pack up our assortment of chairs, rugs and baskets, sleepy children are carried away in parent's arms into tents glowing with gentle lamp light offering a safe haven from the darkness. Those of us in caravans and cabins shut the doors against the dark, safely tucked up inside tubes of wood, steel and plastic.

At dawn, those of us up early enough head off once more to the bush amphitheatre, this time to watch as the galahs leave their tree in a rush of hundreds, their salmon pink breasts flashing in the early light, the branches now standing tall and straight without the weight of the noisome parrots.

Huge flocks of budgies land in the reddish dust beneath the tree, tiny bright jewels in green, blue and yellow flit their wings in the sandy dust. Once they complete their daily ablutions, they sip at the shallow puddles formed from the overnight rainfall.

Large lakes of colour spread all over the ground and cameras start snapping and clicking.

Then the locusts start up and the native birds arrive to have their breakfast, displays of aerobatic manoeuvres now captured on video cameras. Magpies trill in the day; their song flirting with the sun as it blooms life into our day. The sky becomes a brilliant clear blue, clean air fills our lungs urging us to take the deepest breath of intoxicating life. Black cockatoos fly off in disgust at the competition of magpie song, the white tuxedo of the magpie always so smart against the solemn black of the cockatoo.

As the magpies puff their chests to herald the dawn, a musical chorus makes our own hearts want to join in voice with them. A small interval of silence, then the kookaburras take over, which according to Aboriginal legend are the first birds to call at sunrise; their giggling building up until full throated gales of laughter erupt. Our first reaction is to wonder who told such a funny joke, then smiles play around the eyes and mouths of those who are listening. Some of us laugh openly at this daily ritual of happy hour for the kookaburras.

They sit in full view of us laughing with or at each other, a secret shared amongst themselves. There is no other bird in the world like a kookaburra, the mixed brown and white feathers a cover for the wonderful song that can make a small crowd of humans join in. Laughter, both bird and man, now greets the air and rises to meet the sun.

One lone jade-green fruit parrot stares at me, its little black beady eye staring as if to say, 'I'm gorgeous too, what about me!' I have to agree. Its lime green coat and navy-blue band around his neck is handsome. I aim my camera at him. With a sharp whistle it flies off to find others to admire him. The brown creek that bubbles through the grounds closely guards small bunched families of little brown ducks searching for scraps and weed to fill their tummies, a soft muted quacking now fills the air. The ducklings warned not to stray too far away; I notice one stays close by hitching a ride on Mum's back.

My stomach pleads its case, it's my breakfast time, the day's show is over. It's been a magical time for all of us but it's time to move on to another place; our small bus is ready to take us on our adventure.

I've termed this as our gap year; we are finally on our road trip around Western Australia.

Now in our mid-sixties with a small health scare involved, we had decided to put family, work and home on hold. The 'grey nomad' thing? No, this was more than that; this trip was an accumulation of many things, mainly it was time to do a sea change together. I had played with the idea for so long and had this urgent intuition in my chest telling me if this tour was not crossed off my bucket list very soon, it was never going to happen.

Up to five months ago, both of us were busy with our working careers, but now we were carefree and footloose.

The first two weeks it was bloody awful, both of us felt hemmed in because we were with each other day and night, no new adventures or strange places to 'ooh' and 'ahh' over, just the two of us in our house tripping over each other every ten minutes or so. In the past fifteen years, my husband Russ had worked away as a driller on

Pilbara mine sites, his time with me at home in Perth determined by his busy roster. As a mining wife you make your own world, mine was my passion for abstract/creative arts, and as an author. I had a few close friends and created a very independent lifestyle; I had learned to enjoy this way of life.

It is a sad but true saying amongst the miner's wives, 'Love to see them, but love to see them go back as well.'

Russ's life and friends were up north in the mine sites, I knew some of his friends, as he did mine. I had heard this lifestyle could or would cause problems later in our married life but dismissed it as we seemed to be just fine.

Once a year, we had six weeks holidays together and travelled to many exotic destinations. Fun and laughter were always there between us, plus Russ was home every fourth week in the month. It all seemed okay. When he had first gone up north, I felt betrayed and alone. I soon found out it was a common enough feeling for those of us left behind to keep the home fires burning. After a while independence sets in. I had my life and Russ had his. Those not involved in mining did not understand what hard work it took from both of us to live a normal family life at times, especially when the men folk were urgently needed at home. Many marriages had broken up for that reason.

Then a health scare for Russ that could mean the end of his working life hit him right between the eyes. He was told to slow down or take medication, his blood pressure too high to be happy with. It was not life threatening but enough of a scare for us to gather the troops and say we're off before we aren't able to do it.

A caravan or bus that was the question. We chose a small purpose-built bus that suited both of us; it proudly presented itself to us. I had to smother a giggle when the salesman overdid it with the sales talk about the previous owner, we got the full old lady and her car bit, it was second-hand but in wonderful condition and really cute, clean, tidy, with all the mod cons except a toilet and shower. Then again, both of us weren't too keen on going off road, so it would be camping grounds for us. Shopping was so much fun, fitting out the little home on wheels we now proudly owned. A new mattress was the first on the list, it was like shopping for a hobbit house, quite a challenge when you have shopped for a big home and family. It grew on you, the excitement of the unknown out there, the 'great outback' tales started to drift in. Friends, mates, family all with tales of joy and woe, it was up to us to decipher and filter what we wanted to do or not do. There comes a time in everyone's life you have to take a big breath and jump in. We did, and now weeks into our travelling both of us were unsure of what had we done.

The day arrived we felt so free, our face muscles aching with the endless smiles. We were given a fabulous farewell barby two nights before we were to leave, both of us wishing we had kept it very low key, the champagne cocktails still effecting us both or maybe it was one prawn too many. I was glad we were still at home with the bathroom nearby.

Chapter 2

Travelling down the Western Australian coast, there's the most amazing scenery I have ever seen. All the exotic places we had visited did not compare with the majestic turquoise, cobalt, light green and opaque blue as it rolled up onto white sand. The dark-blue Indian Ocean really is eye-popping beautiful; the camera rarely had a chance to get cold. We stopped to watch dolphins cruise by, I'm sure they smiled as they glided without a care in the world. We watched as large white pelicans with tribal facial markings swam past, an elegant ballet of white and black in the turquoise waters, food obviously in abundance here in the beautiful Indian Ocean.

I loved it all, but deep down was a funny feeling of sadness; it had no name, just sat there below the belly button like a tiny smiley face upside down. I dismissed it as being silly. Over a cup of tea, sitting outside our new home on wheels, I realised I was missing my friends, family and home in Rockingham; I was homesick, which took me by surprise.

Russ admitted to missing his mates and work too, both of us sitting outside our bus watching the Indian Ocean change from dark Indian ink blue to pale green with the tide and wind. Both of us far away in thoughts of a life we once had, finally admitting to each other what we missed. 'Okay Tara, you first,' Russ suggested. 'Well I miss our family,' I replied, meaning Jess our grandson and Raewyn our daughter, who at six years of age had changed her name to Rae and should really have been called 'Miss Independence'. I missed the closeness that had grown from her becoming a solo parent; she had come to us for advice and help, forming a close bond in our family.

I missed my friends, the community life I had made for myself with Russ away. All sorts of sad thoughts I had buried followed. Flowers from the garden I had fought the searing summer heat to keep alive, plus my bountiful veggie patch. 'I even miss the stupid chickens.' My voice wobbled with unshed tears. Russ went next, he missed the guys, you could see the faraway look in his eyes when he talked about the Pilbara, the red dirt, wide open blue sky, the camaraderie between them all, 'The beer after work with mates.' I'm sure his chin wobbled as well. I had always felt very left out of his life, as I guess he did mine as I talked about my life in Perth.

We both agreed we missed Rae and Jess, who raced in and out of our lives, our twelve-year old mini whirlwind, we loved him so very much as we knew he did us.

Slowly the little squirmy feeling I had in the tum eased up, it must have showed in our faces as we both burst out laughing,

'I guess we are both homesick,' Russ suggested, both finding solace in being truthful with each other. As we talked, the day closed over, dinner was cooked on the barby and eaten outside on paper plates, just the ticket to feel so much better. As I cleaned up Russ put his arms around me, and one big gulp escaped as I now realised this was going to be a lot harder than I first imagined. The healing power of tears and a good blow of the nose are amazing. Russ admitted to a few tearful gulps himself, but as we held onto each other we knew our life with each other was precious. Not to be wasted or stored for a later day, it was here and now, every day to be lived with a smile. This was our time to rediscover the magic that first brought us together. It did not matter what people called it or what brand they gave it, this was *our* time; the hard work of keeping home and hearth together was over for one year.

The next day we arrived on the outskirts of Bunbury. It seems the smaller towns had to advertise extra hard for travellers not to bypass them. We found a pretty winery not far off the beaten track, buying a bottle of crisp fruity white and a bold red for Russ. Not being huge drinkers and our tums not quite forgetting our farewell party, we popped them into the wine rack for a later date, staying the night in the quiet comfort of a well-maintained camping ground. What amazed us both is how other campers seemed to just pop into other people's vans. It was all a bit too casual for me, so I kept my distance.

The next day was our big travel day, a four-hour trip to Albany. I smile now when I think back to our notion that a big day was four hours' drive. The advertising promised whale watching trips, going to wineries by boat or horse drawn wagon tours, art stores, bookstores, cute little side roads that meander into shops of all descriptions. The main town is fashionable, the couture clothing shops mixed with an element of old hippie culture.

We found the Happy Family Camping and Cabins; our 'spot' was on a small rise overlooking the rest of a long valley sparsely dotted with tents and caravans. The new owners, so happy and helpful, had one of the busiest Christmas times ever, but when we arrived in late February it was almost empty. They were the ones who alerted us to the dawn and dusk bird parade, and it was everything they said it would be, magical.

We did all the tourist things available in Albany, my favourite was a true find–a small bookstore down by a quiet little wharf, the street was cobbled, a bit like in a Dickensian story. They sold hot delicious coffee and fragrant English Breakfast tea with fresh croissants or muffins, the biggest plus you were invited to choose a book, any book, and sit and read while had you had a hot drink, relax, read and savour an hour or two. Russ loved to walk along the sand dunes watching for the elusive flip of a whale fluke. We did both, Russ buried in the day's paper with a black coffee and blueberry muffin, me with a book on caravan cuisine, a hot English tea and freshly made raisin bread.

A much-needed walk along the beach, which always seemed to be windy but exhilarating, seagulls screaming with delight, whooping and fighting over the fishy bits delivered with last night's high tide. The wind whipped your hair, making your face ruddy, the sea air delivering energy to the very depths of your body.

Three days in Albany was really nice, the people so welcoming but it was time to move on.

As we drove back to the camping ground the skies became grey, fat drops of rain splat on the window screen. In the thirty-minute drive from the Albany township to the campground a massive downpour took place. Our little home now looked so forlorn, it seemed to hunch over in the cold rain. We dashed into the office wanting to pay for our three night stay and move on, but the owners looked very stern as they warned us, 'Don't go anywhere as there are warnings out for a huge storm on its way.'

The camp manager's advice was, 'I'll show you to a safer place that's sheltered,' Russ's face showing concern as we followed him on his Ferguson tractor to a safe and sheltered spot.

'You'll be safe now,' the owner yelled above the screaming wind. 'Better to sit this one out.'

Sit it out we did, for four days. If we went to the bathroom it was flip flops, raincoat and a mad dash over to the shower blocks. By the time we got back, the freezing wind and rain had soaked us through. Our bus became a beacon of light, a tiny lighthouse that we headed for and I was never so glad to be inside it. No beautiful sunset or sunrise, just grey to dark and a howling wind that shook our little home as the cold, windy fingers probed for an opening or two. Thankfully, we were snug as two bugs in a rug.

On day four I had enough of being caged up, bad weather or not, opening the door to race over to the toilets, the door whipped out of my hand with a huge bang.

The wind roared inside grasping the air out of my mouth as I fought to keep my balance, Russ hanging on to me and the door to keep his balance. His attempts proved futile as over I went into the biggest lake of icy water ever formed, it was muddy, oozy, freezing water, full of sticks, sand and little sharp stones. I felt like a small child as I wailed, 'I want to go home now.' Russ was doubled over with laughter at me sitting in the large shallow lake surrounding us while I sat wailing like a two-year old full of misery. He grinned all the way to the showers after he had hauled me out, the mud giving up a nasty sucking sound as my lower half was wrestled out of it and the water that surrounded the bus, my pink flip-flops happily bobbing around me.

Russ, between fits of snorting laughter made sure I had not broken or sprained anything and helped me over to the showers. As he held open the shower door for me, I spied my sorry self in the mirror, not just my hair and face splattered with gooey mud, I was covered in mud from head to toe. Very hard not to join in the giggles that kept shaking through Russ. Although my dignity was badly dented, I had to admit, I did look like one of our grandson's imaginary monsters.

The next day bloomed sunny, thank heavens. Birds once again sang and it was warming up but the wind still felt damp with a promise of rain, so it was time to move on. The first problem was being stuck in the mud, so once again the faithful Ferguson was in action. We had to wait for a half hour or so while it rescued another camper, then it was our turn. We were right in the middle of a big brown shallow lake, the wheels of our home sunk into the mud, looking a little dangerous to me as water had crept up to our doorstep. Russ, being a bloke who had experienced all weather on the drill rigs, was not all that concerned. 'Looks like a small beached whale,' he commented. As the Fergie pulled one small bedraggled bus out, I was glad to hear I was not the only one who made sad, sucky noises being dragged out of the mud. The camping bill paid, goodbyes were said and the obligatory, 'Come again, love to see you,' from the staff as we drove away.

That was when I decided to write the name of our bus across her rear end. That night as we dried ourselves out in Esperance, another quaint little seaside village, out came my smuggled pot of black paint and small paintbrush. I painted the name of our new home right across her now clean backside. I called her the *Metal Mermaid*. When finished, I stood back and viewed my handy work, Russ nudging me and handing me a can of cold beer.

'We now proclaim the *Metal Mermaid* our home for the next twelve months. May she glide us safely to wherever we steer her,' Russ announced as he poured a little beer over the back bumper. The name was the cause of many conversation openers as we travelled from Esperance upwards and made new friends at the many campsites. That night, as we both snuggled down in our bed, the sea wind whispered of the adventures about to happen. I truly felt this was going to be both wonderful and the worst time of our lives. I was not wrong.

Chapter 3

A day that dawns with golden sun awaking life all around is a good omen for us all. Breakfast was swift, as Esperance was waiting to be discovered. However, the public toilets in Salmon Bay on the way to Esperance were another story, having to wait for them to open and be cleaned. Thank God for understanding cafe owners. The owner of the Bay Café across the road offered us use of his private toilet, so we both made a dash for them. The kind man even had fresh cinnamon rolls and hot coffee on offer, so we bought our morning tea, grateful for his generosity.

Russ and I both stood outside the Metal Mermaid sipping on hot coffee, reading the discovery maps we had spread across the bonnet. Parked in a small camp spot overlooking the ocean, below us was a small cove of white sand and turquoise sea. I was daydreaming, Russ's voice a pleasant hum in the background as he read about what to do and see in Esperance.

I watched four senior ladies walk down towards the beach. They stood there dipping their toes in the water and I could hear windblown words like 'cold' and 'bit chilly' as they stripped off down to their bathers. By the looks of it, these ladies where serious about going for a swim. All four of them walked into the water till waist deep, all dressed in black bathers with an array of bright coloured swimming caps on their heads making them look like a row of pretty flowers all bobbing around in the sea. They swam from one end of the bay to the other with powerful strokes driving them through the water. 'Come and have a look at this, love,' I said to Russ. No sooner had I said it, two more dark sleek heads joined them.

I was delighted and speechless as two small seals joined the ladies in the water, diving and leaping, rolling, weaving in and out as the women just carried on as if it was a daily occurrence. It went on for a good half hour. The ladies left the water, the seals nowhere to be seen, all ladies laughing, happy and going their different ways. As I put our paper coffee cups in the bin, my head not quite understanding just what we had witnessed, one of the ladies walked into the cafe. I had to ask about the seals. She smiled, replying to my query, 'Every day dear, for the last two years now. They are our mascots, or that's what we call them. We have no idea why, we ignore them, they play around us. When we leave, so do they.'

I asked her why this was not known to others she looked at me saying, 'Why? Life is not about *look at me* it's about look *with* me.' I knew she was right; it was about sharing, caring about one another even if the other was a seal. That wonderful scene set, Russ and my happy buttons were on 'go' as we travelled along the highway for the whole week, the Metal Mermaid humming along happily, not a care in the world.

The other oddity in Esperance were the kangaroos happily heading for the beach for a swim or a morsel of something to eat. The locals thought it was perfectly natural. I was taken aback as we strolled along a bit of quiet coast for a stretch and fresh air as two small kangaroos went hopping past, not at all fazed to see us. They foraged amongst some seaweed then hopped down to the water, quite happy to be there, one of them going into its chest. As per normal I had left the camera in the bus.

We had been on the road for nearly three weeks, and over a home-cooked meal of pasta and fresh salad, we discussed whether we liked being grey nomads, together all day every day. Most of the campers we met were couples that raved about the scenery, the people they met, the places they had been. I was also aware some of them did not like each other's company while others had the content far-off look in their eyes, travel and adventure called them. Some of the folk made the trip a working holiday. One couple I met made and sold soy candles in markets all around this great wide Australia. While we were talking, the woman's mobile phone rang red hot with orders for candles and requests to come back to sell at festivals, some as far away as Queensland. Her partner was an old hand with council road works who found work with different councils wherever they went. Both in love with each other and the nomadic lifestyle.

Another couple sold old silver forks bent into all sorts of shapes sold as wind chimes. They frequented auctions and second-hand shops for these treasures, both absolutely nutty about their passion.

They just went wherever the internet told them there was an auction otherwise they often camped in Bridgetown to make or forge the things they sold in the markets. Good luck to them.

One woman travelled on her own. She really fascinated me; a hippy from way back in a seventies time warp, her twelve-foot caravan smothered in florescent stars. Inside there were charms and beads hanging from every nook and cranny. She smelt of incense and sandalwood, read palms and tarot cards, and her other specialty was as a belly dancer. Not that I'm running it down as I have given the dance a go myself and loved it. This lovely lady was seventy or older, her attitude was, 'Give life a go.' The car that pulled Mimi, her van, was an old four-door station wagon that was her dog, Rancho's, home. She gracefully shrugged her shoulders as I asked, 'Next stop?'

'Who cares! I go with the wind, my dear,' was her reply.

All the folk we had met so far had a story to tell. As we sat there with our meal of pasta, we both discussed how these folks had affected us.

Russ stopped eating and asked me, 'Okay love, so what is our story going to be? Continue on our travels or homeward bound?' We had met a lot of folk coming and going apparently enjoying themselves and the freedom of this way of life. Our question to each other was, did we want this lifestyle ourselves? Or did I feel that the occasional small trip away was the way to go for us? Russ was offering me a way out; to go home to my life as I knew it, or to continue on.

In one breath I answered, 'Onward bound, please.' I wanted to taste, experience, see and do all I could, while I could. I wanted to share this with my Russ. I was now waiting for his answer and could feel my eyebrows up by my hair line. Would he too? Russ is a slow eater and almost deliberates when and if to swallow. Me? I eat, then I'm up and gone. When he did give me his answer, I could almost feel the seconds ticking. 'I think we should carry on and see this bountiful country and what it's all about.'

I had always been the one who booked the holiday, planned, saved and booked the tours when we arrived at our destinations. Russ had left it all to me, now it was up to the two of us to share our destination and be responsible for our actions. It was going to be unsettling for us both at times, but the decision was made to carry on. If only I'd had a crystal ball to foresee what the future was, as I would have said, 'Let's go home now.' I did not, and the adventure together that awaited us was exciting, heart breaking and a real learning curve for me.

I'm naturally inquisitive, my ambition of travelling around the world not quite completed, and it bugged me for years that I had seen a little of Europe and only some of the South Pacific islands. Now was our chance to take off, and still being able keep in touch with family and friends was a plus. Travelling like this was living, seeing, meeting, doing whatever we wanted, whenever we wanted, with no tours, no guides, no timeline, or boat, train or plane to catch.

We both agreed to one year on the road. 'Let's give it a go,' was our answer to each other sealing our vote with a soft loving kiss.

We opened the bottle of white wine to toast our new life and acceptance of whatever came our way. Then out came the maps of all the places we had missed on our way to Esperance. 'If we are going to see Aussie then let's do it right,' Russ said, and I agreed. We could take the road to Kalgoorlie or we could backtrack to see what we missed. It was so exciting; the maps and pamphlets showed us what to do and see, we both knew it would not be what was written for we both had a knack of finding the unusual. That night as we climbed into our bed, the name of our next destination, Denmark, was written onto a stickit note and placed on the dashboard.

Chapter 4

Morning dawned, the camp was full of bustle and the hum of people going about their day, some leaving, some staying, others permanent residents who lived there. As Russ cooked up his Sunday special–a full English breakfast for a good start to our day–I decided to go for a walk around the campground. I found it amazing how people seemed to fit into this world of small homes; some made attempts to live in a van with nothing around them but sand or grass while others had grandeur. One side of this camp had permanent mobile homes; their gardens were nice, it was obvious some owners had the most vivid imaginations with a riot of plants, colour, and carvings; on this side, art of all sorts was alive and well.

As I walked along the well-kept side of the park, I saw the other side where we were camped. It had permanent homes as well, nothing as splendid as the other side but the odd home was well-kept with a small garden, most had a caravan an awning or a hard annex of sorts. One place took my eye, surrounded by large pot plants with healthy palms in them, the pots lovingly mosaiced in tiles, colours of all sorts blending in with the surroundings. The van was a large one with a porch, big double glass doors that lead into a hard annex, and pretty net curtains in all the windows. It looked loved and cared for.

The owner, a tall, attractive, slim women in her sixties, wandered out. She bade me a cheerful, 'Good morning,' as I passed by, her broom making short shrift of any sand or leaves. I stopped to admire her art on the terracotta pots. Chatting to her revealed she too was an artist in abstract, also a prolific writer–recently published, her family scattered all over the world and a husband working up north in the mines.

This was her home. She loved the simplicity of the lifestyle and met so many people she could write about. I mentioned my own large garden and home in Perth. Sadness flitted across the woman's face as she explained she too had once such a place in Perth, but she had been the victim of a prowler ending in a savage burglary, the fear of this happening again while she lived alone was the drive behind her living here. She said, 'I feel safe here; I have created a home for myself and my husband when he comes home.'

Her optimism about where her life would lead her was just what I needed to hear. When I had told her of our intended trip on the road she said, 'Why not give it a go and see if you like it? If you don't go and do it, you will never know.'

Now I know a message when I receive one. How many times had I heard *'give it a go'* in the past weeks? Too many times not to take notice this time.

I could smell our breakfast cooking as I walked towards our bus, Russ calling out to hurry up. Over fried eggs and crunchy bacon, I told Russ of my walk and talk to the residents of the park. He too had met an older gent in the ablution block who told Russ his story. It was a story of sadness and rejection, of heartache and fear. The man was on his own, did not welcome family around and did not want any nosey neighbours. Russ pointed to the man's caravan. It stood stark and bare, a tiny deserted island he claimed as his own. It all looked and sounded just like any ordinary community living day to day with all the problems house owners in suburbia had.

The coat of freedom had now settled quite comfortably on both our shoulders. Dishes were done packed away, bus tidied up, and the Metal Mermaid was on her way again, this time back the way she had come. We drove past the lady who I had just talked to and she waved us farewell, calling out, 'Safe travels.'

Our last port of call in Esperance was the Mermaid Leather shop, how amazing to see all sorts of products made from the skin of sharks and stingrays. The shop owner was very informative about all his products, telling us of the preparation time it took for some of the hides to cure. Then we were on the road to Denmark.

Taking the south-coast road and a turn-off to Mt Barker, we stopped to take photos, noticing locusts were everywhere. Then snaking our way through the Porongurups, we noticed a winding road advertising the most amazing authentic windmill restaurant. We had to stop at this place to take photos, the picturesque scene of dry, sunburnt fields and tall cream-coloured windmill was a creative photo opportunity. The windmill sails creaked and groaned lightly as they turned so very slowly. Inside they served true Dutch coffee and a fabulous homemade apple strudel. We just had to try it all. The hot summer had cooked this place dry, only stalks of plants and skeletons of trees were in the paddocks. Locusts had also been a real problem this summer with two huge swarms, one just recently, the other as we had left Mt Barker not two hours before.

While the restaurant owner, Leo, talked about the summer and his windmill I noticed the bus front bumper was covered in what looked like a yellow paste. Looking closer we saw the yellow paste had wings and long red legs mashed into it–locusts. Our radiator was full of them! No wonder the temperature gauge kept going to hot, then the fan would kick in and it would cool off. We had put it down to the stinking hot day and having the aircon on most of the trip.

Leo offered sage advice to get some sunshade cloth and tie it over the radiator. 'That stops those little suckers from getting in.'

We did just that. Luckily, we had a spare shade cloth in the boot. After sweeping and hosing the hundreds of dead locusts from the bonnet and radiator and attaching the shade cloth, we took off again. We decided the sooner we reached Denmark the better, both of us uncomfortable in the decimated burnt countryside.

Denmark had always been a favourite place of mine for one reason: it had a massive warehouse of dried flowers, and as a floral artist I had always put orders through the internet for these products, especially the gorgeous pods and seeds. We had to search for the source and find it we did late, that afternoon. The imagination ran riot with the colours of dried Australian flowers in this one place, all I could do was turn in circles whispering, 'Oh my God.' It smelt divine as huge sacks of potpourri made on the premises gave off a heavenly perfume. I wanted to bury myself in the delightful smell of lavender and rose; this place dried anything and everything.

Frustration was the overcoming emotion here; I was in a bus, so where do you put huge bouquets of dried flowers when you're away for a year? You don't, was the look on Russ's face, but potpourri was always handy, so I purchased a very small amount to help the Metal Mermaid smell nice. Very proud of my ability not to buy too much, we went off to the tree top walk nearly forty metres above the forest floor amongst towering tree giants. How exhilarating to walk high up through trees thousands of years old, imagining what a giant would feel like.

Next stop was Elephant Rocks, huge boulders of grey rock, that from afar looked just like a herd of the grey mammoths. Putting my hand against one and feeling the sun's warmth on it was like touching the warm hide of the animal itself, you only had to close your eyes and you could imagine the heartbeat.

Again, the folk here were so very friendly and helpful, and used to people like us touring through asking questions of what? How? Where? All answered with a passion for their quaint little village. I was told an international writer now resided there. In fact, many well-known artists had their residencies in the local wineries. Addresses were passed on if we were interested to pay a visit. The road called us to continue our journey so perhaps another time.

Metal Mermaid

The late sun was turning the sky into an orange kaleidoscope, so we needed to find a camping spot and soon. Off road parking is easily missed if not on the lookout or in the know but suddenly there it was; two other vans had stopped for the night our little Metal Mermaid bumped her way into the last spare space. Russ stopped and out we stepped. As always, the other campers welcomed us, with a, 'G'day how ya goin',' the typical Aussie greeting.

While Russ set us up with the portable barbeque, I made the salad. Russ cooked pork chops that sizzled and crackled, the aroma superb. While eating our dinner and discussing the day and what next to see and do, one of the male campers strolled over to ask, 'Where ya headed?' The conversation turned into a lively discussion on the pros and cons of bus versus caravan, his wife adding her opinion to the discussion plus producing a large tray of fresh baked scones. Not to be outdone, I added some of the produce I had made at home. A yummy, interesting debate for next three hours was spent in friendship, the remaining couple with a tired, red-stained caravan didn't bother to join in.

The couple, Blue and Jules, were leaving for Esperance the next day, asking us for any information, Russ told them about road conditions, and I told them about the seals and swimming seniors. The feeling of belonging was beginning to take hold for Russ and me; we could now tell others of our discoveries. This is fun, we both agreed, wondering out loud who would we meet next. The answer was there the following morning.

As I said previously, we didn't have a bathroom, so a bucket had to do. A big red plastic one had been installed for emergencies only and today was that, an emergency. There weren't public toilets in a caravan rest area off the main road and you can't very well knock on another person's caravan door asking, 'Can I please use your dunny,' can you? Not quite the done thing.

I was happy enough to be sitting there on the red bucket, Russ still asleep, the kettle simmering ready for our hot drinks when there was a loud knock on our door. Who on earth? I grabbed the roll of paper trying to stand up and again when a weird suction thing happened to me. One red bucket seriously stuck to my bum! 'Russ wake up,' I whispered as the door rattled again, this time sounding like someone was trying to open it. I grabbed for the door handle trying to hang on while maintaining my sitting position on the bucket. Russ remained in dream land, so I struggled to shift over towards our bed to shake him, but the green carpet and the big red bucket don't get on. I felt myself tipping over and made one mad scramble to sit upright again. *Help!* I'm literally stuck.

Chapter 5

I asked very loudly, 'Who is it?' The reply was, 'We're off now, the other campers want to know if you're going to stay on a bit?'

'We don't know yet. Have a great time won't you,' I replied, silently begging them to disappear and wondering why they would jiggle the door handle. Still struggling with the dammed bucket, I scooted over to the bench, my hand searching for a weapon to stab the big red brute with that had a tight grasp of my bum, anything to let the suction go. A teaspoon was all I could find, so I pushed the end of it between the bucket and my bum. Once again that sucky sound slurped through the bus and I was free. Thank you, God.

Russ staggered with laughter as I retold my dilemma while he slept on completely unaware of my fight with the bucket. 'Only you, sweetheart,' he managed to say before he collapsed in laughter one more time. I was not impressed nor was my bum which now had a deep red circle on it.

The day and our drive to Walpole was about to begin. We also realised what had become a tradition of ours: over dinner we would discuss the day and where to from here, the sticky note written with a destination then popped onto the dashboard, then a check-in phone call to Rae and Jess. We were slowly becoming travellers, thankfully, with a smidge of dry humour.

Russ got out the road maps pointing out that so far, our journey was a zigzag around the southern part of WA. He was happy enough but wanted to really explore this wide state of ours. Before I could answer him there was once again insistent knocking on the door. Our remaining female neighbour obviously not happy with my answer one hour before, was now demanding to know what time we were moving on and if we intended to come back that night.

Russ and I were both speechless at her demanding behaviour, so I said, 'No, we will not be back,' and we hurriedly packed our gear away and left. In the rear-view mirror, we watched as the male of this couple hauled her back into the caravan by the scruff of her t-shirt while she screamed abuse like a wounded cat. It felt like they were waiting for us to leave so they could have a loud domestic. Well, they were almost in the bush, so if they had to have one big argument this was the place for it. The amazing thing about it was they were our age. I guess we are going to meet all types on our travels hopefully not too many like those we had just left behind.

Walpole was great, full of wonderful, happy, helpful locals who were only too willing to tell us the history of their village. Then it was on to Pemberton for brunch, and onward, arriving late afternoon in Bridgetown. This small village was a delight—so English. The chill of the night was setting in, smoke of chimneys lifting softly into a dusky sky. Some of the homes had seen better days and some were quite grand. 'How pretty,' I remarked especially when I spied two huge rose bushes climbing over a trellis in a front yard, the pink and white roses looked spectacular in the dusk, the roses giving off a heady perfume.

I must admit a tiny corner of my heart whispered, 'You have these in your front yard.' Russ must have seen the wistful look in my eyes as that night we left our Metal Mermaid safely locked in a motel's parking lot while we dined on roast lamb at the local hotel, followed by a warm relaxing spa in our motel room. Russ's excuse was, 'Can't forget the luxury of having a break every now and again.' I couldn't say no to that, now could I. As we settled down on a huge king-size bed, Russ produced wine and chocolates plus the road map and a sticky note for our next day. We had seen advertised that Bridgetown was to have its annual Art and Flag Affair.

Russ knew I would love to stay and have a wander through stalls and shops of art and produce and see the Brierly Jigsaw gallery. Wander I did the next day, drinking in all the sights and smells of a country fair, there is nothing on earth to take its place, the fruit and veggies on sale were heavenly. The homemade chutneys, sauces and jams we bought and stocked in our already overflowing larder. The jigsaw gallery was superb, as was the English Breakfast tea we had at a small café in the village. It was time to find a camping ground for the night and then off to another destination. Busselton by the sea or further inland, driving through to Dumbleyung and Lake Grace to reach Hyden? A coin was tossed as both places sounded interesting. I called 'tails' as the silver coin turned in the air, it landed tails up, so my choice, Hyden our next destination.

This was fun. I was now the driver and the open road was tonic in my blood. Off we went, the Metal Mermaid purring along, Diana Krall singing and Russ gently snoring in the passenger seat, the Mermaid lulling him to sleep as we sped along.

Two hours later, we drove through Dumbleyung, deciding to head for Lake Grace to have lunch and a coffee. We discussed the pros and cons of our next stop, Hyden. What we would find there? Most of all, we needed to find a caravan park to have a sudsy warm shower as having hot washes in warm water was fine for a quick freshen up, but we always felt revived by a good scrub in a shower. We realised that by choosing the bus as our home and not having a small ensuite inside was proving to be a drawback for us. To others, it was all part of the caravanning experience; lesson number one now learned.

Waking early to the sound of the country and sunrise simply makes me buzz with joy, galahs with their puffed out chests and their funny little strut across dew laden grass, searching for their breakfast, large crows constantly cawing, their blue black bodies flitting in between ghost gum trees and that smell of freshness, it smelt like no one had ever breathed the air in this place before, it was all brand new and ours to enjoy.

Russ was now at the wheel; it was my turn to take happy snaps and admire the passing scenery as we headed to Hyden.

Hyden Caravan Park and hot showers. Ah! Heaven sent. I had not realised just how much a body could ache with only sitting and or driving but ache we both did. The hot shower and a walk around the camp was a welcome and necessary break. Wave Rock is a famous landmark just out of Hyden, an enormous monolithic superstructure of natural wonder, another in this centuries old land. It amazed me to think here I was standing under a huge lip of rock now known as Wave Rock. It was over 60,000 years old and I'm standing on it, inside it, beside it, making my bones feel very young.

To leave something as wonderful as Wave Rock you want to make sure you have it all recorded, as it just may change in some subtle way; through wear and tear over the centuries, it's colours and structure are awe inspiring. Close by is another wonderful piece of nature, Humpy Rock. Its gaping mouth invites you to peer in, and those brave enough may walk into this cave, where strong native superstition abounds, may feel ripples down their spine, an uncanny or spooky feeling. I tend to respect that feeling in my gut, but Russ dived in, adventure written all over his face. I stayed outside snapping pictures of the wonderful flora all around me, acutely aware of the silence surrounding me.

Tiny delicate white flowers clung precariously to very little soil, so pale but pretty on such an overcast day. A photo opportunity not to be missed, I was getting good at close-ups of stamens and petals, my hands itching to paint what I saw.

Back in Hyden, our Metal Mermaid needed a clean. Those that don't travel may think it happens by magic. I'm sorry but no, good old-fashioned elbow grease is the only way to give your home a good spruce up. Russ suddenly appeared bristling with brooms and brushes tucked under his arms. He tackled the outside, and lucky me got the inside. The only way I could clean was to put everything moveable outside and clean from go to whoa. Russ was busy running from washing the bus, to giving me orders of what and where to put his gear. The poor man was exhausted, stressing about his fishing rods and where I put his 'stuff' as well as washing a bus.

I had to smile and admit to myself that I had a tiny mean streak as I was enjoying watching his dilemma. I literally pulled the inside out and went to work, leaving that certain red bucket to soak with steamy hot water and disinfectant. Then I tackled the washing that accumulates in any family home and the dust that gets in any crack and crevasse, drawers brushed out, wiped and repacked.

By six pm we were both tired, the good tiredness that says, 'Well done, good job.' Our little home was spit-spot twinkling her thanks with shining clean windows, her silver body now sleek and stain free.

The insides smelt heavenly. The clean sheets and aired mattress looked great the whole inside from roof to floor from head to tail shone. A job well done. I suggested a reward for our hard work: a fish and chip dinner from the local shop as I was not doing the dishes in my shiny clean sink.

I decided to let Russ clean up all the equipment borrowed from the camp owners and our own cleaning gear, the ground around us looking like a small war zone.

Chapter 6

It was a ten-minute walk to the shop to buy our tea. While I was there, I met a lady with the same idea of fish and chips for dinner. Her name was Maggie; a South African lady who had lived here for over thirty years. We got talking and her story was wonderful. She was in love with prospecting for gold in the outback, her and her partner had been mildly successful finding a few grams, but nothing huge. 'Our big find was amongst the rocks by the shore in Bunbury,' she told me.

She had decided to pack their metal detector with them on a weekend trip away. One day she was just having fun wandering around rocks when her metal detector started to beep and bleep, to her delight at her feet lay two or three small silver coins. She took them home and washed them off to find they were very old by the dates minted on them. The next day she found a coin collector in Bunbury and discovered the coins had high content silver and were valuable eighteenth century Florins. Maggie went back to the same rocks the next day, again finding more coins, the same as before. She did not say how much they were worth but by the glint in her eye it was no small amount.

The story fascinated me. The details she gave me were very sketchy, and I don't blame her. Who knows what else she was going to find on those rocks? What did amaze me was this brave lady had severe osteoarthritis, her feet and hands so swollen and disfigured it must have been painful every step she took but her smile and happy face said this was an exciting life that she wanted to live every minute of. Maggie was an inspiration to arthritis suffers, me being one of them, but nothing as bad as this dear lady had.

I invited Maggie and her husband, Manny, to join us and eat our meals, the smell of fish and chips and open fresh air always seems to make me hungry and we were all ravenous.

The conversation was gold where and how, Russ's eyes lighting up as another adventure called us onwards but to do this we would need a gold detector and equipment. I was busy adding up sums in my head as Manny told us all we needed to know about purchasing a detector and finding the right place where we could look for gold. Emanuel was a school councillor, work was prolific for him, good for him, yes, but we all agreed it was sad to think the children of today needed so much emotional help. We said our goodbyes as they were off back to Perth the next day for a grandchild's birthday.

It reminded me I had to ring family to check in for the night and Russ and I had to discuss where to go next. I rang Rae, while Russ searched for the sticky note pad and pen, grumbling about when I tidy up, he can't find anything, as men do.

The news from Perth was good; nothing new and everyone was great, well and healthy, I told her our news, where we had been and who we had met. Then Russ spoke to them, Jess wheedling out a promise he could travel with us one day soon.

While the jug was boiling, we got out the maps, over hot drinks we decided where to go next. Keep to the back roads or on the coast road back to Perth or Kalgoorlie? Once tucked up in our freshly made bed that night, I glanced over at the dashboard. There glowing in the moonlight, was a sticky note with our detination Kalgoorlie written on it.

It took some time to reach Kalgoorlie/Boulder a distance of 362 kilometres, the road quite empty of life in many ways. Alison Moyet singing in her throaty voice, Russ and myself joining in with the verses we knew, laughing at each other's attempt to remember the correct words or sing as good as Miz Moyet. Marvel Loch, with its small roadhouse, was a wonderful opportunity to stop, stretch have a cup of tea and buy a sandwich. The store owners so full of information about Kalgoorlie, known worldwide for one of the biggest open-cut gold mines in the southern hemisphere.

Once back on the road I rang a Kalgoorlie caravan park. Yes, there were vacancies, so we booked in. The managers were called Barbie and Ken, I could not hide the smile as they introduced themselves. She must have sensed my amusement as she said, 'No Darl, nothing like the store-bought couple,' and I couldn't have agreed more. These two, although obviously sprightly, were in their late seventies, both small, wiry and full of cheek. They were so nice, Ken, walking us to our choice of parking for our short stay there, said, 'You can have one under the trees, or one by the pool or another alongside a communal kitchen.'

We both asked, 'What do you think?' He said, 'The one under the tree's a shady, quiet place.'

Russ backed in the Metal Mermaid and parked up for the three days we had booked. The first thing we did was shower, the hot water such a reviver to aching muscles. We both decided to cruise for the day, leave our cares behind and do the tourist thing, so we caught a bus that showed us all the top spots, including Lily's, an old-time brothel, once a symbol of shame now proudly displayed in all tourism pamphlets. A blot on respectful society, I once read in a book, written in the early 1900's by a minister's wife. Now it was one of the city's famous icons. What a difference now. All the stables, as they were called, decked out in colour, a visit was encouraged to walk in and experience. A billboard outside advertised an English morning tea with the owner, plus a guided tour. One smart male on the bus calling out, 'Do they serve tarts with the scones and tea?'

Then it was an afternoon tour of a mine shaft and a night-time look at the mine working, the lights on in and around the huge gaping pit making it look like a scene from the movie Mad Max. At any moment we expected Tina Turner or Mel Gibson to come tearing out of the huge gates and start shooting at us. By the time we got back to our little home on wheels it was about seven pm and although there were very few of us in the caravan park for the night, it seemed to hum with a community life of its own. As I was peeling spuds for our dinner, Barbie popped her head around the door.

'Knock, knock,' she said in her raspy voice. 'There's a small do over in the camp kitchen, why don't you join us? Bring your dinner and add it to what we have on the table.'

I raised my eyebrows to Russ as he appeared to be deep into the news on TV. 'Let's go,' he said.

So once spuds were cooked and mashed with butter and my specialty, a dash of Paprika, go we did.

Entering the large camp kitchen, there would have been about thirty of us, and with 'hello's' and 'G'day mate' ringing out to greet us the smell of all sorts of cooked meat and veggies was delicious. We met so many people all with stories to tell, the one that stayed in my mind was of Barbie. She was a cancer survivor who blamed smoking for thirty years for her illness and was brave enough to admit no one had forced her to smoke, her condition was her problem. The pencil-thin white scar across her throat a testament to her struggle, woe betide anyone who lit up around her or anywhere near her. I agreed. 'Good for you, Barbie. You stick to your guns, it's a nasty habit.' Barbie sat next to me at the long camp table telling of her shock to have throat cancer and the near loss of her larynx. The near-death experience she had enthralled me, their decision to sell up in Queensland and take this job, to any one of us listening to her story, was uplifting.

The most amazing thing was about to happen as the food laden table was soon emptied. Barbie stood up and announced, 'Today is my re-birthday. I am now in remission, free of cancer for the past ten years.' We all cheered and clapped; her beaming smile spoke for itself. Ken appeared carrying a massive cake, so many candles it blazed a trail to our table, the tears running down his face as he warbled a happy birthday to his bride of over forty years. Russ and I stood up and joined in the happy birthday song, by then all in the camp kitchen were roaring out happy re-birthday to Barbie.

Russ's hand squeezed mine so very tight. This was our niggling worry, the health scare of a mole going wrong on his back, just caught in time, then a cancer scare with his bowel, again caught in time and all cured. Would he be in remission in nine years' time? Constant monitoring and health checks were now extremely important, and now the high blood pressure problem. My eyes stung with unshed tears for my husband and the life we had been given back to love and enjoy each other, warts and all.

I don't know how it happened, but within minutes all sorts of party pastries, cakes, biscuits, ice cream, cream cakes, a jelly, bowls of chippies and lollies appeared. Once again, the table groaned with food; a party was emerging. Someone found a stereo, good old rock and roll belted out, a real celebration took place and we were honoured to be part of it. Russ and I danced around the floor. He said the same words to me he had said the day we married, 'Here we are dancing together forever.' Tears stung my eyes. I was truly blessed by the company I was keeping, and my marriage. We all took turns in dancing with Barbie, her smile never once faltered; she glowed with gratitude for her reprieve. The camp party came to a halt at midnight, once tucked up in our bed, Russ and I knew just how lucky we were to be here together tonight, as who knows what the wind will blow into your life tomorrow.

Kalgoorlie or 'Kal' as the locals call it, had many attractions and we saw most of them. The nights were always warm, so a dip in the camp pool after dinner was always welcome, followed by a walk around the large, tidy camp greeting others that were enjoying a relaxing twilight. The night before we were to leave, I saw the small yellow sticky pad on the table as Russ cooked our dinner. 'Go through the maps, love. See where you want to go next.' There had been talk of a place called Gwalia to visit; we were to drive the Golden Quest Discovery Trail, first Menzies then Leonora then Gwalia.

Chapter 7

On the sticky note I wrote the name 'Gwalia' and placed it on the dashboard. Russ served dinner, one of his famous garlic filled spag bollies with fresh crusty bread. Yummy! You could smell it a mile away and so could those damned desert flies. Without a fly net over your face, they crawled into every available orifice. I hated them with a vengeance, but Russ was used to them, quite calm and accepting this was how it was.

As we drove out early the next day, Ken and Barbie waved us off, this time with a genuine, 'Come back and see us soon.' Our reply was, 'One day in the near future, we promise.'

Today's morning was a golden promise of another warm wonderful day on the road, with a freedom and adventure only we could share together as everyone sees it differently. Emus, the large silly feather-duster birds, ran beside us as we reached the outskirts of Menzies. Russ cursing them as they often decided running alongside the vehicle was not good enough and veered off in front of the vehicle causing destruction for all parties, their large liquid brown eyes seemed so cheeky. I was very aware of the danger these birds can be to the traveller, so was relieved when they finally disappeared into the back and beyond.

Leonora was a shock to me. Russ had seen it before; the hopeless look in the Aborigines eyes, haunted, lost. One woman really took my artist's eye. She was young, pretty and dressed in a long flowing dress with a woollen beanie hat and woollen cardigan. She was stunning; her large dark eyes seemed huge in her small heart shaped face. I managed to take just one photo of her, she then moved away. The adverts for this township cried out 'famous golf course' but all we saw was dust and more red dust; everything was closed. What a shame. I had seen an advertisement for silk scarf dyeing and had intended to ring the phone number to learn the Aboriginal art of using the natural local plant life. In this fly-ridden heat I thought better of it.

Gwalia finally came into view plus a lunch date with Hoover House. The history book said this was the home of Herbert Hoover who became the 31st President of the USA and had been the Mine Manager. The house felt lonely to me.

Russ said, 'Don't be so weird, it's a museum.' My pragmatic husband would never admit that it did have a weird feeling to it. Our lunch, a picnic, was now unpacked and spread on the homestead's cool, large, shady veranda, I could not help but think, here we are Tara and Russ, two people just sitting where the 31st president of the USA might have sat overlooking his small kingdom. Again, that weird lonely feeling sat within me. Maybe museums do that to me, the ghosts, their belongings on display, their life long gone, just words to remember them by. I must admit the house was superb in all ways, fully furnished as Mr Hoover once lived.

Russ's voice interrupted my thoughts. 'Since we've reached our destination by noon, where to now?' It was time to find a spot for the night. Nothing was advertised here or in sight, so it would have to be off-road. It was almost dusk when ahead we saw a large fifth wheeler caravan drive into a large layby just off the main road, so we followed. Nothing but scrubby plants all around, we pulled up and opened the door, to be met with a blast of hot wind blowing off the desert. A thick cloud of flies headed towards us in a cloud of buzzing excitement, and you could almost hear them chant, 'Oh good, fresh meat.'

The other caravaners had common sense; they both wore fly nets over their hats, long sleeve shirts protecting them as they wandered over to us. They looked like aliens from a far off distant planet with *R&R* written on their van and on their light-blue matching monogrammed shirts. We greeted each other with hearty handshakes.

Rex and Roxanne invited us over into their plush caravan. With all the mod cons available, an ice-cold beer offered to Russ and a chilled white wine for me, I kept comparing our snug little home with this one. I watched Mrs R, as she preferred to be called, put together a small plate of snacks. Wow, what this lady produced from her double-door fridge/freezer was amazing; a large platter of different cheeses, breads, crackers, jams, sauces and dips appeared.

The soft, white leather cushions and couch, heaven to the odd aches in our bodies, I spied Russ removing the sequin spangled designer cushion to another chair. I felt overwhelmed by the opulence of this caravan. Like something out of Aladdin's cave, it glittered and sparkled, gauze net curtains surrounding the round double bed. Every time I looked elsewhere there was another object of creative art, they even had antique framed pictures of their family on the wall. I don't think my mouth closed except to sip my chilled wine. I was awed by all the richness in this caravan and our hospitable hosts with English accents.

After an hour or two of debate on which road to take, the Outback Way or the Goldfields Highway, we said our goodbyes to this lovely couple. Once back to our little home, I could not wait to ring Rae and tell her what we had just seen. Russ called it gossip; I called it outback news. The snack plate we had was very filling, so we decided not to have dinner that night. The giggles from Rae over the phone as I described this couple's caravan made me smile as well; she had a knack of bringing me back to ground zero. 'Mum don't be silly,' she would often say, as one of my tactless comments would often raise eyebrows. This time it was, 'Mum, you don't need all that stuff to have a great time, do you?'

She was right, I had the *I want a bigger better van syndrome* and wondered how come she was so wise in some ways and could be so immature in others. Grateful for her grounding comments, good old common sense won over.

Russ made us both cold drinks, our road map spread over the table, our next destination to be marked and written on the stickit note.

However, a more important date had been set for two weeks' time; Russ was due for his check up at the Geraldton hospital which we had pre-arranged in Perth. We decided to take the Goldfields Highway, driving through Leinster, Meekatharra and Mt Magnet through to Geraldton. We had pre-booked a camp site in Geraldton, deciding to stay for three nights to clean out the Metal Mermaid, restock with provisions, and wash anything that was washable. While I did this, Russ would check over the motor, oiling up, checking brakes, tyres, in fact anything connected to the motor so we didn't have mishaps on our way, and so far she hummed along like a bird, not missing a beat. Plus, with Russ in hospital for his check-up, it meant a twenty-four hour stay, so keeping our minds busy was paramount.

Dawn in the desert is a stunning experience; the advertisements don't do it justice. For each and every one of us the experience is different, for me personally, I would call it profound. As the sun rises higher and hotter and its gold fingers creep over Spinifex and native grasses, the long dark shadows of skeletal trees disappear. With a brand-new day, comes a new story. This morning, Russ came back inside as I was cooking porridge for our breakfast. He looked angry as I enquired, 'What's wrong, love?'

'We have two flat tyres,' he announced flopping down on the unmade bed. 'How the hell do we get them fixed?' he moaned.

As if on cue, Mrs R was standing at our door greeting us with a cheery, 'Good morning, how was your night's sleep?' I looked at the clock; it was only six in the morning.

Seeing our distress at the situation, she immediately asked Rex to drive Russ into Leinster to repair our tyres, Rex was on the ball. 'Of course I will,' he said. 'Got to help one out when one can,' and off they went leaving Mrs R and I to become better acquainted. Two bowls of congealed porridge sat on our bench alongside two cups of cold tea. Mrs R eyed the cold brekkie with distaste, inviting me to, 'Pop on over for a fresh cup of tea dear, whenever you feel like it.'

I preferred to stay in my bus with the aircon on and catch up on some reading and writing, occasionally peeping out the bedroom window only to see Mrs R washing windows, sweeping around their van, shaking mats, then pulling out a portable clothesline to air their blankets and bed linen. It looked like a mini Ali Baba market in Morocco.

All the time my brain was saying, what is she doing it's too hot out there, but Mrs R kept on working; her hair in a French knot with a large diamante clip attached winking at me in the harsh sunlight, her lipstick in place, in fact it looked like a full make-up job had been done as she looked perfect, not one wisp of hair escaped.

Not one rivulet or glob of sweat was evident on her immaculate light blue monogrammed shirt. Her face beamed with joy as she cleaned, re-packed and washed. To my surprise she produced another twin clothesline, and half an hour later she was hanging out freshly laundered washing. I could not believe what I was seeing.

I felt frumpy, old and lazy as she bustled about humming, my tired sense of humour claiming the poor woman's mad, that saying about only Englishmen go out in the midday sun running through my mind. Who was I to point the finger? I carried on with my writing, adding photos from my camera to the computer.

Russ and Rex arrived back hours later with two new tyres. Apparently, the old ones had been fixed but Russ had been advised to buy two extra just in case. I had tidied inside what I could, my competitive side had taken a beating with Mrs R being so industrious. On Russ's return I had cool water waiting so he could have a wash and a cold beer in the fridge. He looked so hot and upset, the cost of two new tyres plus two mended ones were, 'Absolute theft,' he declared.

Chapter 8

We decided to stay another night for safety sake because driving at night was not our forte. Russ went outside to put on the new tyres, mentioning he had talked to Rex about it and they decided to stay another night as well.

Once again, there came the sound of soft knocking on our door, and there stood Mrs R.

'I know you're going to stay another night. Please join us for dinner,' she said, then handed Russ an invite.

I had to laugh at the look on his face as this was going a little overboard, and for some reason this woman for had taken a real shine to Russ, writing *to Russ and Wife* on the invite. My first thought was, 'How rude!' My second thought was, 'Get over yourself! It's going to be a wonderful meal and the night is so warm.' Nevertheless, it was an indirect insult. Or maybe that's the way they did it in the UK? Seven pm the invite said, so on the hour we made the two-minute walk to the camp of R&R.

What greeted us there was a miracle. Surrounding their camp were dozens of fairy lights, twinkling away and lighting the space that had been prepared for our dinner. A long table with a pristine white tablecloth, a large silver candelabra–its long white candles flickered in the warm evening breeze, silver cutlery and pale lemon starched napkins all in place. At the end of the table was a small bain-marie, little puffs of steam escaping from the lids, on the table under a large domed silver meat dish was a golden brown roast turkey with a silver gravy boat filled with steaming brown gravy. Under the table and chairs, a large green carpet. The plastic chairs were covered with a pale lemon calico, large white bows tied at the backs of them.

My brain could not take it all in. Russ gripped my hand as he muttered, 'Is this for real?' as I offered my small, slightly warm limp salad to add to the dinner.

Both of them looked stunning in their clean cream monogrammed shirts and long tanned legs in immaculate shorts, like adverts for the Happy Camper Magazine. I don't think my mouth was capable of closing, it really was a silver service dinner for four in the desert. Again, they offered cold crisp white wine or a bold red for Russ. The smile never left my face as side dishes appeared; pink curls of salmon on avocado slices, and silver finger cups with thin slices of lemon passed around before the main meal was served. Watching the roast turkey being carved made my mouth water, the roasted veggies crisp and yummy, beans and peas so sweet. Then for dessert a small silver dish each of divine cream brûlée.

I could not believe my eyes or ears, all senses on high, a husky smoky voice crooned to beautiful guitar music from a small speaker on the outside of their van, their story told as we ate with Mrs R as the narrator. No health emergencies, no desperate need to travel big wide Aussie like us; nothing to do with grey nomads. The reason they were here was an antique buying trip from the UK to Australia, to take it all back and sell for a small fortune. 'The old homesteads over here have such bargains.'

Both their faces alight with what they had acquired and what was to be acquired. The story continued: they'd advertised in all the local papers on their journey, stating an arrival time. It seemed in this day and age folks did not want their ancestor's silver, gold or jewellery, so R & R offered to buy it for a bargain. The country second-hand shops they visited had no idea of what they had, so again bargain prices.

The conversation ended with Rex announcing, 'What we are eating from and using is a little of the treasure we found while we travelled.'

My first question was, 'Where do you put it all? You can't have that much storage space.'

Rex smiled and said, 'We had this caravan fitted with many drawers that go under the van, plus in the tow vehicle we had a false floor put in.'

So, I was not going nuts, it really was Aladdin's cave.

Russ and I were both still speechless as they told us of their trips all over the world as antique dealers and to top it off we had movies. On the side of the van they projected a movie of some of their experiences all around the world.

This was living: a cool wind in the desert, all replete with a beautiful meal and now the movies, heaven.

It was very late that night as we walked the two minutes to our small home on wheels, my offer of helping to clean up shushed by two very generous and gracious hosts.

Tumbling into bed after a very quick brushing of teeth and wash, we both gave a big sigh about what on earth just happened, then sleep claimed us, too tired for the sticky note to be written. We woke at seven am the next day to find the cosy spot we had sat and dined in last night empty, their van had gone.

A small embossed thick cream envelope was stuck to our door: 'To Russ and Wife, lovely to have met you both, keep well and safe, regards Rex and Roxanne.' A small cream and gold business card with R&R engraved into it tucked in there as well, giving us all their details in London. Written on the back of the card 'To Russ', and once again I was deeply hurt by the rudeness. I had a name. Why on earth would she not use it?

Was I dreaming? Did that really happen? All sorts of questions whizzed through both our heads, our conclusion was that whatever it was and for whatever reason, we had had a fabulous time with nice people. The only way I could tell it was all very real were the tyre tracks in the red earth onto the highway. Making a mental note if I ever saw her again, I would ask her why she refused to call me by my name. It bugged me, and Russ knew it.

I knew by the time we pulled up anywhere, you could certainly tell we had been travelling; baggy shorts and wrinkled tops, our faces travel weary, our bodies not used to all the sitting we were doing. Yet they stayed immaculate, *how?* Russ agreed, 'They did look a bit weird,' as he delicately put it.

I was still confused. Who on earth travels thousands of miles on red dirt roads and comes away super clean? 'Maybe they have a super clean wardrobe in one of those hidden drawers,' I quipped.

Now it was our turn to take off into the wide blue yonder, losing a day with tyre problems was not the end of the world; we had enough time to reach Geraldton and would do it comfortably. Mt Magnet was going to be our next stop, so we decided to stay overnight in the pub there to shower and wash our clothes. While I drove, Russ rang them and booked a room. I was really looking forward to the king size bed and shower advertised on their web site. We also booked a meal. It was going to be just fine, time to relax and enjoy before any hospital tests. Famous last words.

I complained of a headache, so Russ took over driving. I had drifted into a light sleep when Russ called softly, 'Tara wake up, look at this.' He had stopped and was taking snaps of what I would call a macabre scene. On a tall burnt-out tree were four large branches, on each branch was a large black Wedge Tailed Eagle, watching us as we watched them. It was the perfect setting for a horror movie. How could anyone say the outback was boring.

Ever since we met, Russ and I had a code word *Andiamo*; it means *here we go* in Italian. If ever we wanted to leave any situation, we would whisper it to each other. The scene before us had both of us saying, 'Andiamo,' loudly. Russ gunned the Metal Mermaid down the road; shivers of superstition went down my spine. Mt Magnet could not have been closer, and we scurried into the hotel carpark.

The car park was surrounded by what looked like tin shacks, the thought *I hope that's not our room for the night,* went thru my head. To my dismay, Russ returned with the key to one of those awful tin sheds.

Our room had two beds, a table, a broken wooden chair and one green sagging lounge chair. It had an ancient aircon stuck in the window, which I instantly cranked up to the coldest setting to cool down this awful musty tin room. Two single lumpy saggy beds and, oh joy, a flush toilet that leaked when flushed, bubbling into the room between the beds, the smell of wet carpet and urine was gut turning. All I could say was ewww! What on earth was this place? Thoughts of disease or salmonella winding into my now morbid thoughts.

When you showered, there was only cold water and you stood with your arms down by your side because the shower was so small there was no room to move, if you did, your elbows crashed into the sides. We both showered and had a snooze, the room cooling down considerably with the evening dusk and the incessant rattling aircon. Waking up first, Russ went over to reception, to enquire about dinner. He returned looking very amused; in his hand a packet of four sandwiches,

'Our pre ordered dinner has been prepared by the receptionist,' Russ announced. It was foul: warm lettuce and marmite, rancid runny butter, old stale bread. We binned it. I made a very quick trip out to our little home, fetching cheese and crackers and a bottle of pickles plus a cold bottle of lemonade. Dinner over, we read for a while till sleep claimed us both.

I woke to Russ swearing softly. He had gotten up to use the toilet, slipping on his shoes so he would not walk barefoot through the mushy urine stained carpet. He was swearing because he had squashed a huge white beetle that had wriggled into his shoe, one half now mashed into his toes and the other half still wriggling in the shoe. Again, my only word was *ewww*! I could not wait to leave this awful hotel and vowed I would warn my friends and post it to my Facebook page. It was a dump at ransom prices; a small fortune paid out because it was 'high season' for a boiling hot tin hut with bugs in it and a leaky toilet. We could have argued with them, pointed out all the faults and asked for a refund of some sort but the look on Russ's face said *enough! Let's move on as quickly as possible, please.*

Chapter 9

The experience left a bad taste with both of us. We seemed to hurry, our once leisurely pace now became grim determination, we rushed through small quaint villages what should have taken a day or two at leisure took one day. Reaching the outskirts of Geraldton, Russ rang the hospital putting the call onto speaker making sure his times were right, where he was to go to check in. Any calmness and quietness had disappeared from my husband's face, in his eyes a haunted look, it took away the fun and laughter and the wealth of experiences we had just been part of. To top off the day was the receptionist's voice telling him his Perth surgeon was not happy with the last test results; he also wanted a colonoscopy procedure done.

Russ glowered at me over the phone. 'A what?' he asked her. 'Why?'

'Perhaps you should ring the specialist,' she replied. 'Please do not eat for the next two days and be here by the allocated time.' At least something was right, we hadn't eaten for the last fifteen hours.

His voice was angry. I knew it was not at me but at his body letting him down, he had done his best to be healthy and fit.

The surgeon in Perth had already talked with both of us, information given about different cancers and saying in Russ's case it was perhaps hereditary, the cause not always known, and it was early days yet. Leaving Russ to his own thoughts, I arranged with the camp office to stay a full week onsite at Geraldton, my intuition button was saying stay for a while.

No sticky notepad glowed on the dashboard that night, a sandwich for me made and eaten, the conversation forced, food dry and sticking in my throat, Russ wasn't to eat anything at all. An invisible band of 'do not disturb' was around us that night. No one approached us with a friendly, 'G'day.' No-one ventured near us. Even the night was darker than normal. After washing dishes and settling into our bus with a book and a hot cup of tea, Russ went to bed early. I showered, not even the drum of really hot water whooshing over my body could sooth the tumult of weary thoughts rolling around in my head.

Could this be the end of our trip around Australia? Sleep came in snatches, both of us restless, then morning dawned. Our small camp patch seemed to shiver in the air with its cold energy as waking birds preened, fluffing feathers in the tall gum trees that surrounded us. Blowing my hot breath onto my chilled fingertips, I started unpacking the outside storage cupboard, a small but handy extra pantry. I made us both a hot breakfast of porridge and honey, but it suddenly dawned on me, Russ was not to eat today. I dumped it all in the garbage tin, my appetite gone as well. Russ had been up before me, that's if he slept at all, his face baggy with lack of sleep and anxiety. What do you say to your man who has always been a strong and a loving partner to you and any of your problems? There was not a lot I could do or say, except hug him so tight trying to push my love and courage into his chest. My heart wept, my mind declaring *nothing has been done yet to prove any cancer remains, so stop this nonsense right now.* It sounded just like my mother.

We caught the bus into town. Russ checked in for his overnight stay, the efficient staff relieved us of his small bag then showed us to his room. Russ is not one to prolong goodbyes, so I felt like I had been dismissed like a naughty schoolgirl. I wandered down to the harbour alive with seagulls and boats, people walking, talking, laughing, all busy with their lives. I sent up a prayer of gratefulness for the time we had shared asking the good Lord to give us more time together. Such a simple prayer, yet my heart meant every word, 'Please take care of him.'

The bus back to the caravan park rolled up with a soft sigh as if to say, 'Can't wait for this day to finish.' I knew how it felt. There were five or six campers on the bus, all rather tipsy, and I was greeted with, 'Hello Mrs, come and join us.' Again, I felt at odds with the world, so politely declined their offer, their dinner of fish and chips made my tummy roll over. As we bumped along, they started singing this song called Whoopsedoodle. It was a funny ditty, and I had to smile as they roared out the words. I had never heard this song, and although a bit crude in places it was very funny. My first genuine smile of the day amongst strangers, the simple act of smiling felt like a sudden ray of sunshine entering my chest. I felt full of hope and love for my life, my husband and family and all I had seen and done with them.

It was late afternoon before I reached home, settling in with a much longed for cup of tea. I then dialled the hospital number. Russ was in theatre as we spoke, my heart did a small bump, my prayers now mixed with tears. Deep down, my world was a huge part of that man, to be without him at my side was not an option. As I prayed in earnest, a small 'cooee' floated through the open door. There stood a woman who had been one of the people on the bus. 'Honey, saw your face when we pulled up, Anything I can do?' Funny what a kind word can do, and being such a private person, this simple question was the key for me to unload.

Her name was Gilly and she was wonderful at making cups of fresh tea and almost force-feeding me biscuits for some energy. This kind, plump, woman held my hand as the tears came, giving me a tight hug as they ended in hiccups, saying to me, 'Something tells me he's going to be just fine, you wait and see. Tomorrow he will be home and then you'll both have time together.'

Normally I would challenge a comment like that, but this time I let all my fears go, thinking maybe this is the answer to my prayer, maybe this message sent to me is the answer I asked for. Gilly invited me for dinner to her little caravan, and I accepted as I felt safe in her company. She told me her life story, its ups and downs about her family and about her husband who had recently passed away.

Her story sounded sketchy, dragged up but not often talked about.

She sold the family home and everything she owned, including the large sedan car she gave to her late husband's parents who actually grumbled, 'We wanted the washing machine.'

Now why this statement tickled me I have no idea. Gilly was the same, we just sat there and giggled on and off about the stupidity of some people, how the death of a beloved one brings out the worst in some that greed and mischief making became their mission.

Gilly made her mind up that a caravan and travel was the life for her, so she purchased a small blue fourteen-foot caravan with a Jeep to tow it. Gilly had named her van Dusty, 'Oh, after the singer?' I enquired.

'No,' Gilly laughed. 'Named for "eat my dust" as I travel around Aus.' Her aim in life was more fun, more adventure.

I rang the hospital once I was settled. Russ was asleep so I did not bother to wake him. Sleep came quickly and thank God it did, for without this amazing lady's story I would have done nothing but fretted and fussed about Russ all night. It's amazing how a problem shared is a problem halved.

I slept like a baby all night, waking to a bright warm day, the sea breeze gentle as I stretched away the night's kinks in my body. The mobile phone rang. It was Russ ready and eager to come home again. Within the hour, I was at the bus stop to go to the hospital. Russ was there waiting, his arms encircling me as I entered the ward.

'Let's get out of here,' Russ growled.

He looked pale and thin my motherly instincts took over. I was and always will be a mother hen, so it was no use trying to stop me fussing. As we made our way back to the bus stop, a small blue Jeep pulled up

'Want a ride, Darl,' Gilly called out. 'God, you were quick off the mark this morning,' she quipped. 'I pulled up to see if you wanted a ride into town, and you had already gone.'

Gilly deposited us at the Metal Mermaid, both of us very grateful for her generosity. With a toot and wave, she was off, and we watched as she hitched her van to her Jeep and away she went. 'I hate goodbyes,' Gilly had said on our way back from the hospital, 'too final for me.'

I waved as she drove by us to continue her journey. *Bye, Gilly. Take care. Hopefully see you around somewhere.*

Chapter 10

Russ and I both knew it was andiamo time for us as well; hopefully he now had a clean bill of health. The air was fresh and clean, beckoning us to further our trip, so we rang Rae to tell her what we had decided. I could hear the relief in her voice that all was well. Her news was they were off to Bali for a week, how exciting for them. There had been no sticky notes on the dashboard while Russ was recouping, so it was more delving into maps. This time we both wanted to venture far and wide, feeling we had seen the south of Western Australia.

We could travel the coast road up to Monkey Mia or inland to Tom Price where we had many friends from Russ working there for so many years. Tom Price was the one chosen, to be honest, although I love the ocean, I also loved the desert as it changed in colour and shape as you drove along. So Nanutarra Roadhouse was our next stop for a stretch, our destination was Tom Price but there was one place I really wanted to see before we went too far further, that was Kalbarri.

On a sticky note I wrote 'Kalbarri', placing it on the dashboard. A four-hour drive at a leisurely pace from Geraldton, then inland to Nanutarra, crossing to Paraburdoo, hopefully reaching Tom Price in two days. We still had four days here in Geraldton and we both agreed it was best to take our time as anaesthetics in the blood stream could take a while to clear. I could not stop hugging Russ; I was so glad to have him back with me.

It was the information I had received from a shop assistant in

Geraldton that made me think of visiting Kalbarri. A tale of wonder, of the underwater Stromatolites dated billions of years old fascinated me, plus her tale of the pink lakes.

It had piqued my spiritual side as well when she added, 'It's so very special to anyone who's that way inclined.'

According to her, this living sea creature was the beginning of life. In the meantime, we toured Geraldton. I loved it all, especially the statue of a young woman overlooking the harbour as she forever searched for the sight of her one true love, a soldier that went overseas to war. She gave me goose bumps and I found myself searching the horizon with her. Above us wheeled silver seagulls sculpted into a globe of steel, another wonderful piece of art. The shops were delightful and the people so welcoming, but soon the four days were up. Russ was feeling well again, only one time complaining of feeling tired and a light headache behind the eyes. We called the hospital and they said, 'If it gets worse, bring him in.'

He insisted he was fine, so off we drove. Kalbarri here we come. The Metal Mermaid sang along nicely, the two of us happy to be on the go once again with the sea, wind and sun on our faces.

Kalbarri is an amazing place; the ocean booming in over reefs, the surfers living dangerously as the waves would either hurl them out, their boards and bodies cartwheeling in the bright green water or small dark blobs suddenly appearing in the next rolling cresting wave. The bellows of delight from fellow surfers on shore encouraging them to ride it as much as possible.

Russ, an ex-surfer, said, 'Not on your life mate,' to which I added, 'Amen,' but we did watch and bellow encouragement with the other onlookers, my camera catching what I thought were spectacular shots of the sun shining through the sea. One particular deep blue wave had grown into a growling tower of power, cresting with foam that speckled like shattered glass then crashed down into a foaming mass.

Russ was mesmerised by the waves while I talked to the young men, most were from Europe. We started up a conversation with two of them waiting for their turn to jump off a small cliff and go surfing. Both boys smiled when I said, 'Does your Mum know what you're going to do right now?' His Irish accent very strong as he replied, 'No Ma'am. She would skin me alive, sure she would.'

Time to find a camping ground; Russ was tired as most people are after any hospital stay. The nearest camp for us was the Tudor Holiday Park, so we booked a powered site and ensuite and settled in for the night. Russ slept while I read up on Kalbarri and Paraburdoo, the excitement building up in my chest as Tom Price and old friends were soon to be seen.

A small finger of sun shining on the sticky note I had placed on the dashboard was what I first saw as I woke. We cleaned up any clutter we had made, camp table and cups now stored away, when we noticed our neighbours–two senior citizens in a very small tent. I greeted them with, 'Hello, how are we?' and was instantly enfolded into their life story.

Both of them talked so fast I got dizzy looking from one to the other, then Russ popped his head out to say, 'Ready to go?' They then turned to him to rehash their story.

From what I heard they were both in their seventies and from England, now touring Australia. She had first cajoled him into biking New Zealand, both islands thoroughly researched, then biked the length and breadth of the country. I knew of some of the mountainous ranges there and must have looked impressed as she then revealed that now he was seventy-four he refused to bike anywhere.

His story was, 'I feel like I have been biking half of my life I want to sit down and enjoy the view.'

Russ and I tried hard to understand their dilemma. 'So why don't you ride in a car?' we asked.

'Because biking is healthy,' she snapped back in such a bolshie way that Russ and I stood up saying, 'Time for us go.'

He on the other hand was almost in tears, and I looked at their little tent and scant belongings asking, 'How long have you been on the road?'

'Fifteen years,' he replied. 'I just want to buy a car, see what I want to and then go home to the UK.'

To say I was taken back was an understatement. 'You've been biking and living in tent for how long?' I asked, and the poor man's face was so crumpled and sad when he repeated, 'Fifteen years. I just want to go home to our house in the Cotswolds.'

I wanted to wrap him up and send him back immediately; the only thing stopping me offering any sort of advice or help was the ferocious scowl on her face.

I could see the problem but what can you say to a couple who had spent their life bickering about which direction to go in and how to get there? Russ took my hand. 'It's andiamo time,' he whispered and off we went. As I looked back at this odd couple, he was bent under her loud tirade of how lazy he was not to bike Australia. He looked beaten and old, like she had sucked all the joy out of him.

The odd couple seemed determined to make each other's life hell, and as we drove off another, couple had been drawn into the heated discussion of bike or car. For us, new adventures were calling.

The pink lakes and Stromatolites were our next stop. The silence, apart from the sea and seagulls, make you realise that maybe at your feet was the very beginning of life here in Australia. It was a moment for reflection for both of us.

If spiritual means contemplation then the Stromatolites are that, a lot to take on board in one half hour of photo taking, when here at my feet lay three billion years of life. Small coral barnacle-covered lumps in the ocean shallows, it was a shame they couldn't talk, as the stories of man's evolution adventure would have been amazing. Of course, they are protected, as they should be, but to view them just knowing these strange bumps contain our planet's past is almost like meditation.

The pink lakes are just that–a deep pink, the brochures telling us the colour was caused by bacteria trapped in the salt crystals. We finally found a small notice board telling us what to expect; an unusual sight at sundown but this was the mid-morning, and even now it was impressive.

Nanutarra Roadhouse signpost loomed up. We had been on the road for some time that day so I was grateful for the chance to have a stretch and a bit of a walk around–nothing to see–although there was what looked like a camel in a shed, not unusual for this part of the country.

There was a discussion about eating the old reheated greasies (chips and pie's) in the shop for a simple quick snack, or a cold drink and healthy munchies made by me. We opted for the latter, so cheese, cracker's and cold cordial was served up. We sat in the van, door closed, as the flies were horrendous. Funny how you forget about the flies when you spend much of your time in the city.

Our next stop would be Paraburdoo. Russ, now excited, said, 'If we carry on, we can reach Dampier by tomorrow morning. I would like to visit my friends in Karratha, Point Samson and Port Headland.'

'What happened to Tom Price?' I asked. His reply was, 'We are on a holiday. What's the rush?' To this, I had to agree. There was no time limit on us, that was the beauty of the Metal Mermaid and no commitments to anyone.

'I'm game if you are, Russ.'

We camped in a free camping area that night, a small turn-off on the side of the road half-way between Nanutarra and Fortescue, the star filled desert sky truly awe inspiring for anyone who takes the time to just simply sit and watch the night sky. No campfires were allowed but we were happy just to sit, eat our fruit and custard dinner, wrap rugs around us and sit back watching the stars. An amazing blanket of quietness settles around you, your ears and eyes resting, the absence of the noisy day-to-day buzz of modern living, motors, phones etc. You can feel your body quietly relaxing into the hum of the desert as you breathe deeply.

We were up with the sun. A quick wash and hot drinks with toast and honey then back on the road. This time I was driving as Russ still felt tired from his hospital stay over; we just put it down to the anaesthetics still in his body, plus him being a smidgen older than the last time he had been in hospital.

Dampier, what a thriving large township. The last time I was here it was a workingman's town, rough, edgy, wild and simple. Now it was very cosmopolitan.

The once small harbour now huge with ships of all sizes from many countries, all sorting and bustling into some sort of order. The tiny little shopping mall was now a huge sprawling shopping centre with blinking signs, traffic lights, sirens, horns and people, so many people all coming and going about their business, all in a hurry to get there. I looked at Russ in horror. 'What has happened in twenty years?' I asked.

Russ shrugged his shoulders. 'It's called progress, I think?' he said.

'Do you want to stay here?' I asked, 'or do we move on.' I knew I wanted to move on, away from what we called progress, to somewhere I could actually pull over and think, sort out a road map or have a cup of tea.

'Over there,' Russ yelled above the din of this new city. He pointed at a sign reading 'caravan park vacancies' as a red light blinked 'Welcome.'

In we went. They had one small space left right beside the camp pool. 'Gets a bit noisy about dinner time but shuts down around nine pm,' said the manager. I was not that sure about it. For the fifty dollars they wanted for one night, I was really unsure. It was obvious, though, that it was full to the brim everywhere you looked. The manager informed us this little caravan park normally had no vacancies at all, we were lucky to get this one. As for the charges, he was the cheapest in town. Must be a mind reader, I thought. Russ and I walked around our little bus checking for anything that would be amiss; it all looked fine. I decided when we got to Karratha, I would take the insides apart again to give it a good clean up, the red sand gets into everything. Russ agreed he would give the motor a check over then, but today we would enjoy Dampier, visiting places we once knew.

Russ and I had once been to the Dampier Archipelago by boat. The wharf where we left twenty odd years ago was gone. In its place a large floating dock that had two resident pelicans and four very smart fishing boats sitting there, shiny bright and modern. In my mind I pictured the old lugger we once stayed on.

We walked to find the cafe where once we shared bottle of red with the captain and owner of the lugger before we sailed off, but it had gone and in its place was a super store for Asian foodstuffs. Russ and I both felt disappointed that progress sometimes strips away the past leaving only the black and white memories of a wonderful adventure we shared. Russ looked grey, his breathing quite heavy, so we got a taxi back to our little home and settled in for the night. I was becoming very concerned about Russ, his pallor was not good.

'Should we visit the hospital?' I asked him to tell me immediately if he felt worse. He nodded and settled back on the bed to sleep. Not even the foretold noisy six to nine pool party woke him, I settled myself outside in the shade with my book, the afternoon sun warm on my legs.

The teenagers that arrived for their pool party were not all that bad and not all that noisy, and I felt quite comfy staying where I was reading up on Karratha. When Russ woke, I would get some dinner for the two of us. As dusk settled into night the vans, tents and buses all seem to become peaceful little havens with soft lights glowing, the hum of a TV or radio, the smell of cooking now making me hungry, I could have killed a bacon and egg butty right then. What a good idea, I thought, so into the Mermaid I went, bustling about.

'Come on love, time to wake up and have some dinner.'

Russ opened one eye. 'I'm starving,' he announced. They were the words I wanted to hear. He looked great with a beaming smile and making the big stretching noises men make as he got up. 'I'll make the drinks; you cook the dinner.' There is one thing about living in such a small space, you have to allocate what you do or you're falling all over each other.

I made some delicious egg and bacon butties, and Russ poured us a glass of cold light ale to go with them, I had also put together a small fruit salad for a desert. The warm night breeze encouraged us to sit outside and have our dinner.

Russ wanted to do the, 'I remember when… ' chat, so we talked about our trip to the Dampier Archipelago on the lugger and laughed about how young we both were. We accepted that for the cheapest fare we would sleep rough, but had no idea we would have to work our way there and did not even question it or the fact that a leaky air bed on deck was our bed for four nights. I cooked what was in the cupboard. Russ caught fresh fish to go with our meals.

Happy memories clanged into place: how we dived overboard to snorkel in the tepid green water over pure white sand, danger, not even a thought; the old boat wreck we snorkelled over and around, sighting a dugong, huge green turtles and many beautiful sea horses called Lace Dragons that gracefully rode the tide, their tails coiled around seaweed; the deep water providing a wonderful respite after a hot day on deck.

We collapsed in laughter with memories of pumping up the air bed every night with an old pair of bellows we both believed had come from the Ark, making the most delicious passionate groans ever imagined. Of course, the captain ribbed us about our love life, if only he knew we were the innocent ones, it was his airbed and bellows having the passionate affair, not us. The sea air, swimming, plus all the deck work and cooking had put anything sexual on hold, a solid deep sleep was inevitable every night.

What did the captain do? He steered the lugger, his true love as he called her, around the reefs, and ate whatever I put in front of him as long as it had a good spurt of tomato sauce on it and was in a bowl. He ate with a fork that he kept in the band of his straw hat and drank copious amounts of red wine from dawn till dusk. On the deck was a crate of red wine in thick, green bottles with straw around the base of them, very Italian I thought then, even having a sip or two myself with my meal. I soon found I do not like sun warmed sour red wine.

Russ would often crawl into bed in the wee hours worse for wear and slightly hung-over in the mornings. As for the captain, I don't believe he had moved from his cabin since we boarded. In our innocence, not once did we question it thinking it was fantastic to have this sort of adventure, and I guess in those days it was.

Today we would be horrified, both of us agreeing that age and convention changes you. By ten that night, both of us content and full of good food, I got out the sticky note writing 'Karratha' on it. By seven the next morning we had pulled out and were on our way, Russ driving, with Dean Martin crooning 'when the moon hits the sky.' Another gorgeous day, the sun already warm, I felt stress leave my body in excitement of another adventure.

Chapter 11

Karratha at long last. Red dust had settled everywhere, including on us, and the bus was tinted pink with the fine red powder. Our first call was a caravan park for a hot shower, booking in for a two-night stay so we could find Russ's mate, Tino, and catch up with him, plus clean the bus. The weather was so hot, and we knew we were heading in the wrong direction for this season as most of the grey nomads were heading down towards Perth or further south.

Still here we were. We had air-conditioning, so why worry about it. Russ rang Tino, his mate for over ten years. He received such a welcome, and within the half hour Tino pulled up with his wife and six children to welcome us to his hometown. Tino's partner was an Aboriginal woman called Daisy, with the biggest smile I had ever seen, and all six children, 'Tino's Mob' as he called them, were the same with the biggest smiles and gorgeous brown eyes, and I was the honorary Aunty to them all.

We were invited to stay with them. 'Please,' chorused by all of them, so we agreed. Tino's mob were in an old station wagon with their arms, heads and legs poking out in different directions. It was a funny sight as we followed them to their home.

So much laughter and a welcoming feeling, Daisy shooed them all outside, all except for the two eldest who were ordered to, 'Make Aunty and Mum a cuppa and take ya Dad and ya Uncle Russ a cold tinny.' Then I was given the best chair in the house, by the open window, no aircon in here. A large plate of chocolate biscuits appeared; the heat made them run almost immediately and the flies made a bee line for the sugary treat. What made me smile was a small brown hand that snaked through the window, grabbed a handful, then quickly withdrew. Daisy smirked. 'Watch this,' she whispered. Again, the small brown hand snaked through, and she grabbed it, yelling, 'Bang!' The child screamed with fright, the whole house erupting into gales of laughter, the little rascal was rounded up, given a half-hearted wallop on the backside, then a big hug from his mum.

The two eldest girls carried in a huge, old blackened teapot and surprisingly, dainty china cups. Daisy took her tea with three large sugars, slurping her way with gusto, the pleasure of this sugary treat written all over her face. I sipped mine, my mother's voice in my head repeating, 'Manners maketh the man.' She was very stiff upper lip English and would never have even thought about taking tea with this family. Me? I was overjoyed at their simple, fun-loving lifestyle. Dinner was fish and chips from the local take away shop, our plates the newspaper ripped from the huge packet, a massive bottle of tomato sauce was offered around and an enormous jar of pickled onions–proudly homemade–was placed on the table, which seemed to be the start signal for this family.

Suddenly the table became frantic with so many hands diving into greasy chips and large pieces of fish. Tino nudged me, 'Come on Duck's, fill up or go without,' my hand joining the many others coming up with a handful of delicious brown crispy chips smothered in tomato sauce. Not one word was uttered, just many mouths munching with Tino and Daisy making sure everyone got a large handful, and when dinner was finished the smallest child got to lick the paper. 'Family tradition,' Tino said with pride, he was obviously very proud of his beautiful family, and why not? They were delightful.

Newspaper now in the rubbish tin, I was invited to clean up in their bathroom, which was a tin shack outside with a tin bath and toilet. I was glad to rinse the grease off. One particular pretty girl, a teenager, appeared with a clean hand towel. The outside bathroom was not what I had expected but once back inside and again seated in the best chair in the house, I saw the start of a new bathroom inside the house, all gleaming white and silver, tiles with pretty motifs of bush flowers around the walls. The only setback, waiting for sewerage connection which was due to happen any day now.

The pride in their home and family was obvious, and the love that came from this large family overflowed. What a privilege it was to be involved even for a day.

It was dark when we left for our own home parked in their bare, red, dusty backyard. Bed never looked so good. I was so tired I literally melted into it, kicking off my shoes and falling asleep, Russ not even waking me when he put the quilt over me.

Our next day was all about cleaning our home out. The fine red dust was in every nook and cranny, the day's temperature was promising to be in the high thirties, but clean we did. Russ did the outside, I did the inside, blankets got a hot wash, our mattress was dragged out and aired off. By lunch time, I had the whole bus arranged on the one and only patch of yellowed grass. I scrubbed and washed everything; even the curtains were taken down and washed. Russ had cleaned the outside windows and the sides of the bus with their hose.

By three in the afternoon, I had everything back inside our nice clean home. It smelt nice, the bed now made, dishes, cutlery, rugs now all in place. I had borrowed Daisy's vacuum cleaner and washing machine, but try as hard as I may, nothing could stop the family from helping. If I looked sideways, there they were offering to help, and were amazing, carrying, lifting, helping me or Uncle Russ. And when we sat down in the shade with a big sigh and said, 'Man, it's hot,' out came a big ice-cold pitcher of lemon water. Nothing was too much bother for them.

Russ had once again checked tyres and motor stuff I had no idea about. By five pm we were so tired it was boiled eggs mashed on toast and hot drinks of cocoa for our dinner. Tino's mob had gone to catch yabbies in the local creek, miles away from their home. It was so peaceful, plus the heat of the day had calmed down to the low thirties. I truly felt tired, my muscles sore, my eyes felt gritty and I had a migraine coming on. The blasted migraines had been the bane of my life from my thirties onwards, at times lasting for four days, and along with them came nausea, blurred vision, at times facial tics and tiredness and the pain was horrendous.

The specialists I had gone to in Perth offered very little advice and the medication prescribed made me unable to coordinate my limbs, but I was told, 'Learn to recognise the symptoms, take pain killers immediately or whatever worked for you.' Then I got a prescription for anti-nausea medications and paracetamol and told to see them in three months' time.

So, I learned to recognise the signs; first came the slight blurred vision, then a bright flashing diamond for a micro-second in the left eye, followed by a dull ache, tight swollen tummy and nausea. So, at the very first sign it was two painkillers, plus herbal supplements for the tummy. I had also accidently found that by standing under a hot shower helped. You would often find me in a dark room, lying down with a very hot water bottle where the pain was. It all helped instead of being doped up for days.

Today, I felt the cause of this headache was the strong heat; change of weather hot or cold could fire off one of these migraines. Russ muttering, 'It's stress, dear. Learn to relax a little.' I was in no mood for lectures.

Firmly closing the door behind me, I boiled the jug for the hot water bottle, took two pain killers and headed off to my cosy fresh bed for the night. Russ was outside playing on the computer, emailing his friends in Dampier and Port Sampson telling them we were on our way, hopefully arriving within two or three days.

The next thing I saw when waking up was Daisy beside me. She had popped over for a visit to say goodbye when Russ told her I was asleep with a nasty headache. Apparently, she had gone back to their home and boiled up some sort of herbal mix. At first, I was against swallowing the mixture, the smell of boiled desert herbs was awful, my tum reacting with a wretch.

'Come on Aunty, try it.'

Carefully holding my head up, I swallowed a little then sat up and sipped it slowly, it tasted like old mushrooms and wood with a bit of gritty sand mixed into it. Daisy sat beside me, her long brown fingers curled around my hand.

'Gotta getcha betta,' she said.

I have no idea what was in that drink and I don't care because within an hour I was 'betta' as Daisy said. I was up, feeling fabulous, full of energy and my eyesight, which was normally blurry for an hour or two after an episode, was great. When she came back to check on me, I asked her for the remedy. Daisy grinned. It resembled the Cheshire cat in the *Alice in Wonderland* story. 'It's blackfella's stuff. Can't pass it on. Belongs to my Mum.' I do know I slept soundly that night; nothing ached or hurt.

Daisy, Tino and their mob all came over to the bus the next morning. I don't like goodbyes, so felt a tug of sadness to leave our friends in Karratha. Normally, I felt washed out after a migraine, but today it was so different. Russ also noticed my energy levels, a vast improvement from past experiences. So, the twinkle in his eye and a few verbal advances, I winked at him, 'You never know, my friend,' would have to do for now. Something I never thought I would say to my much-loved man.

Last night, Russ had done the traditional sticky note with 'Point Sampson' written on it. The red dirt now become so many different colours from baby pink to deep ochre, with wildlife that took its own lazy sweet time to move. The azure sky truly was amazing; it seemed there was no one else on the road but us, not another person in sight for miles. Stopping off in Roebourne for a refreshing stretch and a cold drink, my energy levels still up there, I made snacks, then offered to drive the rest of the way. Russ was only too willing as he wanted to take some photos of the sunset. Unbeknown to him, I could now see the dark circles under his eyes, his eyelids looked puffy and sore, so what he really wanted was to rest up and close his eyes. Thankfully Point Samson was very close.

Kelly and Alison were there at their gate to meet us. We had known these two for what seemed a lifetime, and they were our age. They had moved here for time together after the mining life had almost destroyed their marriage. Point Sampson, a small seaside village was their saviour; they literally went fishing for a year, tent first then caravan for the winter months, no TV, computer or radio, a mobile phone for calls to family or for emergencies only, nothing that would let the outside world in.

They had both agreed to focus on each other for a year, and now three years in, they had their own home and built a life with and for each other, and extended family, once again. They even became part of a small community. Kelly was over the moon about a new fishing buddy for two or three days and we loved the idea of us girls taking time out to chat about women's stuff.

'Just us ladies hanging out together,' was Alison's request.

Chapter 12

We intended to sleep in our bus on their lawn, but they had a different idea. We'd no sooner parked and had a welcome cold beer when Russ packed up to go fishing and camping for a bloke's weekend. He raised his eyebrows at me as if to say, can I?

'Go and enjoy. I'm quite happy here with Alison.'

I opted to sleep in our bus as I was comfier in there than in a strange bed. My days were filled with meeting Alison's friends; she had a sewing bee at her house every week, a book group was also held here, and at another friend's house was a knitting/sewing group.

The sewers made things for the local church and the knitters made things for the Salvation Army. All this was bundled up together once a month when one of them drove into Karratha where it was delivered to the Catholic Church and Salvation Army. The church ladies' circles would then pass on any wool or material to be used again by these two groups.

It seemed a brilliant idea and was working. I was the gopher in both groups as I did not have a specific job to do; cups of tea, coffee, milo always served with fresh scones and jam, my job was to serve, wash dishes or sweep floors, whatever they wanted the gopher was on hand to help. It was fun and I really enjoyed being part of it.

At night, Alison would cook dinner while I caught up with any emails, or anything else I had to do. One night she said, 'Tara I just have to show you this special place.'

It was a small café right on the beach called Mojo's. We ate the freshest fish I've ever tasted with big chunky chips and drank ice-cold beer. While we watched the sunset, it turned from a bright golden to a soft blue lavender then a deep mauve right before my eyes, the prettiest I've ever seen. God's paintbrush was again working wonders as the ocean matched it in colour and seemed endless. Another amazing photo opportunity missed as Russ had the camera.

On the third night, we got a phone call from Kelly. Would we girls mind if they stayed for the week? The fish were biting and the beer still cold. Alison and I laughed. 'No, go for it,' we both said, as we were having a great time as well.

On the fourth night, two bright headlights turned into the driveway. They were home. 'Why?' was on my lips. What I saw made my heart plunge; Russ was being helped inside by Kelly. 'Come on mate, take a big breath and lean on me.'

'What on earth is the matter?' I asked. Had there been a little too much drinking? Had he hurt himself? Russ sat down heavily, his breathing was not normal, he was panting; his face tinged a grey-green, I crouched beside him asking, 'What's wrong Russ?' He said, 'Don't know love, went to stand up and just lost it.'

'Same as in Dampier when you lost your energy?'

'That's it, love,' he sighed.

Russ looked like an old man of seventy, not the man I started this adventure with.

Kelly's forehead was creased with worry, repeating what Russ had just said. Everything had been fine till the fourth day when Russ said he felt a little tired. Kelly went and put a long line out to catch bait fish for the lines, but when he got back Russ couldn't stand up, felt sick and had problems breathing. They made for home immediately.

I got Russ into the shower and had to stand there with him to support him, both of us now soaking wet.

I insisted, 'Hospital, now.' Russ disagreed. 'I'm okay. Just really tired, that's all.' He was getting distressed at my insisting and it was making matters worse, so I helped him into a dressing gown and onto the bed.

Going back into the house, Alison was also very worried. 'There isn't a doctor on call here. I think he needs an ambulance.'

I agreed but suggested we wait for an hour. If Russ had not calmed down by then I would ask her to ring for medical help.

Russ had a good night's sleep. It seems he was the only one, the three of us all very worried about his health, and all slept poorly. I woke at every grumble or snore.

In fact, once Russ was up and had his breakfast, he seemed very chirpy, most apologetic to Kelly and Alison about his funny turn, trying to explain it away as one of those things. Blaming post-surgery and travelling, the excuses tripping off his tongue one after another. Kelly was very concerned having lost his father to an embolism last Christmas, confiding in me saying he recognised some of the symptoms in Russ.

I rushed out of the house and onto the bus, a hasty goodbye said to our friends, and we were off to Tom Price. A promise to keep in touch soon, and we were back on the road. Russ and I had completely ignored what I wanted to do, which was stay a little longer and ask a local doctor to check him over to sort out what the problem was or determine whether he needed medical help or not. Russ was totally focused on his driving to Tom Price, and in his best no-nonsense voice he used for children, he snapped, 'Stop being so melodramatic and relax.'

Guess what! I did as I was ordered, to his surprise. Normally I would say, 'Stop! Think and do what you must do to stay safe.' This time I shut up and let him go for it, this was obviously his lesson not mine. I did feel for Kelly and Alison, leaving them in a rush like that. This was not the Russ I knew. Why he was being so obnoxious and rude to all around him, I had no idea, but I was determined to find out.

While Russ and Kelly had been on their fishing trip, I had visited the local information centre. I knew I had to gain permission to cross the Millstream Road as it was a private road belonging to the Hamersley Iron Company, so I had paid for the trip across, the certificate now stashed in the glove box. The turn off to the Millstream was not well marked and Russ's driving was fast and furious, the poor Metal Mermaid bumping and grinding. I yelled above the noise of the motor

'Russ, slow down we are about to reach the turn off.'

With what seemed a huge sigh from him we slowed down to a decent pace.

'What is your problem?' I yelled again, to which he just stopped the bus and said, 'I'm going to be sick; I have one hell of a headache.'

He had become pale and clammy, his eyes bloodshot, and claimed he was dizzy. He threw up on the side of the road till he was on his knees dry retching, and from where I sat it looked like Russ was experiencing his first migraine, but why?

It took one whole day to drive to Millstream. The long snaking trains full of iron ore from the mines are the only life around. The most beautiful flower, the Sturt Desert Pea, was in abundance. The red dirt of the road broken by the odd greenery, and half-way across was an oasis of silent beauty–white ghost gum trees surrounding a small freshwater billabong. It was mid-afternoon when we reached this little haven of shade.

I had been doing the driving as Russ was in agony, so I simply turned off as near to the trees as possible for shade and ordered him to bed for a sleep before we got to Tom Price.

With very little fuss, he did as he was told. I made us both ham sandwiches with a cold drink, his face blanched at the thought of eating. I knew how he felt, so left him to snooze, offering him a hot water bottle for his head.

My husband was in a lot of pain and sadly, there wasn't a lot I could do, so I sat quietly reading, answering any emails, saving them as drafts, intending to send them once we had a connection.

I rang our daughter, Rae, but the connection wasn't good, and trying to discuss her Dad's dilemma, her reaction surprised me. 'Good, maybe now he will understand how it feels for once.'

I was very surprised, as this was a one hundred per cent Dad's girl from very early on in her life. I heard Russ moving around, so went inside to see if he was okay. One blue eye opened. 'How about a cuppa,' he croaked through dry lips. That was a good sign; he was on the mend. A cuppa was made, a piece of bread and butter eaten, and finally, he looked almost normal.

Time for explanations. Russ was as bewildered as I was. 'I suddenly felt super tired when fishing with Kelly. My chest hurt, and when the headache arrived, I panicked, thinking if I just get on the road and concentrate on something else, it will help it all go away.'

I demanded he see a GP or visit the hospital at Tom Price, and he agreed. Dusk arrived. We were tucked up in our cosy home early, Russ peacefully asleep beside me. The last thing I did was write 'Tom Price' on our sticky note, attach it to the dashboard and gratefully close my eyes.

When daybreak cast its golden glow over the Metal Mermaid and the billabong we were up, washed, had breakfast and back on the road. Bette Midler sang 'The Wind Beneath My Wings' as we pulled out onto the main road, both of us eager to get to our destination.

Russ still had a very mild headache, but his tum had settled down with medication. I drove again, my mind mulling over headaches. I had Googled his symptoms on my laptop but there were no answers only maybes.

Not coming to terms with Russ's erratic behaviour and driving, I opted to drive, whispering a mantra, 'Today is going to be a good day,' wishing Tom Price would miraculously appear.

I drove carefully, aware that Russ was not in a good way; our situation did not feel comfortable at all. I no longer wanted to be a grey nomad driving through the desert without a care in the world. All I wanted was safety amongst a community with people I trusted.

The Metal Mermaid was chugging along in time with my internal mantra, 'Please keep us safe.'

Brian and Winn's house at Tom Price could not appear soon enough, and once we were there, solid arms surrounded us both. Alison thankfully had rung ahead and informed them of our dilemma.

I felt like I was ten years old again, tears once welled up now escaping as I sunk down into a comfy couch and told Winn and Brian all about Russ's health scare, the hospital visit and what happened at Kelly and Alison's house.

The loving care we both got there was amazing. Brian took charge, making me sit and talk to Winn while he drove Russ to the hospital, and we were to follow him as soon as I had calmed down.

A hot shower and change of clothes for me, the sobs now transformed into the odd hiccup. As I walked into the small medical centre, Russ was being ushered into the doctor's room to be examined, again being helped as his legs could not support him any longer. Russ was in real trouble health-wise and we both knew it.

Chapter 13

My heart sounded like a big drum in my ears as I sat there with Russ's hand in mine, ready to hear why he could not physically function properly. His tired dizzy spells, nausea, painful headaches and trouble getting lungs full of air was baffling to us both, and now he said his right leg was painful.

Two days passed in hospital. They had asked him to stay in for another night, next day more tests would be done, and all tests were being sent to and examined by specialists in Perth. Russ still very weak; his legs just giving out and his breathing becoming gasps if any exertion was needed, his lips now had a tinge of blue to them. Doctor Benson came into the room, his face lined, tired and serious.

'Russ,' he announced, 'we have found something a little serious that may explain why you're feeling so sick.' Russ gripped my hand so hard it hurt. They had found a large blood clot in the aortic vein in his right groin, suspecting tiny fragments had been breaking off and travelling through the blood stream towards the brain and heart.

Dr Benson said, 'Luckily for you we can deal with it through medication and a small keyhole operation, but the only hospital that has immediate surgery available is in Perth.'

We both sat there stunned. 'How dangerous is this?' I asked, my gut already knowing the answer.

'Very,' the doctor said. 'If the whole clot moves or breaks up, then it could reach his heart causing a fatal heart attack, or if any of the clot breaks free, even a minuscule amount, it could pass through the heart valves and straight to the brain causing a major stroke.'

I felt like my heart was beating inside my very dry mouth as I asked, 'How has this happened?'

His answer, although not satisfactory, was, 'Who knows? Internal haemorrhaging could be hereditary, or it could be caused by recent surgery. There are many reasons, but the point is he needs to have this seen to immediately, I am arranging to fly him out this afternoon.'

Russ and I were floored by all this information. He was critically ill and needed medical intervention to survive. Russ was put back into the ward to await the Royal Flying Doctor service. This was a medical team flying all over the outback saving lives from infants to seniors; they were renowned throughout Australia for their heroic life-saving flights.

This organisation was always in need of financial support, it was only the many generous gifts of charitable people or caring philanthropists that really kept them afloat. At this time and in this place, I would have given everything I owned to keep my Russ safe. As most women, when faced with major decisions, calmness now crept inside my chest. I never questioned this part of me as it was the accurate decision maker, the 'let's deal with it now' part of me that took no nonsense from anyone.

I gave Russ a hug saying, 'I will be back in an hour.'

I had some arranging to do regarding the Metal Mermaid, our life on the road now on hold for a while. The medical staff told me the medics would be here by one pm, so I had three hours to make arrangements. My first call, to our daughter Rae, I explained our situation, asking would she be there for her Dad, to which she agreed to meet the medics in Perth. Then it was back to Brian and Winn's home to tell them the news. Arranging somewhere to put our little home till we could bring her back to Perth. Winn offered her help in any way and Brian offered us the use of the old lean-to in their back yard 'For security, mainly.' I took this warning on board as a deserted bus was fair game for some folk.

I gratefully accepted his offer, backing our little home onto their once grassy back yard; the summer heat had killed what was once a pretty green patch, now dried out red. Little Willie Willies made pink twirls by kicking up the red earth as they wound their way across the back yard. Winn's comment, 'At least you will be home for Christmas,' was a shock. I had forgotten all about Christmas coming in three weeks' time. I then booked my fare home over the internet as I was unable to fly with Russ. Rae would be there to meet her Dad at Royal Perth hospital, I still felt unnaturally calm about it all.

Packing my case and one for Russ, I locked up the Metal Mermaid, I almost wanted to hug her. She had been my safe cocoon for so long, but now I was needed elsewhere and would be home in Perth for Christmas with my family. Strange how it all was panning out, how unforeseen circumstances were affecting us in a huge way, from a general check-up at our local doctor six months ago to this major health problem now, and our amazing friends opening their homes and arms to help us get back to our home in Perth.

Winn and Brian's kind faces looked worried as they drove me to the hospital to say bye to Russ. He was sedated so did not have a clue what was going on. We watched as they wheeled Russ onto the plane. It rumbled down the manmade landing strip and took off into the bluest, cloud-free sky that suddenly cracked into a kaleidoscope of silver blue, just as the tears in my eyes finally took over my vision. Being brave and strong is okay in front of the people who love and want to support you, but the moment they leave my side I become a mess. All I wanted to do was curl up in a ball and cry.

Then it was time for me to board my plane. Winn gave me a hug, Brian put my bag through, and I was enveloped in huge hard hug, 'Take good care of yerself, Tara. Give Russ a good kick up the arse for me.' This was an outback man that loved my husband, so it was said with concern and love for his friend; his rough words bought a shaky smile to my face.

Paraburdoo Airport hummed with the miners going home. My plane was ready to board, the miners showing concern for me. Russ was a popular figure in this world having worked with and trained many young men in their job's as drillers or as a driller's offsider. He was also known as a practical joker.

This was once a tough world, a man's world that was changing. Among the men now stood women who drove massive dump trucks carrying the iron ore. It was unusual for me to see a woman standing there with the men, drinking a cold beer discussing work with the blokes before take-off, but they treated me with respect considering I only knew two of the folks in line. It was no surprise that Russ was considered one of them, and as I was Russ's 'Mrs' as they put it, they made sure I was okay.

The news of Russ and his health travelled fast. Rides to the hospital once I landed in Perth where offered, messages of, 'Get well soon, mate,' were genuinely given to me for Russ. How wonderful to be treated with respect and kindness.

Two hours later we landed, and I saw Rae and Jess waiting at the baggage carousel. We just hung on to each other, Jess squirming in between us. 'Give me a hug, Nana,' he demanded. Suddenly I realised just how much I had missed this little man and my daughter, the tiny niggly hole that had been there in the corner of my heart suddenly closed up. My family were here for us and we were going to be fine. My arms were now full of the people I loved, and although I was shown so much love and consideration from friends and met some wonderful folk on the way, there is nothing like the familiar touch of your own family, children and grandchildren.

Our first stop was Royal Perth hospital. Russ had been admitted and tucked in, and Rae had helped with all the details the hospital needed. He was still sedated when we reached him. I was told the clot had moved a little, that this was an emergency in a big way and the specialist was now scrubbing up. Rae and I sat beside Russ, talking to him in a calm voice that belied how I felt. I wanted to sob and cry out, 'It's not fair.' I promised him we would be there for him when he was out of theatre.

As Russ was wheeled through the theatre doors Jess called out, 'See you soon, Ranrad,' his baby name for his Grandad.

I felt numb. How this would turn out was anyone's guess. Please keep my Russ safe, bring him through this safely, I prayed. Thank heavens for the hospital coffee shop as that's where I spent the next two hours. Rae had taken Jess home to prepare a meal and tidy up the spare room as I was staying in for one night with them before going back to my own home.

Finally, Russ was out of theatre, the surgeon saying all went well and they had caught it in time. There had been a bit of damage to the vein in his right leg, but they replaced it with a vein from his arm.

'He will be a confused and very sore,' the surgeon said. 'I will call in later and explain the procedure to him.'

I rang Rae with the news as I sat and held Russ's hand, all the tubes and beeps from machines making me feel very inadequate, as these machines were his lifeline. I then rang our friends, Brian, Kelly, Alice and Winn, to tell them the news that Russ was going to take some time to recover at our home, but then one day we would definitely come back and visit, or if ever they were our way to please stay with us. These friends had been invaluable with their support for us both.

I then rang Tino and Daisy, telling them what had happened. Russ needed as much support as possible now. 'Anything you need, love, just let us know.'

Russ came around, his blue eyes shadowed in pain. 'What's happened?' he mumbled from under the oxygen mask, so I told him what I knew about the blood clot, not adding about the operation on the arm as I felt the doctor could do that much better than me trying to explain. Time for me to go to Rae's home, so I rang her once on the bus. 'I'm on my way now.' Jess met me at the bus stop, his little hand holding mine. 'Come on Nana, come home with me.' I almost sagged in relief. 'Yes please, let's go home.'

The next day, I moved back into my own home. I literally sank down in my chair not wanting to move one muscle, I felt so tired. My head ached and my heart ached for Russ, who I missed incredibly. This was not the home coming I had dreamed of.

Rae had kindly brought in all the groceries I would need for a day or two and had made me a meat pie for my dinner that night; I had no need to go out till tomorrow. *Home* what a magic word that is. My house looked and felt huge next to the little bus we had called home for the past months.

Durant House was our home for the last twenty years, the name taken from some sort of ancient manuscript the family had found in the family estate from the 1800's in England. I found the name charming, so we christened our home the same name.

This house was instant love for us both. Once we both saw it, we knew it had to be ours. It had old world charm that made us feel we belonged here. Rose bushes of all colours grew around the perimeter, as did blue and white agapanthus, native grasses, palm trees and royal mauve agaves. The wide bricked paths that led around the bull nose veranda cooled our home in summer and protected it in the wild Perth winter storms. The backyard had a wooden swing with old gum trees giving shade, a cracked rock pond was found, cleaned up and kept, and over time, whatever needed a watery home resided in this much discussed backyard oddity as no one knew what lived there. Come night in summertime the frog song was timid, but it was there, so obviously some liked it.

Chapter 14

The garden had an old aviary which Russ had made into a nursery for his prize orchids. He also had a passion for dainty native ferns, and these were now running wild with joy at not being cut back regularly. I sighed as I added this job to the to-do list growing in my head, mentally making notes as I sat and looked around me.

Inside wide and cool rooms—very modern for such an old home—the one thing I adored about this house was the French doors that opened from the kitchen to the veranda to create a huge, open room. The many barbeques, parties, family get-togethers had such fond memories for all of us, and our little girl was conceived in this house and born here.

There had also been a son, Ross. He had lived for six hours before he broke our hearts by passing away from a hole in his heart. Not detected till he was born, he fought to breathe, he fought to live, his tiny baby fingers clutched mine as he battled with life, then he gave in and drifted away in my arms, his daddy's arm around us both, as we said our heartbroken goodbyes to our little man. My eyes settled on a small white plaque by the fernery with 'Ross' engraved on it. I was home.

I woke from a deep slumber as the sun was setting, the lounge now basked in its golden glow, dust motes floated in the air. My mobile phone ringing was the prod I needed to get up and move, if not I would have slept here for the night. It was Rae, concerned if I was okay being on my own or if I needed her to pop over and stay with me. 'I'm fine, honey. I intend to have that pie you made me, a hot bath, then sleep till tomorrow. I will ring you once I have been to see your dad.'

'Just ring if you need me,' she replied.

I did as I had said I would; a hot shower then dinner, although hungry I was not, then ringing the hospital to see how Russ was doing. He was now in the ward, stable and comfortable was the report from the nurses' station.

Sleep is the most healing thing the body can do. I woke to a bright new day, feeling refreshed as I knew Russ was coming home soon and we would all have a wonderful Christmas together. Well that was the plan I had dreamed of and felt would happen. In the meantime, it was once again ring the hospital, check Russ was feeling better, and speak to him if possible, which he was not according to the staff. Then put together a list of things he might need for his stay while there, and then tackle this dusty house till I could visit my husband. The phone started ringing, stopping any housework or daydreams of happy ever afters. Friends, family, extended family all asking, 'Just heard. How we can help?' or, 'When can we call in to see him?'

The days passed quickly, with Russ mending well. Any sign of blood clots now gone, and no sign of any other health scares. In between hospital visits, I spent a lot of time in the garden pruning wayward roses and plants that had decided to wander off and do their own thing.

I decorated the house with Christmas decorations, even ordering a tree so the smell of pine would drift though, Jess and I both decorating it, Jess with the gusto of a twelve-year old. Once finished it resembled a huge exploded party popper, very little tree showing under the tinsel, streamers and baubles of all colours. Our superb combined art piece now had pride of place in the lounge.

Then the day came for Russ to come home. Rae was picking him up once the doctor had given him clearance. The car driving up the gravel driveway alerted me to his arrival. Russ looked pale, bandaged on one arm and leg, he hobbled into our lounge and seemed to deflate onto the couch, putting his feet up and closing his eyes. He was out to it. 'Welcome home, my darling,' I whispered.

We left him there, a light throw rug now covering him, and Rae and I sat out in the kitchen having a cup of coffee discussing what to cook for Christmas dinner and what to buy for Christmas gifts. Her excitement that her parents were going to be home for Christmas was contagious.

It was all going to work out. Russ was on the mend; all his medical reports were encouraging. I even had thoughts of us carrying on with our travels in the New Year when he was better. With this in mind, I decided my gift to him would be road maps and a new GPS. What he needed now was encouragement to feel confident about resuming our trip. While he healed, we could plan it so much better than before as I felt we both now had the experience to caravan properly. One of my ideas I knew would cause hiccups, so I would leave it till he was much better. Roll on Christmas. I was feeling excited about all of it.

When Russ woke up looking so much better, his one sentence was, 'Hey there, how are you doing?'

I did the nurse thing, plumping pillows, making coffee and afternoon tea, asking what would interest him for dinner, dishing out medication. While he was feeling pain free and comfortable, I told him what happened to the Metal Mermaid.

I told him it was as safe as it could be as Brian had offered to guard it with his life, if need be. I suggested once he was feeling better, we could fly up and collect her, driving it back down here or perhaps head to Broome then carry on around the top of Australia. Russ smiled. He knew this had been a bucket list thing of mine for years that had dimmed over time due to life happening. We had both travelled all over the world, yet the top end of Australia was still a mystery to us both. I had declared many years ago, 'Once I have visited this mysterious land of magical tales, I will be content to stay at home.' Famous last words.

'Whatever you want, sweetheart,' his tired voice rasped. Now this was the part that always scared me the most, when loved ones actually sound like they have given up on the joys of being alive. I had experienced relatives when they had given up, so my job was to make sure Russ took an interest again and felt the motivation to do so.

Russ stayed in bed most days refusing to walk as it hurt refusing to take part in our family get togethers. We had to go to him if we wanted to discuss anything, and there was an endless stream of family and friends wearing a path on the carpet to the bedroom. It annoyed me, as that was our private domain, so I had to be the bad cop again and move a rather grumpy Russ into the conservatory, making up a day bed for him. At night I would support him to reach our room, but then I got smart and bought him a walking stick. He improved slowly; he was now smiling at our private jokes and taking short strolls around his pride and joy, the fernery. I went over the memories of our recent trip and the folk we had met, anything to encourage him. However, the big dark circles under his eyes stayed, the tiredness seemed to suck the life out of him, and by midday nearly every day he was back on the day bed.

I checked with our doctor that the medication was not the reason for Russ's behaviour. He visited us, checking on Russ's wound and talking to Russ about his symptoms. The doctor asked me to give it another fortnight of resting, then if no better, he would look at changing the medication Russ was on. He also offered to send Silver Chain round so I could get some help in bathing and re-bandaging the wounds because they deep and needed cleaning twice a day. I accepted gratefully.

Robin from Silver Chain arrived in two days. Very professional, and a kind, a no-nonsense person, she was allocated two hours every second day to help Russ, shooing me out of the house. 'Go out and have a coffee or meet a mate,' she would say. 'He's going to be just fine, I'm here now.'

Russ and Robin hit it off immediately. He had no choice, she informed him in no uncertain terms. 'Do as you're told, young man, and we will get on just fine.'

So, out for a coffee and meet my mates I did go and enjoyed it immensely. Their tactful humour always made me laugh. To my delight I also achieved some Christmas shopping. I bought road maps, a proper diary for daily comments and destinations etc. The new navigator was a beauty. I knew Russ would love it, and inside this little package I put in a bright yellow sticky note pad that had a huge smiley face on it.

I have always enjoyed preparing for Christmas; the baking, the smell of Christmas wafting through our home as I mixed spices and added rum to the Christmas cake and pudding. Slowly, Christmas gifts started piling up under the tree. We had agreed three for Jess and one for each of us, well that was what Rae and I settled on, but now we were home could we not spoil him a little? Russ nodded in agreement when I enquired. Russ adored his grandson, there was no-one better for him and Jess was a good tonic for his grandad as well.

'Let's get the Grasshopper (his nick name for Jess, since he was born) a mobile phone as his gift.'

I was delighted with the idea. We read many pamphlets, Russ finally choosing the one he wanted to buy. He rang and ordered it, making sure it was the correct one and confirming the delivery date.

As Russ improved very slowly some days were great. He shuffled from our bed to the day bed or armchair, demanding a coffee and the newspaper, and as normal I would tell him where the paper was and he could get it while I made the coffee. Other days were not good at all; his breathing shallow, his face pale, the arm wound causing the most pain. Russ would want my attention nonstop when he was unwell, but there were times I had to bite back a hasty reply. It left me wondering why a major hospital stay or a health setback caused him to become so needy. My Dad had been the same; he had aged badly. If not for me taking over at times, Mum would have been worn out before her time to go to God. On the positive side it was close to Christmas, so hopefully Russ would be much better on the day. I was well and happy enough, so I could pamper this good man as much as he needed to become active and well and part of our family once more.

Chapter 15

Christmas day arrived. Jess and Rae had stayed overnight, we both knew it would be an early morning start and we were not wrong with Jess hurtling out of his room yelling, 'It's present time,' at five am. Russ had a role he loved to play–Mr Scrooge incarnate. He would appear dishevelled and very grumpy, dawdle, moan about the early hour, making the family and friends in previous years yell at him, 'Come on old man, get a move on.' I intercepted our grandson in the hallway. 'Wake your mum up first,' I suggested, then realised something was wrong. This time Russ was not in our bed for the first time since we had married. It was Christmas day and Russ was not beside me, it was a strange feeling. I made the coffee and heated fruit mince pies thinking he was asleep in the conservatory as recently Russ would get up and hobble into the day bed so he would not wake me, the pain making him restless, and he would read or snooze in his armchair to let me sleep.

While everything was brewing, I quickly dressed, then called everyone to the lounge where the Christmas tree twinkled in semi darkness. There was my Russ, asleep in his armchair, his sore leg up on a footstool, his head laid back on the chair, his soft grey curls still all ruffled from a bad night sleep. Jess was so excited Rae poured the hot drinks while trying to calm him down saying, 'Jess, this is Grandads job, to give out the gifts under the tree.'

I filled up a plate of Christmas goodies, taking that and coffee over to Russ, and said loudly, 'Come on sleepy, time to be Santa,' shaking him lightly. I had no response, so I gave his arm a shake again. This time his head rolled forward. I looked at Rae, her eyes mirroring mine, 'No!' Walking over to her Dad she gave him another shake saying crossly, 'Come on Dad, it's not the day to kid around.'

I just stared at my strong husband, 'This is not possible!' screaming in my skull. I knelt beside him, my fingers on his neck pulse, but nothing. I shook as I placed my head on his chest, listening for the comforting bump I had heard for the last forty years, nothing.

My Russ was dead. I have no idea what happened after that, all I could think was this was a joke, any moment now he would get up and yell, 'Fooled ya.' Russ was almost famous for his silly practical jokes; this surely was one of them. I have no idea how, why or who came that day, all I know was I wanted to hold onto him and never let go. I wanted to scream 'NO!' but the cry remained bottled up inside me, and I do not remember much at all but having to accept my husband was dead. A man I never met before gently pulled my arms away from Russ, helping me into a nearby chair, my legs buckling under me as I tried to stand up, his voice and hands guiding me to sit down.

When I looked up, they had put Russ on a gurney going into an ambulance. It was too soon! The cry I had kept bottled up inside me erupted into a moan that came from so deep inside it hurt. I don't recall much at all. I said stupid things, did stupid things, telling Jess that, 'Grandad was a silly man. Fancy doing that on Christmas day!' I don't recall wandering in the garden weeping out for him, my neighbour Perry hearing me and coming over to help, taking the secateurs out of my hands as I began cutting back the roses. This kind man understood my grief, having lost his wife Nancy a few years back.

Perry just sat with me and let me cry it all out, I did not have to be brave with him. He wiped my nose and rubbed my back crooning to me, 'Let it go, just let it go.' Rae was inside, I could hear her sobbing. Jess was nowhere to be seen. What had happened to this bright and beautiful day? Why had this happened to us? There were no answers,

Perry saying, 'It was his time. Thank God he went peacefully.'

Then my brain kicked in. *Did he?* What if he cried for help and I did not hear him through me asking him to sleep in another room when he was in pain? What if he was in pain, and through my selfishness, he felt he could not ask for assistance? The guilt now set in.

Rae was as bad saying to me, 'If only I had said something different when you said Dad had a migraine. I feel awful Mum. I feel he was asking for help and I failed him.'

I held her in my arms, it was my turn to be the comforter. It was such a hazy time for us both; the hospital wanting an autopsy to prove there had been no medical mistake.

Finally, it was the day of the funeral, the day we said goodbye forever. The small local church packed to overflowing, there were folks standing outside. Russ, in his will, had requested no flowers and any money offered for wreaths was to go to a charity of my choice. On his coffin was a simple posy of his orchids from home with as much of his green ferns as we could find. Jess and I together had done this final act for his Ranrad.

Our brave, sweet twelve-year old grandson handling the situation like a man, his little chin trembling with the need to sob his grief out. Jess took pride of place at the front of the pall bearers, too small to handle the coffin, he marched in front of them as the coffin left the church.

Russ would have been so very proud of his Jess in his new black suit, would have teased him, then hugged him telling him, 'What a good-looking man you are, you must take after me.' Jess opened the car doors for us both, making sure we were all tucked in, Rae and I both pale with fatigue and grief.

Little Jess was now the man of our family, not having a dad himself, Russ had taken over that empty spot. They did so much together, his blue eyes—so much like Russ's—shimmered with tears, only released that night once he was in bed. I heard his crying and went into comfort him. Jess cried, 'What am I going to do now, Nana? I loved him so much. I miss him. I want him back.'

'Me too, sweetheart. Me too,' I said. I ached for Russ's arms and his tummy jiggle when he laughed.

I don't believe in ghosts or spirits, but I swear I felt the soft touch of a hand on my shoulder as I held our grandson close.

The funeral director rang to say the death certificate had been released and would I like to pick it up personally or have it delivered to me. I chose the latter. I did not open it once it was handed over; I left it on the table by the phone. I did not need a piece of paper telling me my right arm was missing. Rae insisted we open it together. I did not care. 'Whatever.'

She said, 'They say here "embolism" but that's not right, Mum, they took the entire clot away from him.' Rae was ready to take her anger and frustration out on the medical system. I gently took her hand away from the certificate. 'He's gone Rae, he's gone. That's all I can deal with right now, okay.'

It took nearly a year for me to regain the logical side of life, of getting on without my husband to chivvy me along, or to try not saying, 'Oh, I must tell Russ about this,' when something funny happened or a piece of news filtered through I knew he would enjoy. Time is a healer and it was only time that was slowly healing me.

It was almost Christmas the following year, all of us dreading it because of the painful memories it would bring back. One week before I had still not done anything about presents or a tree; it was all too much.

Jess was disappointed with me; he had bounced back full of life as young ones do and Rae had met a man and it looked like love was in the air. How do you say it's too soon for change? I needed or wanted to keep everything the same, when honestly, we had all changed dramatically.

I was dozing in my armchair when there was a knock on the door, thinking it was a friend or my neighbours, I called out, 'Coming!' To my surprise there stood Gilly, the woman I had met in Geraldton. She was hesitant when she said, 'Hi, remember me?' She then smiled, and as I swung the door open in amazement, she held out her arms. 'I only heard about Russ last week. I'm so sorry.'

Gilly was the trigger I needed to start my life once again.

'Come in, come in please, I'm so glad to see you.'

Gilly came in, and then under strict instructions from me stayed for the Christmas week, sharing my family, fun, laughter and a week of friendship. Gilly made us all laugh, her bubbly personality dragging back the curtain of gloom that had settled on me.

I woke with something to look forward to; she brightened my day, the once lonely day that dragged on now filled with 'female stuff' as Russ would have put it. Gilly gardened with me and made her version of a Christmas pudding that would blow your head off with the amount of rum and brandy mixed into it; Jess was under orders to eat Nana's pudding only. She encouraged Jess to decorate the Christmas tree they had both sourced and dragged home, it exploded with every bit of tinsel and garish ornament they could find, beg, borrow or steal.

Gilly's presence helped make our Christmas wonderful; I loved having her around in the house, her little caravan now tucked up in the driveway, 'Parked away for the festivities,' as she put it.

Chapter 16

I even put on a New Year's Eve party, the first one in years as Russ hated them with a vengeance, inviting all neighbours and friends that could attend. Rae bought Jono, her new man, with her. She looked stunning; slim, elegant with long tanned legs, and so very happy, her man a tall, dark, handsome Greek. Together they made a stunning couple. The house bulged at the seams with everyone turning up. We had such a fabulous time dancing, laughing, eating and singing in the New Year with 'Auld Lang Syne'. Gilly got quite drunk, doing some sort of weird dance in the corner of the room, calling it 'a Fijian love dance'. I hid my smile.

What fun we all had, and by one am the next morning all that was left of the party were streamers, dirty plates and glasses.

While I sat down and got my breath, enjoying an amazing feeling of liberation, I was now into one year without Russ. Enough of being sad and gloomy, I still had enough life in me to live life to the fullest while I was well enough to do so.

Rae opted to stay the night with me, and I invited Jono to stay as well. Thankfully, Jess was at a mate's place over night. Gilly had offered to sleep in her caravan for the night. The spare room was there in case any of my friends had over indulged. After the party had finished, I had nothing to do but wish them all a happy New Year and go to bed myself. Ahh... peace! The night was so silent after the music, the loud chatter, laughter and clink of glasses. Sleep took a while coming as so many thoughts where running around in my head, the major one was about Russ. I felt very disloyal to his memory but honestly, I was remembering the arguments we had had about having parties. He liked small, intimate dinner parties where he would shine as the dinner host. He disliked and discouraged any sort of large gathering in our home; more than six people were too much for him but would willingly accept invites to large gatherings in others' homes.

He only picked Aussie blokes for his girl, Rae, so she rarely brought her boyfriend's home if they were of any other nationality than true-blue Aussie. One memory came back: the embarrassment Russ caused when Rae brought home a young Indonesian student she had made friends with. I was going to invite him for dinner when Russ intervened with his opinion, leaving both Rae and I in an awful situation. Luckily, the young man sensed the animosity and left with excuses of getting home on time. Rae was furious, Russ smugly said, 'My home, my table.'

This was not the only problem we had and bicker we did at times, especially when he was home on a trip from the mines. If I had agreed to go out with one of my social groups, he would sulk, or sarcasm would drip like honey from his toast in the morning. 'Had a good time, did we?' he would say in a falsetto voice trying to imitate a female, then he would giggle, fluttering his eyelashes. He knew it would make me angry and, yes, I did let it get to me; I was not a child. Russ liked me to himself and had a jealous streak. I admit I was also at fault, as I had given in. 'Anything for a peaceful life,' had been my motto.

Rae, however, saw it differently and they would argue day was night. From a young age she would yell at him, 'You're not the boss of me!' then it became, 'My life, my body. I will date whoever I like,' the argument ending as she stalked out. This last year I had a small taste of freedom and it felt wonderful to have my head out of the gloomy bin, realising Russ had always had very big say in my life, and I had let him as head of the house.

I had built my own independent life when he was away but once he was home, we all catered to his demands. Still, I loved him. The fun times far outweighed any bad times, and there were so many wonderful times together, his memory still so very much in my heart, but I was an independent woman now with a life of my own to love.

Sleep claimed me quite late, so when I woke it was nearly ten in the morning.

'Good morning, sleepy,' Gilly called as she went from bathroom to kitchen. 'Hi Mum, cuppa's on the table,' Rae called out, her and Jono's arms around each other's waists. And what a glorious morning it was; sunny, warm and full of promise. Looking at the two new love birds made me smile. Russ would be blue in the face if he knew I had actually permitted his daughter to sleep with a man and under our roof as well. When the two of them saw me smiling they had no idea what I was smiling about.

Gilly was busy packing her bag as she intended to leave within the next day to go south and visit some friends; her plans were to head back to Melbourne.

I was dreading her going as it meant an empty house again, Rae and Jono said their goodbyes and off they went to get Jess. I decided to clean up the lounge, take down the tree and do all the dishes, winding so many coloured streamers up in my arms. It's funny when there is no one watching how you can act out what a child would do. I ran around the lounge making whirring noises and winding the many streamers quickly around my arms until a huge ball of the colour was formed, my heart bumped out.

'I miss Russ.' Anything to keep busy, keep a smile on my face while Gilly made us breakfast.

'What's up?' she asked, staring at the paper ball in my arms. How do you say, 'I'm going to miss you,' to a woman you do not know all that well? I'm not one for silly excuses either, so I dived in the deep end saying, 'I don't want you to go so soon.'

Gilly's face was worth a thousand words. 'I feel the same way,' she admitted. By dinner time that day we'd figured out what we could do together; she would return in a week, then I was going to show her my beautiful city, Perth, loving the idea of being a tourist in my own town. Then we would fly to Tom Price to scatter Russ's ashes and bring the Metal Mermaid home.

Rae, Jono and Jess arrived, so we set the table for three more, leftovers with chicken pie on the menu. Rae then told us her news. Jono had asked Jess and her to move in with him. Rae was ecstatic, Jess unsure, and it showed. Time for a Nana and Grandson talk, I thought. Excusing us from the table we went to the conservatory for a chat about life in the New Year and what it was going to mean for him as this little boy was a huge part of my life, so any decisions I/we made also involved him. I told him about my planned trip to Tom Price and he immediately brightened, 'Can I come too, Nana? You did promise last time you went away I could do a trip with you.'

'So I did,' I said. 'Let me see what Mum thinks and then we can discuss it properly.' Rae was all for it, all agreeing it would make things easier for them when moving if Jess was occupied.

Gilly went back to her home. The week dragged forever.

Perth shone its best for my new friend Gilly; our first tour, close to home, was Penguin Island at Safety Bay. We took Jess with us, all of us delighting in these very cute tiny penguins, then a boat cruise around Penguin Island to watch the seals. Ice creams on the Rockingham foreshore and a movie for Jess. He chose 'The Warhorse' by Stephen King which I must say, I loved as well. Returning a very tired young man to his mum, we went home ourselves to sort out what to pack and take with us. I had left most of my gear in the Metal Mermaid while Gilly had all her things with her, so we decided to pack one large case and a box of goodies from the pantry.

The next day our Perth tour continued. It was quite exciting as we went to the Royal Mint, rode the double-decker bus around Kings Park, which had its best summer hat on so it was picture perfect, then a Swan river cruise watching dolphins swim along the boat's side as we enjoyed a delicious salad for lunch.

We caught the train home, my feet hot and sore as I had not walked so much or so far for a long time. Back home, we collapsed on the couch, Gilly offering me a foot rub if I made dinner. Ahh... heaven! I sank back as she kneaded my tired toes back into life.

The next day we went to the zoo and it was like visiting a wildlife park or was I seeing all of this through tourist's eyes; Gilly's enthusiasm about Perth was so contagious. The next day we visited Government House, the Perth Museum, walked along St George's Terrace taking snap shots of all the wonderful bronze statues along the way, and then London Court where ye olde world curiosity shops still thrived.

Fremantle was just as exciting; taking a trip on the tall ship, the Leeuwin, the white topped waves splashing into our faces while seagulls screeched with laughter at us both getting so wet. The Fremantle markets next, then the movies to relax in icy air-conditioning away from the forty-degree summer day.

Next day, Subiaco markets to meet friends of mine, an Argentinean couple called Carlos and Margarita who owned a food stall there, feeding us up on their spinach pancake specialty. The next three days were spent combing the city on trains and buses, enjoying our time together, getting to know each other better.

On the weekend we drove to the Kalamunda markets where golden jams, homemade candles, jewellery and fresh fruit from nearby orchards could be found, and then through to York where a hot air balloon ride took us far and above the beautiful golden landscape.

On our last day at home we made chutneys and jams from the fruit and vegies we had brought, topping up the pantry and packing some of this produce into the box for the trip north. I did the banking and bill paying late that night, emptying my home of vases of flowers, plus vacuuming and washing while Gilly cleaned out the fridge and cleaned the bathrooms. Ten days had sped by so fast; suddenly it was time to head for the airport to fly to Paraburdoo and then on to Tom Price. We made a time limit to return in two weeks, there was one very important duty I had to do—send Russ's ashes up with the wind in his beloved north, the small wooden box packed alongside my clothes.

Jess was beside himself; he was at long last going on a trip with Nana and his new best mate Gilly, who it was obvious returned the feeling.

Rae warned me, 'Be home in time for school, please,' but their attention riveted on each other, mainly. Gilly and I could have had blue spots on our faces and all Rae would have done is smile and say, 'See you Mum, have a great time,' and floated off with her man. Was I ever that in love? Did I ever have that sort of glow about me? I was really happy for our daughter; at long last she was silly, giggling, smiling and in love.

Chapter 17

Up and away we went, into that endless blue-sky Australia is known for. Jess was sitting at the window giving us a running commentary on whatever took his fancy—this being his very first flight—everything including the toilet was a fascinating amusement, and his loud comments on what a big whoosh the toilet flush did caused the whole plane to titter. Only a child could say what he did and get a smile. I was quite happy to let him ramble and he did just that, him and Gilly chatting away like old mates. My quietness was caused by memories of Russ coming up here as a young man so keen and eager to conquer it all, very much like his grandson. I felt sad I was going to greet all our friends once more, only this time without Russ at my side. I felt a tear slide down my face, as no matter how independent I felt, he was still my Russ. This was our last *andiamo* together.

I hated the name widow; it was a black name to me. Some ladies I had known in the past gloried in widowhood wearing it like a mantle. Me? The label 'widow' sounded like the spider waiting for her next victim. I was anything but that. Russ, and forty years of being together was it for me, another man would need extremely large feet to fit his shoes.

The plane glided to a halt. Jess was unbuckled and standing before the motors were switched off, my hand on his shoulder as I told him, 'Jess, calm down.' I needed to stay focused, I found his excitement disconcerting. Thank god for Gilly who squeezed my hand and took over, looking after my grandson. Brian was there waiting for us, his face told me how sad he was, and I could feel him tremble as we hugged. 'It's alright Brian, really, it's alright,' I whispered, both of our eyes shiny with tears. This was Russ's right-hand man, working closely in all the mines they had worked in. I felt for him, he knew Russ as well as I did, the difference was he knew Russ the working man.

Our ride into Tom price was a fairly silent one. Winn, Brian and I had some time out together. They told me of the memorial that Tom Price mine had put on for Russ at the mess.

So, it was here, Tom Price, that I decided to let his ashes fly with the wind on top of Mt Nameless. That night in their home was spent with smiles, tears and the, 'I remember when Russ said or did... ' It was a peep into the past to understand what a firm friendship these two had formed.

That night, I slept on my own in the Metal Mermaid for the first time in fourteen months, Gilly and Jess bedded down in the house. I sobbed myself to sleep as our journey together had finished, no more twosome, no more squabbles of who stood where so we could dress or eat or drink, yet it still felt wonderful to be back. Our Metal Mermaid was made for travel and adventure, but where would I go on my own dragging my memories with me? I also felt a little guilty as just before Russ had died, my fabulous idea was to sell this one and buy a bigger caravan with our own ensuite, calling her the Metal Mermaid II.

Could I sell this pretty little home on wheels? We had so much fun in her, or would I keep it as a mausoleum to treasure our last days together? My eyes closed with exhaustion pondering this question.

Morning arrived with Jess knocking on my door. 'Come on sleepy, here's your mug of tea.'

As Jess entered, his eyes were enormous. Everywhere he looked were reminders of his Grandad; the shaving mug and razor Jess had given him for a birthday present one year, a large framed photo of all four of us on the wall above the table, Russ's aftershave. Jess's chin wobbled. 'I miss him Nana.' We both ended up hugging each other, again with tears, which was fine with me; it was our healing time.

The first job this morning was to ring our friends Tino and Daisy; I knew the bush telegraph would have already informed them of why I was back. I still felt the need to tell them that the memorial I intended to hold on Mt Nameless was in a day's time. When Daisy heard my voice, she gave a cry of joy, yelling out to the others, 'Russ's Mrs is on the phone.' I gave her the details.

She said, 'See ya there,' crashing the phone down in my ear. Then it was off to the Shire of Tom Price to see if I could actually do this. I had a sneaky feeling it was against Aboriginal Law.

My answer was, 'No, I was not allowed to do this. It was a sacred women's place,' so I opted for another favourite place of Russ's, the Billabong at Millstream where I stopped when Russ first got ill. We had loved the little retreat and I had enjoyed the peace of it as well. I decided to ask his closest friends Brian, Kelly, Tino and their wives to join Gilly, Jess and myself there. I intended to drive the Metal Mermaid out there as I wanted to stay the night, to say our last goodbyes, and our friends could meet us there.

We all arrived, very aware of what was going to happen. It was dusk and a light wind blew. I didn't offer a prayer, more of a, 'Thank you for our life together, go with the wind my darling.'

Daisy keened an aboriginal song to send safely him on his way, Jess, now holding the box of ashes, came forward solemnly, his cheerful banter now silent. I put the box down on the earth and waited for the wind to take the ashes away and on queue a small willy-willy formed around us, a small red whirl of dust tipped the box over and away went the ashes up into the dark mauve sunset.

'Goodbye mate. See you again one day,' his friends called out.

'Bye Russ. Love you,' was my silent call.

Jess, suddenly silent as his best friend's ashes floated off into the dusky sky, just held up his hand in a last farewell.

Our faces looked into the deepening dusk as Russ became one with his red desert forever. Our friends went on their way home giving many hugs and requests to please call in on our way home, then silence, car motors and head lights receding into the night. The three of us stayed on to spend one more beautiful star filled night at the billabong.

I drove back to Tom Price the next day pulling into a service station for petrol. I had misgivings about calling into Brian and Winn's again, I wanted closure now, not, 'I remember… ' or hugging the past, not moving on. I asked Gilly what she thought, and she agreed with me. Stopping outside a Vinnie's second-hand shop, I cleaned out all of Russ's clothes and anything we did not need. Jess claimed the photo of the four of us, which was fine by me.

Then onto the highway, but first a gift given to our good friends, who had looked after us so well when we had needed them. I wrapped up Russ's fishing gear, his fishing hat, tackle box and knife with a large thank you card to Brian. For Winn, I bought a huge bunch of flowers from the gas station. I knew they would be at work so I popped them in the shade in their kitchen; they would know who it was from.

'Time to go now,' I said to Gilly and Jess, who readily agreed, and off we drove, the Metal Mermaid once more on the road and hopefully many adventures ahead.

Which way to go? Well I had never been farther than Point Sampson and Gilly admitted she had never been to Broome. 'Broome it is,' we all agreed. The Metal Mermaid chugged along quite content to be back on the road again. I'm certain my home on wheels could sniff out adventure; she was also prone to flat tyres, once again.

One flat tyre meant I stopped on the outskirts of Broome, those bloody little flies sitting on us everywhere. I'm not good at lifting and changing tyres and belonged to the RAC, so why try to do it myself? I rang them, and one hour later the yellow and black truck showed up and fixed it. It was now very close to lunch. Jess, being an active twelve-year-old with hollow legs was ravenous, and what Gilly and I had packed was not enough for a teenager to munch on.

Gilly had a heat headache, so we opted for a caravan park for our stay in Broome. Jess wanted one with a pool so he could swim all day. Gilly wanted a hot cuppa, painkillers and sleep. I wanted to find a caravan park so I could stop driving.

I saw a sign advertising the Palm Grove Holiday resort, with the all-important pool, trees for shade so Gilly can have her nap, and close to the beach where I would have an hour just to myself. Wonderful. I booked for five nights, paid the bill, made sure Jess was fine; even though he swam like a fish in water and an adult in attendance was important if anything did happen. I made sure Gilly was alright, and she was out to it.

I almost ran to the sand hills, found a spot where no one would find me, laid down in the warm sand, had a wander in the shallows, picked some tiny shells up off the beach and literally caught my breath. Time to breathe, time to exhale, then slowly breathe in the ocean air, and time to ask my heart, 'How are you today?' Time to watch the beginning of a sunset, time out as the wind briskly whipped up sand and sea. It was my time, and I needed it.

No tears, just a huge sigh that said it's over, done. *Andiamo Russ. I love you, always have and always will.*

Chapter 18

How other women handled a loved one's death, I have no idea, but I had dealt with it in my own way. I rang Rae and told her what we had done about her dad's ashes and his belongings, where we were for five days and that we'd be back home in hopefully eight days as Jess started school in two weeks. Her news was also exciting; Jono had proposed. A pregnant pause for a nanosecond, then I smiled and said, 'Rae you were made for love and happiness. As long as you're sure, I'm fine with it.'

'Oh Mum, there is so much I want to tell you as well,' she replied. 'Save it up for when I get home, honey. Now do you want me to tell Jess, or do you want to tell him?'

'Let us tell him, Mum, it's going to be a shock for him.'

She had no idea. I was surprised myself it was so soon after all that had happened, or was I being silly about all of this, maybe a little jealous?

Once back at the caravan park I was pleasantly surprised as Jess was there in his cotton PJs showered and ready for bed. Dinner was almost cooked, a glass of wine sat on the table set up outside, all done courtesy of Gilly.

'Wow, I can get used to this,' I said, admiring a gorgeous crisp green salad and fish frying on the barbeque. What a heavenly smell.

'Now, my friend,' Gilly announced, 'you have a job to do.'

'I do?'

'Yes, sit down and enjoy this meal and let's sort Broome out.'

'You have a deal,' I laughed, and there it was–I was me again, no tight smiles; a genuine laugh that made the other two people now in my life laugh with me. Broome watch out, we have arrived.

All three of us had a list as long as your arm of what we wanted to see and do in Broome. Over dinner, we all put our ideas forward, coming up with a mixed, colourful bag of what would be fun if it all worked out. I for one wanted to visit all the art galleries and knew Gilly and Jess would not enjoy it, so it was compromise time. I also knew I enjoyed some time out from life in a small bus and Jess's enthusiasm. Gilly felt the same, and to my amusement, Jess said, 'I need my private time as well.'

We all agreed to do our own thing once back at the Metal Mermaid, after sightseeing for the day. Gilly did her photography, Jess was in the pool and I was writing again, this time poetry. Once settled on the sand dunes, the ocean and sky provided inspiration, and I could feel the stirrings of excitement of what I could now do with my life. Maybe even a write a novel or small poetry booklet, a skill I had loved to play with in the past. Russ disliked it, said it was a, 'Waste of time rhyming lovey-dovey words,' so I hadn't bothered till now. The words literally poured out of me onto my notebook.

Gilly clicked her way through the day with pictures of people, I'm talking real people, real characters, for her yearly calendar that many shops throughout Western Australia bought from her.

Gilly had recently received an order from a cruise ship company for over two thousand calendars. Her main theme was the older population, her photos tastefully empathetic to those who agreed to be photographed. How clever and artistic she was, her time out spent sorting out or discarding what she liked and did not like.

Jess whooped it up at the large camp pool, meeting two other teens, the camp manager keeping a close eye on the energy released by three teenage boys.

During the day we saw the sights, and what a fun time all three of us had. Chinatown, with all the pearl shops, galleries, cafes and the culture, was amazing, as was the museum where we learned about the divers and the diverse cultures here; Indonesian, Asian and Aboriginal people working side-by-side. We went on the bus tour to visit the home of 130-million-year-old fossils and booked a camel ride–Gilly and I hanging on for dear life while Jess wanted his camel to go as fast as possible.

We wandered about the markets in the day and night, watching the fire eaters and jugglers in awe; the juice of fresh mangos running down our chins tasting the many dishes on offer, some hot and fiery, some so delicious you wanted more. I booked a surprise for us all; we went whale watching in the morning and in the afternoon, Jess was dropped off at a kid's fun parlour, his one craze was electronic games and this place had them all. So, for two hours, with Jess given the strictest of instructions to behave, Gilly and I had a pamper afternoon five doors down from the games shop; the phone number of our whereabouts emblazoned on Jess's mobile phone. *Good idea Russ, thank you.*

Oh bliss, as the oils seeped onto skin that was dry. The masseur's hands started on my feet, and I woke when she called my name and said, 'All done, dear.' I felt sleepy without the pressure of having to do or say anything. It was pure bliss. Gilly looked like a sleepy gecko when she floated out of her little room. A lukewarm shower was next, our hands and feet then buffed, and toenails painted. What luxury. Then time to pick up Jess and go home, our stay in Broome nearly over.

I was up very early the next day, our sleeping arrangements weren't the best but would suffice for a holiday, Gilly had the spare bed, a concoction of the table fitting into the seating arrangement around it. Jess and I topped and tailed, a small bolster dividing the double bed, so he had his side and I mine, both content with a sheet on top. Broome in the summer with temperatures in the thirties and awful humidity was uncomfortable. Thank the makers of aircon as it certainly worked overtime with all three of us inside. This morning I tiptoed out, not wanting to wake anyone.

Cable Beach is so pretty. Today it was calm, the white sand and turquoise water was amazing almost yelling at me come in for a swim. There was no-one about so the beach was empty. Dare I? All I had on was knickers and a sarong, but I dipped my toes in the water, my heart egging me on to be a child once again, the inner me saying, 'Go on have a swim, it won't hurt anyone.' By then I was up to my waist and in I went, my arms and legs splashing in the gorgeous warm water. I swam till I was really puffed, stopping and bobbing along in the gentle swell, then heading back to my sandy spot to sit and meditate. As I swam slowly back to shore, enjoying the feeling of water against my body, I heard a noise that sounded like opera, getting louder by the moment.

Suddenly, a senior citizen trawled past on his back, his strokes strong and clean, singing Bocelli at the top of his voice. I was gobsmacked, so much so that I had to stop and tread water, swallowing a little and spluttering. As he swam by, he stopped singing and looked in my direction, 'Morning Ma'am,' and off he went again.

Back on the sand, and having nothing to change into, I sat down enjoying the feeling of salt drying on my skin in the warm sea air. The senior had come ashore—stark naked—casually walked over to his clothing held down by a picnic basket, towelled himself off, wrapped a sarong around himself, then strode off along the beach singing at the top of his voice, and it was beautiful.

I walked back to the bus, a smile erupting into a laugh when I told Gilly about it. 'You should have woken me,' she cried. 'I could have photographed him.' I promised if I woke early the next day I would do just that.

We visited the Crocodile Park and I succumbed to buying two

large really beautiful Trochus seashells, one for me and one for Rae.

Jess asked a favour of me. 'Nana, could we please have another camel ride?' I hated to say no, but my bum was still sore from the last one, so I asked him, 'Jess, would you like to do it by yourself?' Silly question to ask a twelve-year old.

Once he was on and settled, he was off for a half-hour ride along Cable Beach. Gilly and I wandered along the sand. We spotted two people sitting on a rug in the sand, a small instrument in their hands. She was winding furiously, while he parted coloured thread and fed it to the machine. I just had to stop to ask what they were doing.

'Reta and Steve from Switzerland,' he said in broken English as he shook our hands. 'We are on a trip around the Australia.'

The machine they were using looked like an old-fashioned eggbeater, so I hunkered down beside them both to get a closer look. 'That's an old eggbeater,' I declared. Sure enough, they had modified an old eggbeater, one that had the old large blades and wooden handle from way back in the 1940's; my gran had one and so did my mum. What they were doing with it, though, was pure magic. Somehow, they inserted a large steel ring and clamped it tight, then by hand, Steve fed the coloured string into the beater while Reta wound the handle, first slowly then faster. Steve picked colours at random, inserting them while she wound. The finished product was amazing: a multicoloured ring like a very tiny dream catcher. Steve snipped the thread and Reta pulled out a small pair of pliers, putting a silver earring hook on the top of the ring. I held out my hand and there lay the most perfect bright, multicoloured earring.

Chapter 19

I invited them to my bus for dinner that night so we could learn more of their travels; we both found these two rather interesting.

We raced back to the camel pick up point, grabbed Jess as he had just arrived back, then went food shopping, much to Jess's disappointment, his face sulky because his afternoon swim was cancelled, all because Nana and Gilly were fussing about food.

My answer was, 'Tough, sort it out. I'm going to be busy. Either join in or go to bed.' Jess knew I was getting annoyed by his sulky attitude and thankfully chose to join in. His job was afters, choosing some creamy cheeses with crackers and mint chocolates. 'Good choice,' Gilly and I chorused. We had bought food to make a spaghetti Bolognese, Gilly crowing her 'Spag boll was to die for.' What she didn't know was I'd become really disinterested in cooking. Gilly my friend, you go for it.

Reta and Steve arrived at six that night. Jess and I had set the outside table with a plastic dinner set, a blue and white check tablecloth set it all off. Gilly proudly dished up her meal and I must admit it smelt lip-smacking good and tasted wonderful. Jess bought out his dish all perfectly displayed on a small plastic tray, just right to set off the meal, and we all enjoyed it and praised his efforts. The night air was cool, and we had good food and company, or so we thought.

Steve told us all about his adventures and the way he met Reta, who demurely blushed as Steve told us of their meeting. It went something like this, 'I saw. I liked. I chased her, and she was mine.' Wow, some love story, I thought.

'What about the courting, the cuddles and the lead up to a life together?' I queried. Reta was so shy with us it was painful; she hardly spoke and looked overwhelmed when Steve took over any conversation.

'No need,' he said. 'She likes me. I like her. The end,' so abrupt and dismissive it stopped the conversation for a while.

These two looked the epitome of a hippie lifestyle; his long, braided hair, hers long and swept up to a top knot, rings covered their hands. Steve had a nose ring and tattoos covered his arms, Reta had a tattoo on the back of her neck, and she wore a pair of her earring creations that shone with metallic thread.

They both looked healthy and tanned, their lifestyle obviously agreeing with them. I could not stop thinking about what Russ would have said.

Reta offered to show us some of the thread jewellery they had made, but Steve strongly objected. Reta quickly shoved it back in her bag. Steve changed the subject by saying he had often found many small objects to add to their jewellery, some of them were old and valuable, so he sold them to an antique dealer adding the money their own coffers.

'Don't you hand them to the police in case it's lost?' Gilly enquired.

'No finders, keepers,' he snarled, half slapping/snatching them off Reta, tucking them away in his leather satchel.

I saw a dark, bullying side to this man who believed dishonesty was okay and at someone else's misery or loss. This was not part of me or mine. Something snapped inside me. I stood up and said, 'Please leave my camp site immediately.'

Reta was in tears as he roughly took her arm and shoved her in front of him. 'Put the fuckin' torch on!' he screamed at her, giving her a push. Reta stumbled into the sand, and he slapped her hard, then marched on ahead, leaving her behind softly crying out for him to stop. I rang the camp manager asking him for help. When he arrived, I told him what had happened. He took Reta into their home and rang the police. Jess had seen a nasty side to life he had never witnessed before.

I had some explaining to do to my grandson but was just as shocked as Jess when Gilly said, 'Well look who's growing balls.'

I felt good to be in control, and of whom I shared my company with. I explained to Jess that saying 'finders keepers' was wrong, and nothing must ever convince him to steal another's property.

I also addressed bullying; it was wrong full stop. What Steve had done tonight was wrong, to deal with another in such a mean way showed others what sort of person you are inside your heart.

Gilly and I sat outside in the cooling night air. Tomorrow we would head home to Perth. I admitted I was not ready to go back, and she agreed.

'Always ready for an adventure,' she said. She slipped a postcard in front of me. 'Ever thought of doing this?' Emblazoned across the front was New Zealand and a picture of Mt Cook, its dazzling top bright with snow.

By now, I knew of her Kiwi background, her parents related to the Maori people. She always said she had a ton of family she had never met, adding, 'My plan was to come back to Perth with you, sell up my small caravan, move back home, and buy another van and tour New Zealand.'

I looked at her face; it was one huge smile. 'Come on Tara, I'll sell mine if you sell yours.'

'Sell up the Metal Mermaid?' I spluttered. She roared laughing, 'It's not the holy grail, pet, and you yourself told me this had been one of your ideas when the big guy was alive, so why not now? Let's do something really fun, sell it all and buy another bus or caravan over there. Let's go on a real adventure.'

Could I do this? I thought. Could I leave it all behind and just up and go? What about Jess and Rae? What about the house? What about my life I was slowly putting back together in Perth?

'We should do this slowly,' Gilly advised. 'Once we are back at your house let's look at both our finances and the possibility of both going to New Zealand for one whole year.'

Phew! That sounded better. 'Yes, let's do that.' I agreed. 'Let's see what I can do, then make plans once we are back at my house.'

'Do you mind if I stay in the house with you?' Gilly queried.

'I won't have it any other way,' I replied. Her next statement floored me; I'm not often speechless but tonight my mouth hung open.

Gilly told me there were some things I needed to know about her, that after her husband had died, she went and stayed at a friend's house.

'That's right, I remember you telling me,' I said.

'Well, pet,' Gilly leant forward saying, 'we did more than stay together.'

You did? A weird feeling was in my gut.

'We became lovers.'

'So, you're a–'

'Yes, I'm a lesbian.'

I had never met one, let alone sat next to one. Immediately I was full of questions, plus a feeling of *not for me* was forming in my gut. 'Gilly, I don't know what to say.' My very new friend looked sad.

'You're quite safe, Tara. I'm not diseased and I don't fancy you.

You're my friend and that's how I intend to keep it.'

That night I went to sleep with trepidation lurching around inside me. We had talked to the small hours about how to make this new adventure work, both agreeing, 'If we can, we should do this together,' and, 'Why not, before we cannot?' But I still felt a little shocked, silly really as she hadn't grown horns or scales because of her sexual preference. The problem was mine.

The next day I was up and showered, dressing in the ladies' shower room. Normally it was a struggle for all three of us to find the clothes for the day and get dressed, amongst much laughter of whose legs and arms were in whose face.

It was duly noted by Gilly. I too felt really bad. Here I was judging her, and I had not bothered to ask myself why. If she had not told me, maybe I would never have found out. Part of me said brave lady, the other part said foolish lady. Would I really let this new curve ball ruin any adventure I was offered? Or did I have a small heart that only allowed the nice things in life to be seen? This was a real eye opener for me as I thought I was an open-minded person but obviously, I needed to work on that.

Chapter 20

We were on the road the next morning by eight am, deciding to have breakfast on the way. About two hours out of Broome we spied two hitch hikers trying to get a ride. It was Reta and Steve. Gilly looked at me and I shook my head. *No!* I was not becoming involved with them again. We drove past, Steve shaking his fist at us, Jess pulling faces at them, shouting, 'Loser, scum bag.' 'Jess!' I said, 'Enough, let it go.'

It took two days of driving, shared between Gilly and I, to reach my last stop up in the Pilbara. Arriving at Tino and Daisy's home in Karratha, the mob tumbled out of doors and windows like mini acrobats to greet us. I had one last gift to give away, this was to Tino. It was Russ's hardhat. The story attached to the hat was that Tino had saved Russ's life once and this was the hat Russ had worn that day, now kept as a memento of the mine's stupidity and greed. A ten-tonne missile of stone had fallen from an unsafe rock wall, Russ and Tino only just jumping clear as it completely crushed their drill rig. As it was told to me, Tino was responsible for pushing Russ out of the cabin ahead of himself. Tino's eyes held soft memories.

'I'm so sorry, love,' he said enfolding me in his arms. Daisy was there beside us patting us better with her warm brown hands. I struggled not to cry, instead introducing Gilly, then Jess, who was by now in full play mode with the mob.

'Please stay,' they said. 'Stay over and have a cuppa.'

'No, I need to go,' I answered, time for us to get Jess back home, any excuse not to go over Russ's death one more time. I held Daisy's ever busy hands, acknowledging her need to make me better as well.

'I can't stay. I'm sorry Daisy, I truly can't. I'm responsible for getting my grandson home to his mum.'

It was time to go.

'Come on,' I called to Jess and Gilly. It was then I know I heard *andiamo* whispered on the warm desert air, the hair on the back of my neck rising. How silly I am, I thought. It's a lovely memory, that's all.

I opened the driver's side to clamber in when Darcy, their eldest girl, slipped her hand into mine. 'He says travel well, be safe and do what your heart calls you to do.'

Tino had overheard his daughter. 'Don't ask,' he said to me. 'It's something to do with the Aboriginal background.' I knew exactly what she meant.

As I left, Daisy had asked a favour of me. She gave me a large gunny sack of food to drop off at her auntie's place, no address given. 'They will find you,' she said. I was dubious. I intended to drive as much as I could all day, Gilly taking over when I got tired, plus three nights camping out was what we had planned.

I also had a huge amount of questions to ask Gilly to see if this trip she suggested was viable for us both to do emotionally, physically and financially. Although I was not broke, I certainly could not afford to throw money away; I honestly had no idea funerals were so expensive. Russ was insured, but the months we had taken off work had certainly taken a big bite out of our savings. I felt drained just thinking about it all.

An old Aboriginal woman sat in the middle of the road. Sounds like the start of a story or poem, but that's how it happened. Jess was sitting in the passenger seat; Gilly had succumbed to sleep with the brain numbing rumble of the bus and the long ribbon of red road ahead. Michael Jackson was singing, Jess and I laughing about Nana trying to reach the high notes when he yelled, 'Look out, there's an old lady on the road!' and sure enough there she was, just like you see a mirage appear. She suddenly stood up and waved us down. I slammed the brakes on, Gilly yelling, 'What the hell!' as we swerved to miss her.

My heart was in my throat. 'What are you doing?' I yelled at this little wrinkled up old lady who calmly wandered up to the side of the bus.

She was as bandy as a drunken sailor, a gummy smile one mile wide, dressed in baggy blue work overalls with the sleeves ripped off, a woollen beanie on, flies crawling everywhere. I knew this was the Aunty I was to look out for; no one else lived out here for miles. I passed the small sack through the bus window.

'Me Mabis,' she said and grabbed my hand, shaking it sideways like a wet dog.

'Hi there, Mabis. Nice to meet you,' then the smell of what the sack contained hit us. My gag reflex set in; flies, zillions of them, were everywhere.

I let the sack go. It plopped onto the red sand and Mabis hurriedly opened it, checking out what I had presumed were groceries. Now why was I surprised when a small dead, skinned animal was pulled out? This trip was proving full of surprises.

Mabis smacked her gums in expectation of this meal she was about to enjoy. I pulled away with all of us waving, and half an hour down the road, I hurriedly pulled over again and threw up, the smell was in my throat, in the bus, everywhere. It was Gilly who spied the small puddle of bloody goo where the sack had been sitting. Once it was disturbed, it stunk to high heaven. We both poured disinfectant over it and Jess found the paper towels. Our scrubbing took some of the smell away, but it still cloyed its way into the back of your throat.

For some reason I felt exhausted, so Gilly took over the driving and Jess played games on his phone. I went into a deep sleep till Gilly pulled into a small gully of sparse trees and red dirt. We're here for the night she said, turning off the motor. She made us all a cuppa and a tomato sandwich, then taught Jess how to play poker. I went back to sleep feeling light-headed and so dammed upset. *Why?* I had no idea. There were now times it all seemed too much for me to take in.

'Good morning, Nana,' Jess whispered into my ear. 'You slept well. Do you want a cup of tea?'

He had learned to use the gas stove in the bus and now it was a cup of tea at every chance he got.

My little grandson. I hugged him tightly to me, the sweet smell of sleep on a child still clung to him. 'Yes, I would love that cup of tea honey, then what say we find a roadhouse for some breakfast?'

Knowing it would be greasy finger food, I did not care. I just wanted to get home and feel safe within my own four walls. I must have mumbled out loud, 'And no more surprises for a while please.'

'Famous last words,' Gilly chortled from her bunk. 'What about a cup of tea for your poker mate over here?' she asked Jess.

I learned they had played till one am that morning, Jess had found the game exciting, the match sticks had piled up at his end of the table. It was Gilly who called an end to it saying, 'There's always tomorrow night, Jess.'

It was time for some map reading. We were on the outskirts of Barradale, another red, dusty, hot, two-shop town. I stopped there, going in to buy all of us some breakfast, the store owner still very sleepy as it was only seven am. All he had was ice creams for sale. The three of us sat on an old wooden bench on the large, cool, shop veranda, eating our breakfast: huge three-tier ice-creams, big runny ones of yummy, chocolate ice cream. I started a game of 'I spy' as we ate, which turned into a raucous argument between the three of us as we accused each other of who said what, then wild accusations of changing the subjects. It was the zillions of flies that drove us back into the bus, we passed around a cold flannel to wipe off the sticky ice-cream from hands and faces, Jess being the worst affected. I swear he dived into his ice-cream headfirst.

We decided to reach Carnarvon by night fall. 'I'll drive for four hours, then you take over,' Gilly offered.

'All right by me,' I said. I was so glad she was along with me; I don't think I could have done such a huge trip on my own.

The day was a hum of motor, red dirt and scraggly trees. The termite mounds were huge, Gilly snapping photos of the ones that resembled castles or mountain ranges, then stopping off at Minilya Bridge Roadhouse for gas and a much-needed toilet break. A half-hour there with stretches and cold drinks and fresh sandwiches, then all back inside the Metal Mermaid, Carnarvon here we come. This time I was driving, Jess and Gilly starting up another round of poker. Finally, I got a glimpse of the sea, then the sea wind and Carnarvon appeared. Now to find a caravan park for a night. Jess spied the pool first, his excited cry of, 'There's one, Nana,' so into 'there' we went.

A small caravan park this quiet was scary. 'Where is everybody?' I queried the manager. He said in the slowest Aussie twang, 'Gone south lady, too damn hot here for anyone in the summer.' I had to agree, this had been the hottest day so far.

We all headed for the pool, a crystal blue wonderland with a waterfall, and once in the water sounds of pure bliss escaped from all three of us. I dunked myself right under, my head felt like it was steaming under the lukewarm water. Jess swam up and down the pool, never out of energy, more seal than human at times. Gilly sat on the other side of the pool under the waterfall, her head back, eyes closed, relaxing as the water cascaded over her.

I allowed myself to study this woman who had become my friend. Who was she? Why a lesbian at her age? Or had she always been one? Why did she choose me as a travel companion when I'm obviously Mrs Straight Lace? Gilly was in her late fifties, a small woman in stature, a little plump, short curly blond hair now glinting with silver threads, blue eyes that had a fine mesh of lines around them or laughter lines as she called them, her face still very attractive but like me she was showing her age. I was the opposite; tall, short spiky silver hair, hazel eyes, slim, also with a web of life's lines around my eyes, and a twin furrow between my black eyebrows. My interests were the arts, community and my family. I knew of Gilly's family feeling sad for her, but I had no idea of her interests apart from photography. She caught me staring at her and smiled, her even white teeth making her skin looked tanned.

'What do you see?' she asked. 'Anything scary?'

'No Gilly,' I admitted. 'I see nothing scary; I see you and I'm very glad you're here with Jess and I on this trip.'

'Sounds promising,' she laughed. 'I've been waiting for the heave-ho out of the bus and your life.'

Our swim in the pool turned into, 'Who we had met.' It was fun, helping us relax with each other once again. Jess had overheard most of this conversation, claiming he was going to travel the world when he was grown up and meet everyone just like us.

'Jess,' both Gilly and I said together, 'this is only the beginning for you,' then looked at each other grinning. At least we had one thing in common—we had begun to say things at the same time. I put it down to the travel together in such a small bus, it was bound to have an effect on us both somehow. The swim had done us all good cooling us down, the tight stress in my chest and shoulders had lifted. Somehow, the fact Gilly was a lesbian was not that important anymore or that I had to get Jess home soon, or that there were plans to be made if I was to take this trip with Gilly to New Zealand.

Somehow the water had calmed it all down to a slow chatter in my head, not the scream it was before. It had felt like shock but now

I was a lot calmer. And the anger I had felt? Well, I put that down to Russ and giving him up to the red desert once again. I had always felt he belonged up there; it was a huge part of his life, and when in Perth with me or our family was the butter on our bread.

With Russ, just one whiff of a job up north and off he would go, nothing I could say convinced him otherwise, backpack on and that smile that said, 'I'm off, see you soon'. I knew he loved us, we were part of his family life and I knew we were a huge part of his heart, but the Pilbara had claimed his spirit.

Maybe I was the jealous type after all; I did not want to share him with anyone let alone a bit of red dirt. I put it down to me; it was who I was, always a knee jerk reaction to shock, then after two or three days it would all calm down. I was the same with Rae. I could be very jealous at times with her success, hiding it well with smiles and love but it was there lurking in a corner of my being.

Right, it's time for change. I do not want to be a lonely old lady who's afraid of others because they are different to me or my morals and beliefs. I do not want to be a sad old woman who disliked others who chose to be different and lived their life with optimism and happiness. Amazing what introspection does for a heart. Time for change starts right now. Marching up to Gilly, I put my arms around her and hugged her tight, apologising for my behaviour when she had been completely honest with me. Gilly's face beamed, her eyes bright with unshed tears, and she gladly accepted my sincere apology.

'I may not be your way inclined,' I said, 'but I enjoy your friendship. I love the way you interact with Jess and I'd like to call you my friend.'

Jess noticed the difference in the bus straight away, 'Someone had good news?' he asked.

'No Jess, it's just your nana feels so much better today, that's all.' What more could I say? 'What am I going to cook for dinner?' I said out loud. Jess and Gilly both crying out in unison, 'Fish and chips tonight, please.' Off to the fish and chip shop we went, thankfully in this heat it was only twenty minutes walking distance. We opted for the walk, then to sit on the rocks facing the ocean munching on our dinner. We watched four pelicans calmly bobbing along not a care in the world, floating gracefully and more interested in finding their own fishy tea than three silly humans sitting on the rocks eating out of newspaper.

Seagulls flashed past almost crashing into each other to pick up any titbits we tossed into the water, little windblown splashes of the sea wetting our feet. It felt good to be here relaxing, talking to Jess about his new school year about to start, if he had enjoyed the trip with Nana and Gilly, what were his favourite places, his experiences. His answers were not what I expected. His favourite place was the Pilbara where we had said goodbye to his grandad, he talked about the red Pilbara with such passion I wanted to say it took Russ away from us, but instead I just nodded in all the right places. After all, this was his trip as well.

Chapter 21

Night time fell quickly, I no longer wanted to sit outside and ponder who did what today, I wanted my bed. By eight pm it was a quick wash and a good night to all, the three of us settling down with books. Soon we were all fast asleep.

Our next destination was Monkey Mia. I wanted to show Jess the dolphins, and this time the tourist advertising came in very handy. It was not a long drive, and we went straight into a caravan park for an overnight booking, the office full of information on what, where and how to do it all.

Gilly wanted to watch dolphins as well, so I thought why not all three of us go, and we went to watch these beautiful mammals at feeding time on the water's edge. We fought for a space between the overseas tourists who pushed, shoved, yelled and slapped the water trying to attract them their way. The poor ranger was so busy trying to keep one particular lively Asian family at bay. They had started bombing the water with huge hunks of bread and didn't have time to notice one very small dolphin behind them eating the fish bits that floated out of their container. It was so tiny it seemed no-one else had noticed it. I took Jess by the hand and led him into the water we waited quietly, hoping for one small encounter.

The dolphin swivelled over on its side and looked me straight in the eye, its face was amazing. Jess stroked it and I put my hand under its chin and held it, my voice just above a whisper, talking to it as if it was small lost child. I have no idea how long we spent doing that, I just knew it had touched my soul deep inside. It backed its way out of my hand, its little tail fluke working furiously, then off it darted to hide in the depths somewhere reminding me of a small child who had been caught with its hand in the cookie jar. I could have sworn it smiled at me.

Gilly's voice broke through my daydreaming. 'Geez, you're sure lucky being able to have that sort of karma with dolphins.'

The ranger overheard and said, 'What dolphin? I'm still trying to call them in for the feed schedule.'

I looked at Gilly and Jess, shaking my head and leading the way back to our home. My heart was in heaven. I could not believe what had just happened and I felt ten feet tall, any sad heaviness had gone, none of us sure of what just happened but happy with the outcome.

Jess skipped all the way back to the bus, 'Nana, I patted a dolphin, and no one saw us.'

'Well honey, the dolphin must have known how special you are.' I repeated the story I had heard about how a dolphin knows when you're very sad, hurt or lonely and swim up to you to make sure you smile again, after all, it did have a huge smile on its gorgeous little face, enough to share for the three of us. I had to admit amongst all my adventures this was one I would never ever forget.

A small place called Dongara was the plan next day, then maybe two more days to home in Perth, and to Rae and Jono.

Dongara another small seaside town with quite a bustling community around it. Time to shop for tonight's dinner as tomorrow night we would be in Perth.

'Do we stop here for the night?' Gilly asked as she pulled over.

'Yes,' I said. 'It's one more night on the road then back home to Perth,' her face alight with excitement. Soon we could be planning our trip to New Zealand but it depended on how secure I felt in all aspects. This time no pool, no eating takeaways for dinner; it was scrambled eggs on toast, a hot shower, make up the beds, read books and sleep for an early take off next morning.

I love the skyline of Perth, you can see the tall buildings from afar, and to me the, silhouette of the Bell tower is perfect. The streets are wide and clean, most of them lined with trees, and within twelve hours I would be seeing all that. I felt content and safe to be going home. I loved being on the road, but I knew I loved being in my home as well. I imagined driving down the Graham Farmer freeway onto the Tonkin Highway, a main artery into Perth, then one hour from the city was home in Rockingham. I was so excited about it all and could not wait to plonk my bum onto a non-moving seat, put my feet up and relax with no added twelve-year old responsibilities. Did I love my grandson, Jess? Big time. I guess I was just tired.

And there suddenly was Perth in the late afternoon sun, all the dreaming of coming home now a reality. Finally, I was driving along the Rockingham foreshore, drinking in the sights and smells of where I lived. I'm sure the Pelicans knew of my return, as a large V shaped flock was in the sky as I turned into my driveway. I turned off the motor and ran to the front door.

Standing there with her arms out to me was Rae, her smile wide, her face glowing with health and happiness. Jess bounded out of the bus, almost knocking her over with joy. He wrapped his arms around her, his adventure already pouring out of him. Four weeks in a bus with Nana and Gilly, the kangaroos, eagles, lizards, people he had met, what he had seen, his time with the dolphins, red earth of the Pilbara, and the fun times and sad times he'd had.

Rae gently put her hand over his mouth. 'Shush honey, let's wait till we are home then we can go over every little detail, plus I have some news for you,' she winked at me. 'Everything okay, Mum?' I nodded; my brain already busy with things to do.

Gilly walked inside and put her case in the guest room again, then went to the kitchen and put the jug on. Rae looked at me with surprise. I offered no explanation only, 'Talk later.' I watched her and Jess walk down our driveway, noticing the way Jess patted the bus as he passed. 'Bye Mermaid,' he said.

I watched as they drove off to their home, then I sank down into Russ's favourite chair looking out towards the garden we both loved so much. As the sun set, I smiled thinking how much I loved the way the sunlight played on the garden. I adored getting up, breathing the clean fresh air and early wide-awake birdsong, everything fresh and new, remembering Russ was the complete opposite. He would lie in bed for ages, then come dusk would sit in this chair enjoying the sunset, telling me every five minutes of the changes of colour in the sky as the sun went down, the way the wildlife settled onto branches and into the gardens nooks and crannies to await another day, the way the world quieted down. 'I miss you so much, Russ,' I whispered into the dusk.

'Cuppa, pet?' Gilly's voice interrupted my thoughts, and a welcome one at that. I knew I could sort it out with Gilly but for now I just wanted to sit and put my feet up in my comfortable home, 'I'm home,' singing in my mind.

A relaxing sleep in my bed was bliss and when the sun peeped through my curtains at five am the next morning I was up, did my yoga stretches, then as quietly as possible opened my home up to the early morning breeze. Today was the start of a new day. I was full of energy, now feeling I was able to have that much needed discussion with Gilly before I flung my lot in with hers and waved my home and Perth goodbye for a year.

Gilly was always a late riser, so I made myself an herbal tea and peeled a gorgeous fresh mango, compliments of Rae, as I wandered outside with my diary, juggling tea and juicy mango and trying to balance it all. I sat on my garden swing and wrote down all the things I wanted to discuss with her, all the jobs I had to do around the house if I decided to join her, and most importantly who would look after my home. Did I leave it empty or rent it out? The thought sent shivers along my spine. Some stranger in my bed? I don't think so.

I suddenly realised it was the end of January, tomorrow was the first of February. Where had the past year gone? What had I done in that year? The wind ruffled all the bright yellow stickers that stuck out of my diary as if saying, 'Look what you've done. Look how much you have grown.' I opened my small, red book on our life and travels. It was full of small road maps, small sketches of roadhouses we had been into, stunning bare trees that fires had denuded, still strong and standing their ground, and all the scribblings of the day's accomplishments. I also noticed two entries from Gilly, which annoyed me greatly as my diary was off limits, full stop. No one read my thoughts and feelings except me.

I decided to say something when she was up. But for now, time out for me to ponder and meander amongst my plants, thinking of a few things I would like to do to improve this overgrown garden, pick a few roses and put them in water, and scribble a few lines of poetry.

I had also written down some plans. I wanted to show Gilly around Rockingham, wanted to saunter down the café strip and eat a gelato ice-cream, sit on the boardwalk watching dolphins or pelicans swim by as dusk slipped into navy blue night, show how the stars here seemed reachable, the sky so clear. I wanted to show off Safety Bay via my favourite fruit and vegie shop, the Malibu Delicatessen, to buy the most decadent fresh fruit, then drive to the pond in Safety Bay where multicoloured sails of wind surfers flew across the blue water and watch in awe the aeronautics of these folk who braved the waters, or encouraged the learners who wobbled their way through the shallows till they took off.

A memory of Russ and I popped up. How we would get out of the car and cheer them on as they floated over the small white topped waves, their faces a mixture of horror and excitement? I wanted to show why I loved this place so much; the people always friendly, even the local chip shop welcomed me like a long-lost friend.

'Haven't seen you for yonks,' the Maori woman who owned it would yell out to me. I guess 'yonks' meant ages. I always smiled and waved back to her.

Another place I adored was Dwellingup, one hour from Rockingham, with its mix of past and present in the cafes and homes. The bed and breakfast villa where we stayed with its delightful trapeze bed in the master bedroom upstairs. We soon discovered every movement we made we swayed and laughing made it worse. I simply refused to make love, terrified we would fly out the large window opposite the bed. The grounds of this beautiful place were fabulous, full of bushes, and trees home to a very tiny marsupial that was almost extinct, a Black-Gloved Wallaby. Also, in Dwellingup, they had the Dinner Train that wound its way through bush with a five-course meal and wine, then you got back to the station after three hours eating, drinking and enjoying your meal, the bed and breakfast owner's car there to take you back. Russ and I had such a fun time. I knew I had to make a decision. Do I stay here in Rockingham safe and secure with family and friends, or go to New Zealand with Gilly for another adventure?

Chapter 22

First of all, some toast and a morning read of the newspaper. I knew I was putting off the inevitable, but who could resist the fresh warm morning air and a relax on my garden swing. I for one could not. I'm very glad I took this time out just for me. As soon as I went inside to make some toast the phone rang and that was it. An avalanche of rolling emotions was now in motion.

The phone call was from Rae. She had told Jess about Jono's proposal of moving in together, then after a while, marriage. Jess's reaction was the biggest tantrum she had ever seen; he threw things around his room until she went in and calmed him down. I had no answers to give her, I suggested she leave it alone for a while.

Then Gilly was up and showered ready with toast and coffee in hand to discuss our trip. We sat together until late that day writing down the pros and cons of New Zealand, leaving Perth and family, and being away for a year. She didn't have commitments but was certainly helpful in her suggestions, so what was stopping me?

It seemed silly such a small answer of yes or no could put into action such huge consequences. The day turning to dusk and still no answers, I admired Gilly's patience, I was impatient with myself. Why couldn't I throw my hands in the air and say see you all later, I'm off?

Gilly's blue eyes looked into mine, 'Because you care, because you have spent forty years building up this life for you and Russ, because you are who you are. It's okay to say no, you're not hurting anyone.' Gilly got up and hugged me,

'Tara, I'm leaving tomorrow. Let me know what you're going to do. I'm selling Dusty and intend to leave for New Zealand in one month, if you want to contact me you know my phone number.'

I wanted to cry.

'Thanks, Tara, for the wonderful trip up north to the Pilbara, and thank you for sharing that adventure with me. Keep safe and well, pet.' Then she packed her bag, leaving me to sort myself out. First, I felt put out as Gilly had insisted we share the costs of the trip up north, and so far, nothing was offered. I chastised myself mentally. *You need think differently now. You offered, she accepted, end of story.*

Gilly was leaving and I was just standing there numb. She threw her bag into her Jeep, backed it up, hitched Dusty on, clicked it all into place, attached this and that, waved to me, then drove off.

Suddenly my home was all mine again, my intentions of showing off Rockingham blown up in smoke, the bare patch where she had parked Dusty, empty. Just me, my house and the Metal Mermaid. I was all alone. Once that had hit me, I almost had an anxiety attack.

On the table lay Gilly's note with her number, so I stuck it on the fridge door. 'Thanks for everything, Gilly,' I murmured as tears ran down my cheeks. Why am I crying? I thought, but cry I did until it was all over. I sat at my kitchen table and cried until no more tears left. I was gut tired, so tired of feeling torn about what I wanted to do, my legs wobbled down the hallway to my bedroom, falling asleep almost instantly when my head hit the pillow. When I woke it was one am. I have no idea why I woke up, but suddenly I was wide-eyed and feeling brilliant.

I knew what I could and could not do. Somehow in my sleep the answer had fallen into place. I knew with such clarity what I would do and knew it was the right thing to do. I woke again at nine am, leapt out of bed and rang my daughter. 'Can you meet me at the

Dickson street library café in an hour?'

'Sure Mum,' she replied. 'What's up?'

'You'll know soon enough,' I laughed. Then I rang Gilly, her sleepy voice answered, 'Hello, pet. Did I forget something?'

'Yes, you did. Me.' I told her of my decision.

Gilly crowed, 'Brilliant, I'm going back to Brisbane for two weeks, do you want to meet me there?'

'Why not?' Once I had made that decision my plans for travel blossomed into reality at long last. It had been a few years since I had visited Brisbane.

Rae looked stunning: fresh, pretty face, dark tan and in very short shorts; meeting Jono had really upped her self-esteem. We hugged and she said I looked tired. I admitted I felt tired, then told her of the dilemma I had been through with Gilly's offer and how I had struggled with her sexual preference, to which Rae laughed, 'Gilly? No really? Oh, Mum you're not thinking of coming out are you?' A friendly slap on her hand shut her up.

'No Rae, I'm thinking.' Then taking a big breath I said, 'Why don't you, Jono and Jess rent my home? I hate the thought of any strangers renting it, and it's also part of you.'

Her eyebrows nearly shot off her face, 'Mum that's brilliant! We have been searching for just the right place for us all and found nothing but apartments.'

I suggested, 'Maybe Jess will be okay with Jono and you together if he is on familiar ground.' Then it was time to tell her of my plans with Gilly and New Zealand. Her arm shot around me, 'Mum you're fabulous,' she cried.

'I know,' I chortled. 'I surprise myself at times.' We agreed to all have dinner at home that night to discuss the finer points.

My next heart stopping chore for the day was go to a caravan dealer see if he was interested in selling the bus for me. I drove back to the dealer where we bought it. Yes, he was interested, things were slow and there was a backlog of caravans but not a mobile home. He offered to come out the next day and give me a price, plus his commission. Then I had another great thought. Why not sell Russ's Jeep while I was at it? Once home, I rang the local newspaper and advertised Russ's four-door, gold-coloured Jeep. I remembered his voice so well when he bought it, 'Hey Tara, electric leather seats that will keep your bum warm.'

He had loved his Jeep but sadly it was of no use to me. I arranged the advert to go in the local paper for Friday, today was Tuesday. Then it was outside with mop and buckets to lather up the Metal Mermaid inside and out until it shone.

I took the inside apart, cleaning it all, putting it all back into place; I was taking all the priceless memories with me in my heart.

Rae, Jono and Jess arrived at six pm as I was putting all the cleaning gear away. I had already prepared a salad and asked Jono to barbeque the steaks. Rae handed him a beer, pouring the two of us a cold white wine. Jono had heard the news, so had Jess, both of them really excited. Jono thanking me for trusting my home and family to his care, Jess stood beside me his arm around my waist, 'Do I keep my old room, Nana?'

'Of course, Jess, you're to help looking after our home for me while I'm away.'

'When can I come to New Zealand?' he asked.

'One day soon I promise, but not this time.'

So, it was settled. I entrusted my home to my daughter, her partner and grandson and all I asked was the amenities were paid, the garden looked after, and the house kept clean. Someone that loved it would be living in it, and I had no mortgage to pay, so had no worries there.

Jono and Rae where beaming from ear to ear. 'Will I tell her, or do you want to?' Rae said. My heart did a little thump as Rae said, 'Mum, we are getting married when you come back from your trip.' Wow! Things were moving along at a fast trot. 'Good for you,' I cried, and we had another glass of wine, this time toasting her dad and much-loved departed grandparents from both sides. Rae, her humour always offbeat, commented, 'You'll soon be departed as well, Mum.' Where did she get her off-beat humour?

Chapter 23

I attempted to sleep that night but was so excited. I was woken by the front doorbell; flinging on my dressing gown, mumbling to myself, if this is those Jehovah's Witnesses I'm going to slam the door shut. Instead, at the door stood my neighbour, Perry. It had been ages since we had seen each other. 'Perry, come on in, I'll put the jug on.'

Perry had been a godsend when Russ had been away, saving my bacon so many times with home repairs, kids and transport, and I had helped them as well; it seemed we had been neighbour's forever. We had the occasional meal together; they did not socialise too much as Nancy, his wife, was not well for a very long time. They had been a lovely couple.

Perry had arrived on my doorstep with news; he was moving on, selling up as his home was too big for him now. His other news stopped me in my tracks. He was going to buy a caravan and do a bit of travel, he had met a woman, Frances, and she was going with him for company. I felt sad at his leaving the neighbourhood; he was a true gentleman. We finished our chat but just as he was leaving my brain kicked in, 'Perry,' I almost shouted, the poor man's very large white eyebrows went up. 'Do you want a caravan or a bus? Mine is for sale.' He stopped and pondered.

'That's an interesting situation, let me ask Frances. I'll get back to you.' My intuition told me they would buy it from me, and sure enough late that afternoon Perry and Francis both came over to have a good look at the Metal Mermaid. Frances was so petite, like an ancient doll with curly white hair, and deep brown eyes that held a naughty sense of humour. She was ever so slightly bent. 'Back problems,' she said. I felt like a healthy giant next to her fragility. I showed them the bus telling them about the quirks and how much I had enjoyed driving her.

Then we discussed the price, without having to pay any commission it was fairly cheap, or so I thought. They thought it was a bargain, so for five hundred less than we had paid for it, it was all signed and sealed over a glass of port. They asked why the name 'Metal Mermaid'. I told them of my memories; the lake of mud we got stuck in at Albany, how she had floated and been waterproof all the way, no matter what weather hit us. Suddenly it struck me that they might change her name and I wanted to cry again, my eyes saying what I could not for fear of sounding like a two-year old. Frances saw my face. 'Metal Mermaid it is,' she said.

I was now a lot wealthier than when I woke this morning and rang Gilly to tell her.

'You don't waste any time, do you?'

'Gilly, with the time I have left to me, I want to live as much as I can.'

'Good for you, pet.'

'Oh Gilly, one more thing: please stop calling me "pet", my name is "Tara".'

'Righto, no worries P– oh sorry, "Tara" it is from now on.'

I rang Rae and told her of my progress.

'Hell, Mum that was quick! You are meant to go, aren't you?'

'Seems that way, honey.'

Rae asked me if it was alright if they moved in as soon as possible, paying rent was sucking their savings out from them. 'That's fine with me,' I said.

Metal Mermaid

I was soon to have a houseful again.

My day had started and ended with one major obstacle out of my way. The Metal Mermaid now sat next door and I could hear Perry and Francis rummaging about inside, delighted I had left almost all the gear in her. I sat down feeling like I had run a marathon. Relaxing for me was not on the agenda as no sooner I had sat down when the caravan man arrived to look over the bus. I had forgotten all about him.

I was most apologetic as I told him it had already sold. As he walked away he spied the 'for sale' sign on the Jeep. 'How much?' he enquired. I told him what I wanted, and he went over it with a fine-tooth comb.

'I'll be back tomorrow to see it in the daylight,' he said. Fine with me, I thought, I just wanted to lie down, I had no energy and a headache.

I poached eggs on toast for my dinner then rang all my friends and the clubs I belonged to, telling them I was going away for one year, most of them agog or jealous I had made such a big decision

'What has happened to the careful, steady Tara we all know and love?' the president of my art club asked.

'Time to change,' I answered, 'or I will never go anywhere.'

This lady I truly admired; she had travelled around the world, crossed so many continents, her art now in museums all over the world, her deep infectious chuckle came over the phone as she said, 'You are so right. Enjoy! I will see you once you're home again.'

Time for my bed and to breathe deeply, today and yesterday had gone with a whoosh.

As I settled back into comfy pillows with a book and hot Milo, the phone rang. 'Clark from Clarkson's Caravan Sales here, Tara. I will be around tomorrow to definitely buy the Jeep. Will you be home around ten in the morning?'

'Why yes, I will make sure I am,' I replied.

'See you then,' he replied.

Sleep? What's that? In two days, I was thousands of dollars better off. I wanted to dance and sing, excitement building at my future. It's midnight, you silly woman, I chided myself. No one's awake at this hour. Go to sleep. I'm sure the clock smirked at two am when all I could do was lie there and listen to its ticking, thinking to myself this is not happening and I'm going to wake up and it's all been a dream. I hardly slept at all, so when Gilly rang at seven am, I was feeling quite jittery. She rang to tell me her lover Wendy was out of town, her mobile phone number disconnected, her voice betraying her tears. What do you say to a fifty-plus woman who is heartbroken and who is very different to you? Simple, I guess, it's the same feeling worldwide; one of despair, abandonment and sorrow. Gilly needed a shoulder and I was here.

'Why don't you fly back here, stay with me until we have it all sorted here, then we fly out to New Zealand from here? How does that sound?'

The relief in her voice was obvious as she thanked me for my generosity. To me, a friend in need was just that. Gilly texted me her flight details two hours later, arriving tomorrow on Qantas flight 476 at two-thirty pm.

That day was a mad house. Rae turning up with boxes of things and stacking them in her old room. Jono almost tripping over as he ran in and out with boxes of gear from their villa in Armadale, stacking them in the garage. Jess sorting out his room. Clark turning up taking the Jeep for a test drive. My next-door neighbours, Perry and Frances, coming over to ask about water storage and how it all worked.

The drive to the airport was peaceful. I had opted to take Jess with me, not telling him who was arriving, I decided to keep it a secret, his questions answered when he saw who it was. 'It's Gilly!' he said, rushing over and hugging her. She pushed him away saying, 'Come on, mate, it's not been that long.'

Jess looked hurt at the rebuff. I also thought it was a strange action from one who claimed she was his friend. Gilly looked tired and sad like the wind had been blown right out of her sails; I felt she was grieving for a lost love. Even though I would never understand her passion for the same sex, I still knew what grief felt like; my heart went out to her.

On the drive home I warned her, 'It's nuts at my house today, Gilly.' Then Jess took over the conversation until Gilly snapped, 'Okay, I get the picture.' Again, the rebuff hurt him, and I was now concerned.

'Are you sure there is room for me?' she asked.

'Of course,' I answered, rearranging in my head the sleeping arrangements, thinking an airbed in the lounge or my room for Jess won't kill him so Gilly can have his room. Problem solved until we get ourselves sorted. Hmm… Not quite that simple.

Once home, I found all of Russ's clothing now in the garage. I had carefully packed them all, storing them in the spare room. It hurt to see his clothing just dumped outside.

I also found my dining room furniture rearranged in my home, and large pot plants now dotted over the lounge floor with no protection from water leakage under them. This annoyed me even more. Jono was an electrical enthusiast and was ensconced in my lounge, plugging in his network of wires into my TV, silver boxes of all shapes and sizes scattered over the floor. I could hear Russ now, 'Oi! Hang on mate, you could ask before you take over,' that is if Russ would allow Jono in our home. As I said, Russ was quite racist in his view of each to his own country, so when Rae suggested she and Jono take over my room as it was the master bedroom with an ensuite, it was the last straw. I blew up in front of all of them.

'There is no way young lady you are taking over my home while I'm still living in it, so furniture back in place please, your pot plants in the patio area or outside, and Jono, please remove all your stereo gear from my lounge room as Jess is sleeping in there.'

Jess squealed, 'Nana, I want to sleep in my room.' Gilly looked shocked at the tempers flaring. Rae flounced out muttering, 'Overbearing sensitive mothers,' Jono moodily dumping his boxes into a large cardboard box with a surly retort of, 'Thought I was welcome,' while Jess slumped sulking in Grandad's chair.

'Happy families, Gilly. Welcome to the fold,' I said.

Enough, I thought. If anyone was going to have a temper tantrum it was me. I slammed the front door and shouted, 'Shut up the lot of you. This is my home, full stop. When Gilly and I leave, then you can play musical bedrooms, but for now, show some respect or leave,' to which Rae said quietly, 'Gilly and you now is it?' I was shocked into silence.

'How dare you be so rude,' I said.

'Oh, come on Mum. Since you two met it's been Gilly this and Gilly that. We all know what's been going on, you're beside each other as much as possible.'

'You rude, dirty girl. Get out NOW! And take your family with you. I will pack your things myself and put them on the driveway for you tomorrow.'

I had never spoken to my daughter like this before, it even shocked me as the words fell out of my mouth. Gilly was now sitting in the dark conservatory.

'I'll find a motel,' she offered. 'Could you drop me off there?'

'You will not! This is my home and I'm still the lady of the house. Stay.' Wow, I thought. I've got tough in my travels. Once, I would have melted with the fear of disapproval, trying to pat people better.

Metal Mermaid

The family had left leaving the front door wide open. I slammed it shut, thinking to myself, good, learn some respect and manners, Rae.

I saw an envelope on the foyer table addressed to me. It was a cheque for the Jeep; I had completely forgotten all about it. I felt shocked I had not even missed it in the garage as I was so incensed by Russ's clothing. I hadn't completed the transfer papers, and the note on the envelope said, 'Pop them into the caravan sales park tomorrow please.'

Gilly helped me pack and sort out Rae's belongings. The next day both of us very quiet knowing this was a serious situation for my family. I waited until mid-afternoon, my heart squeezing tight with disappointment in my daughter.

Gilly helped me carry their belongings and put them all down the end of the driveway. Every time a car went by we both went to the window to see if it was them, or that no one was stealing their things. When they did arrive, not once did Rae or Jono look up at my windows and wave, they simply packed their things in their car and left. I knew my daughter. By now she would have rung and apologised, so why not now? So many *why's* racing through my head.

The silence between Jess, Rae and I was awful. We normally rang every day to say, 'Hi, how's your day going.' Four days went by and nothing. I carried on making the bookings and plans as I had promised myself, banking the cash for everything I had sold. The garden now trimmed right back thanks to Gilly; she had worked very hard. 'Got to earn my bed and brekkie,' she claimed.

I had decided I was going to lock up everything and just go, this was my time now. We had talked almost all through the night of the family blow up, Gilly saying very little, just kept asking me if I was sure I was doing the right thing. It infuriated me that my daughter could walk in and take over, relegating me to the spare room, telling me in no uncertain terms I was gay and her rude boyfriend was just as ignorant, both carrying on like spoilt children when I had made a generous offer. 'Gilly, for the last time yes, I am sure I want to do this and want to travel with you, end of story.'

In less than a week I was leaving for New Zealand, Gilly and I went to the travel agent and collected all the information on camping sites in New Zealand we could find as I did not want to stay with her family or backpack. I made flight arrangements over the internet using my credit card. We were flying out in one weeks' time and I also paid for Gilly's fare on the promise once Dusty had sold, she would definitely pay me back. If I had a niggle of doubt, it soon disappeared as the Salvation Army truck arrived taking away all of Russ's clothing, the furniture in his study and anything else I could add to the pile.

There was one thing I kept from the pile that was growing with an alarming rate, Russ's winter anorak. I had bought it for him on one of our overseas trips, Gilly had seen it and advised I keep it, as we would be spending some time in the South Island where there would be snow.

Still no apology from Rae and Jess. Frances and Perry came over one night at my invitation. He had sold the house, a certain shift in our perspective of life as we knew it. I raised my glass. 'Cheers,' I said, 'May the Metal Mermaid take you safely wherever you go.' Gilly raised her glass, 'May we all find what we want at the end of our rainbows.'

Frances and Perry raised their glass's and quipped, 'May our glasses always be half full.'

It was the end of an era for us all.

Rae had her Dad's stubborn streak, her righteous, judgmental streak always causing trouble at school and work until she was in her twenties. I had hoped she had learned to shut her big mouth before she caused irreparable damage. My phone never rang with an apology, hoping when I answered the impatient ring I would hear 'I'm sorry Mum.'

I made sure the alarm company knew I was going away for a year and we put dust sheets over the lounge and dining room furniture. The bank manager showed me how to make automatic payments on the quarterly rates and how to change money around on my new mobile phone. Yes, I was now one of the cool people with a new mobile phone that does everything but cook dinner.

It was locking up time, *andiamo* time. As I pulled the key out of the lock, next door gave one last beep of their horn and off they drove. 'Happy camping folks,' I whispered, watching as the taillights of the Metal Mermaid disappear around the corner. My heart did a little creak of sorrow, the dream of Russ and I adventuring together was gone forever.

No apology happened, not even a phone call just to say, 'Hi Mum, how are you?' So I gave in and rang Jess on his Mobile. 'Nana?' he whispered.

'Yes, honey it's me.'

I could hear muffled voices then, 'I'm not… ' It went to dial tone, the disconnection beep cut into me deeply. Obviously, Jess was not allowed to talk to me either. The only contact I received was an envelope in the letter box with the spare house keys in it.

It hurt like a paper cut and went through and around my chest, repeating over and over, *you should have tried to contact her to say sorry for being so cross*. On the night Frances and Perry were over I had told them about my family's behaviour and accusations. Their advice was, 'Why should *you* apologise? You opened your home and heart to them.'

'She's my daughter and Jess is my only grandson,' I said.

'Makes no difference' Frances advised. 'If you accept this abusive behaviour it's condoning it, first and foremost,' and added, 'You have a right to be who you want to be, and if you have chosen to be gay or a scotch egg, then so be it.' I knew she was right.

It was five am, and Gilly and I were at the airport. With one small suitcase each, we checked in, our cases now on the conveyer belt and us on the escalator going up to the duty-free department. I was overwhelmingly tired, and it showed, huge dark circles under my eyes. I wanted to slump in a chair like my grandson, Jess, had done. I wanted to whimper in pain. It hurt not to say goodbye with 'love you' and 'see you in a year'. Then anger stormed in and said, *Tara, if you're friends and neighbours can come up to you and wish you well and safe journey, what the hell is wrong with your daughter?*

There were too many confusing emotions. Gilly handed me a hot coffee, her face was beaming, the smile so wide it lit her way. 'Guess what?' she cried. 'Dusty has been sold.'

'That's marvellous, Gilly. When?' 'Yesterday, I guess,' she said. 'I just opened my messages, and there it was, the money is in the bank. Yahoo, we can go to New Zealand without a worry now.'

'Oh my God, Gilly! Do you mean to say you have been relying on the sale of Dusty to get by on?' I almost choked on the words.

'Gotta have faith, sister,' she replied.

Gilly's actions at times worried me. My thoughts of doom and gloom about family where now replaced with what if she had not sold her caravan and Jeep, would she have relied on me to finance this trip we had planned together? Gilly said, 'I can now pay you back for my fare once we arrive and I'm on the internet.' My brain clicked into gear. 'Why not now, Gilly? We both have the same internet services on our mobiles?'

Gilly had promised to pay for her fare every time I broached the subject, but I had not seen a cent for staying with me for over a month, plus now the airfares. Gilly's face darkened to deep red, 'Are you asking me to pay you back immediately?'

'Yes, I am, Gilly. We have the time, don't we?' I thought she was going to explode, her face now scarlet.

'Tara, are you calling me dishonest?'

'No, Gilly, I'm not. I would like you to repay me for the airfare that's all.' My gut was churning. Gilly stomped off tapping at her phone, then holding the phone in my direction yelling at me, 'There's not much left now.'

Gilly, it's not my problem, I thought. Please be an adult. Too late fate cried, *you are about to be strapped into an airtight metal vessel and your holiday is about to begin.* My gut rolled over, 'Oh no, I can't be sick, not now.'

Chapter 24

It was well known among our circle of friends and family if Tara was super stressed then Tara threw up. I knew I had to breathe deeply, listen to the plane music and relax those muscles as I watched the people wandering in and finding their allocated seats. I knew I could not leave without telling my family, 'I love you.' I grabbed my phone and texted, 'I love you both, bye until we talk again,' and pressed send. I sent the same message to Jess, then switched it off for take-off.

'Too late for regrets now,' Gilly said. 'New Zealand land of the Long White Cloud here we come,' nudging me when the very good looking young female cabin attendant leaned over her to ask me to place my bag in the overhead locker.

'Gilly behave,' I mouthed, my face flaming at what her nudging and eye rolling suggested, I was old enough to be her mum. I was going to have to watch this friend of mine or I could end up in trouble. Five hours in a metal tube is not comfortable at all. Being stuck in the middle of two other people as I was, is not comfortable either. Gilly was quite at home; she had the aisle seat, getting up and down like a mad fiddler's elbow, I found her annoying.

Her constant flirting with the female crew was embarrassing, her giggle wandering around the plane. Shouting, 'Let me off now, please,' to a hundred plus people was what I really wanted to do. Instead I tried to doze, watch the TV or read, but one thought kept trickling though my mind, 'what have I done?' I gave up on sleep. Wandering off to the bathroom I spied an empty row of seats at the very back, perfect for me to do some writing. I asked one of the crew members if this was possible? She was standing in the galley making a coffee for one of the passengers, Gilly was also in the galley flirting and chattering nonstop to who she obviously hoped was her next lover. I felt awful thinking things like this, but she had made it so obvious, cornering this young lady every chance she got and talking at her.

The crew member I asked about the spare seats looked at where I had been sitting, then looked at Gilly, looked back at me and nodded. 'Of course you can.' I went and got my small onboard bag and settled down right at the back, on my own. Ahh peace. Gilly was asked to return to her seat by the hostess she was flirting with, a distinct no-nonsense tone to her voice; Gilly complied looking so angry, the way she stormed off then plonked down into her seat was not pretty. This space was what I needed and the words flowed like music on paper like never before; I did not even notice the cabin crew preparing to land until I was asked to move back to my designated seat and buckle up.

We had a two-hour stopover in Sydney, so I went and did some duty-free shopping, stocking up on my favourite perfume and body cream at the L'Occitane shop. What heaven; you can feel the body relax as the heady perfumes invade your nostrils like butter on hot toast as it sinks in and you just want to gulp it back into your lungs.

When I last saw Gilly, she was fairly optimistic about her new friend on the plane. Now all I saw was that scowl that preceded her bad temper, not knowing what had happened, my thoughts wary, what do I ask? I wanted to comfort her like a mother, but another emotion kicked in, a warning that this was Gilly. Any sort of rebuttal, refusal or in plain speaking *if it did not go her way, her life was crap*. I seemed to be on my guard lately, a lot of appeasing her or patting better. Yes, she had helped me when Russ was ill and I was very grateful for her kindness, but I owed her nothing. In my book, kindness and love is something you give, no one can force it from you and I was getting tired of the posturing and brain games she played. Maybe New Zealand was a bad idea. I thought, oh well give it a go. If it does not work out, then so be it, I will do something else. I was financially secure so could do whatever I wanted to. I remembered one of the sayings Russ had when he was driving in the outback, 'I'm living the dream babe.' Hopefully I could say that as well.

Buying the new 'Eat Pray Love' book by Elizabeth Gilbert, I put my nose firmly into it, waiting for our departure call to New Zealand. Gilly could sort her own mess.

Our plane was ready and at long last we were boarding. I noticed we had the same crew as the previous flight, the young hostess who had let me sit at the back greeted me with a smile, it was not flirtatious, it was more like a 'hello again'.

Gilly saw the exchange between us and fumed, her wise crack as we sat down and buckled in was nasty. 'What's the deal between you two?' she nodded at the hostess. Now was the time to speak my mind while she was belted in. 'Gilly, if you continue like this I'm not too sure of our holiday together. I've been through so much this last year, for God's sake, give your hormones a rest please.' Her mouth gaped.

'I mean it, I've had it. You're acting as old as Jess and I won't stand for it. If you're going to be my travel companion, then try to be reasonable; we've agreed to travel together for a year, or we can call it quits right now before we are in too deep'.

My intuition spoke *you're already in too deep;* we were in the air, on our way to New Zealand.

I was not spoken to during the take-off. Once in the air I got up out of my seat and again approached the hostess to find out if there were any spare seats. 'Yes,' she said pointing to the middle row of four seats. With one passenger sat on the very end, I could have the other end. 'Lovely, thank you.' I grabbed my gear and sat down, away from the black, fuming Gilly. At least I could write and read here in peace, the man at the other end was asleep.

My sense of humour took over I wrote a poem called Silly Gilly, knowing she would never read it as deep reading was not what she liked to do. Maybe a glossy magazine for one short article, or my diary, but I had noticed boredom set in quickly. Gilly craved attention, that's why Jess loved to be with her; they were great play mates.

As we flew out of Sydney the pilot called our attention to an unusual cloud formation. There in the sky were three huge tornado shaped columns of golden clouds, the colour caused by the glow of bush fires and the sun. The pilot gave us all the run down on what sort of weather caused these formations, saying they were harmless and quite rare to see this late in the day, my camera busy clicking these truly beautiful formations. Then as dusk deepened and we flew over the Tasman Sea, the blinds drawn for a snooze by some passengers, another announcement was made, 'If you look to your right, ladies and gentlemen.'

Staining the night sky, were deep crimson, blood red clouds reflecting from the fires. It was a scary thought that folks were dying, losing their homes, animals burned and in pain and I was off on a holiday. There is nothing I could do but send money to a charity to help, once I had landed in New Zealand.

Time for walk and a stretch around the plane, two hours to go before we land. I touched Gilly's shoulder as I passed her, like a child she flinched away, tossing her head away from me, almost turning her whole body in the opposite direction. I sighed; this was not good.

I walked on around the plane and back to my seat, not once did Gilly offer any sort of smile or recognition, her body language screaming 'go away'. Once landed, we were off to immigration. Huge totem poles with Tikis carved into them greeted us, and once through, we went to collect our luggage and then after customs, the exit door slid open.

I was now In New Zealand, but now what? Gilly nowhere in sight, she had either walked ahead or was lagging behind, avoiding me. Then Gilly walked past me, and I ran after her, my case banging against my leg. 'Hey there!' She walked on. 'Come on, silly. I'm on your side, remember?' I said.

Her reply was, 'Fuck off, Grandma.'

What?

She walked towards the exit doors outside, waving to people that were obviously there to greet her. Then she was gone, and I was left standing there with no one to ask, 'What the hell just happened?'

To say I was stunned was not the correct word; I was paralysed. I was in New Zealand, a stranger in a country I knew nothing about and didn't know anyone but Gilly, who had just flicked me off without a backwards glance.

I was literally on my own. My first reaction was terror, the world tilted for one second. I quickly sat down, common-sense and logic skittered around my head, and taking a big breath I instructed myself, the time is midnight, what can you do, Tara? Come on girl, think.

I walked to the taxi rank and asked the lady driver could she take me to a decent hotel. She was an older Maori woman. 'Sure love,' she said. 'Hop in.'

As we sped off onto the Auckland motorway heading for the city, stopping at blurred red lights, the tears so close I just wanted to sit in a quiet room and cry. The driver kept looking at me in the rear-view mirror, finally asking, 'Anything I can help with, love?' I told her I was stranded in New Zealand. She looked shocked. 'Why not join me in a cuppa love, see if I can help you?'

I agreed to stopping off, which we did in a place called Mangere. She stopped outside a quiet coffee shop that was about to close. We sat in her taxi with cups full of sweet hot tea and I told I had agreed to travel together with a friend around New Zealand for one year; the hot tears now slipping down my cheeks unashamedly, ending my tale with, 'I had so far financed the entire trip to be told to "F off" at the airport.'

All she did was listen, sip on her tea and then said, 'Well that makes a change. I expected a man somewhere in the tale. Let's get you into a room for the night then tomorrow is another day. I'm Margi, what's your label?'

'Tara,' I hiccupped.

The hotel we found was cheap but clean. Margi gave me her business card saying, 'Call if you need a ride,' and off she drove.

Tomorrow is another day, I thought as the hot shower water hit my sore back, tomorrow is another day as the hot water poured over my aching head, but it's already tomorrow was my last waking thought.

What on earth do I do now? Then, thankfully, sleep claimed me.

.

Chapter 25

Is it wrong for a sixty-plus year-old woman to burst into loud sobs? 'I just want to go home.' Well if it is, I'm guilty, as that's what I did when I woke up and freaked. I wanted to catch the plane back to Perth as soon as possible. I rang the airport from the hotel's reception desk as my new phone was playing up and could feel the panic building up inside.

'I'm sorry madam, all our flights are fully booked until Friday. I would be most happy to make your booking now, or you can use the internet,' was the reply to my request.

Okay, I'm here for four days until Friday, my thinking jagged but becoming clear. I'm safe in this little motel, so I will have a look around Auckland, find an internet café or mall and book the flight home. I felt a little brighter now I was organising myself, doing something proactive. I had breakfast, showered then went to reception, 'Could I book my room for the rest of the week?'

'Yes madam, will you pay with cash or credit?'

Next step, ring Margi who was more than happy to taxi me around to a car hire place. Her smile was so welcome, 'Hello there Tara, you look a little better not like a possum caught in the headlights.'

Margi was so large, as was her magical chuckle that made her whole-body wobble, but I was still not able to laugh; I felt like I had been side swiped.

On our way to the car rentals by the airport, Margi gave me her opinion, 'I thought about you last night, that friend of yours needs a darn good kick up her rear.'

'I could not agree more, Margi,' I said. She continued, 'You're better off without trash like her leaning on you for a year, you don't need her. Why don't you just go and do what you came here to do? Tour New Zealand. You won't be sorry; you may never have this time again.'

It was a light bulb moment for me. 'You're right,' I said. 'It's not the end of the world for me, I guess I was in shock that she would do that to me.'

Margi stopped her cab. 'Well, what's it to be? Wanna have some fun first or wanna go home to Aussie?'

I chose the first option, 'Fun please, I've had enough of tears.'

'Righto, let's sort you out,' she said. Margi was worth her weight in gold, and we decided that for a fee, she would drive me all around the tourist spots in Auckland.

'It's cheaper than a hire car,' she said, 'but no one believes me when I tell them.' I did not care really, I was grateful for her chatter, her knowledge of Auckland and suburbs, and if it cost twice the amount of a hire car well, so be it, I could afford it.

Auckland was very busy; we visited so many places, some I got out and took photos, some I told Margi to drop me off and pick me up later, and some we bypassed with her sage advice, 'You don't want to go there love.'

In four days, I had seen most of Auckland. Margi arrived at the hotel at eight am and I was dropped off by six pm.

'Gotta feed the kids on time,' she would say. I learned she had eight kids and an old man for a husband.

Margi was simple, honest, looked at life without blinkers on and called a spade a spade. On the Thursday, she picked me up as normal only this time yelling at me, 'Hurry up, get in fast, I have to show you this.'

Off we went to a caravan sales yard and in there was the smallest caravan I have ever seen.

'Perfect for you girl,' she cried; Margi was determined I was going to see her country.

I stumbled and stuttered, 'Gee, I don't know, Margi.'

'Ah, come on,' she said, 'be a devil.'

Oh boy, a devil is not what I am. I'm Tara from Rockingham in Western Australia I thought but go in I did. I looked at it carefully inside and out, all the time trying to channel Russ's advice about buying a lemon.

Margi offered her husband, Tom, to look underneath it and check it all out. She rang her home, barked an order, and half an hour later the old man turned up and looked underneath, looked inside and believe me, if this man–another large person–could fit inside it, well that proved it was shock proof for me.

'All good lady,' Tom said.

I offered him payment for his time, he shyly refused, his bulk struggling back inside his car, then he drove away. Now it was down to business with the dealer, Mark. If I did see shark written across his forehead, I was not worried; I had my personal bulldog with me, Margi. I knew she would stand up to a cyclone to get the best deal for her best customer, as she called me. Mark proved to me that not all you see is what you get as he pointed out it was a teardrop van made popular in the 1950's. This little gem was one of the last ones in New Zealand from that era. It had been fully upholstered and refurbished, it smelt clean and new, there was nothing to fix. He showed me the little pull out kitchen that slid out from the back, so all my cooking was done outside. Inside was basic containing only a large single bed with a small light above the bed. In the roof was a large ceiling vent that popped open if I chose. In a tiny cupboard was a space for a toaster, plus they had made a small semi-lift base on the bed to store gear in, basically a bedroom on wheels. I loved it.

I could manage this all by myself, it was so light weight; a deep silver in colour and at the back I could imagine Mermaid II written across her tiny bum. I asked as many pertinent questions about the van as possible, trying hard to remember the questions I should ask. Margi made me smile, she wasn't too worried about the caravan. I signed on the dotted line and handed Mark my cheque. Emotions raged inside me, I wanted to snatch it back and say, 'I can't do this.'

Logically I knew I could, all I had to do was think through my situation, not react to my situation.

Oh no! What have you done, my mind said as my heart gave a little skip of joy. Mark gave me one warning, 'Don't overload it, she won't like it.'

'Can I leave it here for a day, until I find a vehicle?'

He produced a large red *SOLD* sticker, putting it across the teardrop van.

'My pleasure,' Mark said.

'Now,' Margi announced, 'all you need is a little car to tow it.'

I will be forever grateful to Margi. As we trawled car market after car market she bullied, harassed, told off and argued until I stepped in stopping the haranguing by saying, 'Margi, I really like this little Jeep.'

It was a bright red, two-seater, manual–perfect. It had room in the back for any extra gear I might need. Again, Tom was rung, orders given and he duly arrived, heaved and huffed his way into the Silverdale car yard, went over the Jeep with a fine tooth comb and gave me the thumbs up.

I bought the Jeep. I started her up, my hands sweating, my head thumping, my stomach rolling over. Oh no, not now, I thought, and sure enough I had to stop and throw up. Margi sat in her cab and patiently waited for me to climb back in the Jeep and follow her to the caravan dealer. Mark was surprised at the speed I had bought the car. He was very kind knowing this was my first attempt at caravanning on my own. He went over the Jeep as well, and once satisfied it would tow my Mermaid II he showed me twice how to hook up my little van. He even filled the gas bottle the water tank for me, wonderful! Thank you.

Margi then said, 'Where to now?'

'I have no idea Margi, back to the hotel, pack my gear, find a shop I can fit out the van, then I guess I'm away.' It had all happened so quickly.

That's exactly what happened. I packed my gear up, threw it into the Jeep, gave Margi a long hug thanking her for all her support, and paid her what I owed for my narrated sight-seeing tour around Auckland. She held me by the shoulders and belted out, 'We Are Women, Hear Us Roar.'

I burst out laughing and there I was, Tara was back again. Margi pointed to the right, 'That's Northland, beautiful country where my tribe, the Ngapuhi people, are from.' Then Margi pointed left, 'That's south. Keep going and you come to Wellington, then it's across to the South Island. Enjoy my country, Haere mai, welcome, to Aotearoa.'

She touched my nose with hers; this Maori Hongi is their greeting, then said, 'Haere rai, farewell, keep well and safe, and keep in touch please.'

I promised I would, driving out onto the motorway and turning right. This was now my journey.

I was as excited as I had been on my wedding day, all nervy and twitchy. I was on the road on my own and I was going to see New Zealand from the cape in Northland to the bluff in the South Island. My very first stop a camping store I had seen, almost next to where I had bought the Jeep at Silverdale just out of a seaside village called Orewa.

The store owner must have thought all his birthdays had arrived at once. I bought way too much, I know I did, I was making sure I was warm and fed; I had been told about the huge amount of rain New Zealand has even in their summer. The store manager guided me to Orewa where I joined the Automobile Association for car and caravan insurance, like the RAC back home. They advised me to go to the licensing place to make sure all was good with the license plates. I did this finding the van and car was legally registered in my name and good for the road. One very kind traffic policeman popping out and checking it all for me, he pointed out it was, 'Nearly five pm, heavy traffic time, so why not stay overnight in a local camping ground to be safe and get used to the roads, and set yourself up,' he advised.

I also got a huge number of maps for Northland where I was heading courtesy of the information bureau. Finding out all the pros and cons of caravanning in New Zealand was exhausting, especially since I had expected to purchase a car and van then toddle off with a friend in tow with no problems. It was a real learning curve for me as Russ had attended to all the legal jargon the first time we had an adventure, but now it was up to me.

One camping ground found, one night booked and learning to reverse my little van in was a breeze after five attempts. I will get better at this I vowed. I parked, then unwrapped and put all my new gear into place. I could almost hear, 'Well done, sweetheart.' Phew, Russ if only you knew, I muttered to myself. 'Oh no, now I'm talking to myself.'

That night I warmed up a tin of soup and listened to the sea crash onto Orewa beach. I had purchased a very small bottle of white wine and was sitting back in my new camp chair enjoying a half glass and the night-time chorus of birdsong when my phone rang. Rae's name came up on the screen. My heart skipped more than a beat, it trembled. Should I answer with a friendly hello or a simple yes?

Her outburst beat me to it. 'Mum, I'm sorry,' she said. 'I wanted to tell you we both want you to come home, we miss you.'

'I miss you too, Rae, both you and Jess, but I'm not coming home for a while honey, not if I can help it. You will have to sort out your own life.'

The resignation in her voice turned to hope when she asked, 'I understand Mum. Please ring me lots and tell me how you are getting on.'

I promised I would do just that, my face and heart smiling as I was in touch with my family again. We chatted about my trip I told her about Gilly. She was furious. I told her about Margi, and we laughed at Margi's old man, Tom, and laughed about my recent purchases of the van and Jeep.

'I would love to be there with you, Mum.'

I replied, 'I need to do this on my own for now.'

'Why? When you are so secure, loved and safe in Rockingham.'

'I have no idea, Rae. I just know I'm not ready for the retirement home yet.'

'I doubt you ever will be, Mum. Goodnight, sleep tight.'

I noticed not one word about Jono and again I thought, her life, let her live it. I felt funny about our conversation, relieved we were talking again, but there was something else my intuition was picking up, or was I just tired? I curled up inside my little home, Mermaid II, and must have gone to sleep with a smile on my face as I certainly woke with one. It was bird song that woke me. They were everywhere; no cawing or muttering like our crows and parrots but cheeping and peeping. How wonderful; the ocean a quiet murmur in the background.

As I showered in the camp bathrooms and changed into clean

clothes, my phone rang again, this time number unknown came up. I bet it's either Mark or Margi, I thought. 'Hello, Tara speaking,' was met with silence, so I switched off and potted around making some toast, boiling eggs and a big mug of hot tea for my breakfast; this Kiwi fresh sea air certainly made me super hungry. The phone trilled again, 'Hello Tara speaking.'

'Tara,' a small girly voice spoke, 'it's me, Gilly.'

I went silent, so did the other end, then I thought, stuff it, I don't need her unbalanced behaviour in my life. I said in a bright happy voice, 'Gilly, fuck off,' then switched my phone off.

Bubbles of laughter erupted until I was bent over, laughing and spluttering until my face ached. I chuckled right though my breakfast thinking, 'man that felt good.' I felt liberated; at long last no hangers on whining, 'pat me better now.' I was going to see New Zealand and from there on who knew where the wind would blow me. Packing up my home, off I went on the road, who knows where or when I would stop. I did have one more stop to make, a music store to buy some CDs. Orewa had a music store on the main road and it did not take too long to buy thirty CD's and big bar of dark chocolate, then I was off.

Chapter 26

Waiwera came into view, another seaside township with a huge water fun park and thermal pools. It looked packed with people, so I decided not to stop. Driving over the winding hills to Warkworth was more like it. I loved it; quaint olde-world-looking and a pretty camping ground. I asked for a site, one I could park in for two nights. The manager walked me to my site under huge willow trees by the river, it was fabulous. This time I cooked a stew and it simmered on the little gas stove at the back of my van while I packed away everything I bought. I had simply dumped most of it on the bed and in the back of the Jeep, now tucking it away in the right places, the little cupboard soon filled. I then packed all tins and packets into a large plastic box and put them under my comfy bed. I was as relaxed as I could be with a life-time's experience of knowing just when the stew was cooked and settled down to eat my dinner, the Jeep radio softly playing Beethoven. I read my book outside until the light would no longer let me see the words then went inside to read, play on my laptop and sleep.

I downloaded images from my camera onto my thumb drive, feeling very grateful I had those computer lessons at the local Autumn centre in Rockingham last year. I stayed for two nights, enjoying this pretty little place with all its little shops, the river side café and the million ducks, all vying for that one last crumb you just might toss in the water to them.

Just out of Warkworth is a place called Goat Island Reserve, a marine reserve. A little out of my way, but I'm so glad I drove out there before I left the area, driving through small country towns, surrounding me all the way were green hills. Goat Island was beautiful. I waded in the cold Pacific Ocean, the most amazing brilliant blue fish called Blue Mau Mau nibbled at my toes and the tourist ride in the glass bottom boat was amazing–the only word I knew to explain the fish of all types; huge, fat, healthy, and inquisitive of us as we were of them.

The beach was almost deserted except for two couples. The two men were in the water scuba diving, the ladies sat on the beach under a large striped beach umbrella reading magazines and chatting. I sat and watched the antics of the men in the water, laughing at them as they mucked about. And as people do, the two women and I got talking. The older of the two asked, 'Where are you from?'

'I'm an Aussie from Perth.'

'Me to,' she cried. 'I'm from Gosnells.'

They invited me to join them, I had not much else planned, so why not? As we chatted I ate wonderful fresh sandwiches offered, feeling very cheeky as I had brought nothing with me.

The two men arrived. It looked like they had stepped out of a comic strip; one was very short, a little chubby with a bright red beard showing under the dive mask and snorkel, the other was the other end of the scale–very tall, skinny, and a black beard showing under his mask and snorkel. What made me stare was the very tall skinny one because he had on a silver wet suit that was obviously too small for him plus it was a women's wet suit. He saw me look more than once, then explained he had borrowed it from his mate's wife so he could dive at the reserve. The short one with the red beard had masking tape wrapped around the outside of the wrists and ankles of his wet suit. He also saw my surprised look and explained the dive suit was old and leaked.

They both looked like poor relations of Jacques Cousteau, but if they were happy puttering about for the day in the ocean who was I to judge.

We all chatted about Perth and touring New Zealand; how different it was to Australia, how small and close all the little townships were and how close the sea was to both sides of the country. Then it was time for me to go, thanking them for their hospitality. I was on my way, the cares and woes of my world that once felt like a log across my shoulders had gone, I was really and truly foot loose and fancy free. What a wonderful feeling.

Back to Warkworth to hitch up my home and onto the town ship of Wellsford. I drove through slowly, finding it a place of such loneliness where people seemed to wander without any hope; it reminded me of Mt Magnet in Australia, and didn't bother to stop at another little place called Maungaturoto as it had one shop and a gas station. Then onto the Brynderwyn ranges. I had been warned about them; they are narrow, windy and scary. I was not used to these roads and the steep curves, but the scenery was fabulous. The off-road parking gave me the opportunity to pull over to take as many photos as possible.

I drove past Marsden Point turn off, as I was warned by a lady in Warkworth it was not a place for tourists, now I headed to Whangarei.

It was a four-hour drive and by the time I had found the Whangarei Falls Caravan Park, I was buggered. The lawns and trees were so green and the waterfalls sounded so nice, so I enquired about parking my van. Yes, I could stay for a week if I wanted, something inside said stay. When I reversed I was still a bit wobbly with parking, but I did it, then prepared myself for a trip into town.

Unhitching the Mermaid, putting chocks under her wheels, winding down the jockey wheel, putting on the brakes; I can do this, I thought. Then changing into fresh clothing and into the jeep, Whangarei here I come.

Clapham's Clocks were still open, so I visited there then walked along the wharves watching the fishermen unload their catch. Across the street was a market with gorgeous fruit and veggies for sale, so I wandered through purchasing and eating a fresh locally grown persimmon, deep orange coloured juice dripped and stained my clean t-shirt.

I walked back across the road congratulating myself on resisting too much of the produce; all I had bought was the persimmon and a bag of Kiwi fruit. Before I got into the jeep, I spied a little café on the opposite side of the fisherman's wharf. I walked over the bridge along the boardwalk, settling into the café, the smell of baking bread floating out was divine.

It reminded me of our holiday in Paris; walking along the Seine, sitting at sidewalk cafés, watching the French live their everyday life. My bag contained the notebook I often did light sketching in, so why not now while I sipped my hot chocolate, enjoying the sights, people and activity as the day became late afternoon. I wrote beside my sketches, 'Can't believe I'm here and doing all this on my own.' I listed all the things I wanted to do in this town, then I was going to head up North to visit small townships. Everyone said go to Russell, so I added that to my bucket list as well. The blurb on Keri Keri and surrounding districts was interesting, and as before in Australia, I not only wanted to see all the big towns, I wanted to visit the out-of-the way places no-one bothered with.

The café was putting out its dinner menu boards. Why not? I ordered reef and beef with a side salad, an enormous meal, the need for a doggy bag obvious. I got halfway through the meal and could not eat another morsel.

I asked what entertainment was like around here. The manager said pubs, night clubs and movies, so I opted for my van and bed as tomorrow was another day. I'm not a club or pub type, so why bother? Once back at the park everything was in darkness, no lights showing. Was everyone asleep?

The waterfall roared in all its splendour, sending up a light mist. Frogs croaked greetings to each other, night birds tweeted in their trees, and I heard an owl, a Morepork by the eerie lonely sound it made, the only friendly sound was the click of my light switch once I had found my way inside my van.

Lonely yet, Tara? Came the internal whisper. *No, I am not going there, not tonight*, mentally giving myself a good shake, muttering to myself, I'm fine thank you. I read my book trying to ignore the fact that yes, I was lonely, very much so. I missed everyone. Tears formed and fell.

Being a Sagittarius, I'm a gregarious type. I loved company, I loved entertaining and having my friends and family around me. What on earth am I doing here in a small caravan alone in a strange country? I'm also known for my tenaciousness, so I'm giving this trip all I've got. Amen.

I slept lightly that night, on top of the bed, the weather hot and humid with rain forecast for tomorrow. I woke in the late morning feeling heavy, hot, nauseous and not all that well, my one thought was, I can't be sick, not now.

That day was a blur as my temperature shot up. I went out to the back of the Mermaid to boil water but ended up dry retching, having to sit on the wet grass; the rain had arrived overnight soaking the ground. The wife of the camp manager noticed me sitting there, not moving as the world was tilting too much to stand. 'Can I help?' she asked. I was about to say, 'I don't know. I can't stand up,' when a massive stream of hot sour vomit erupted, down her front and mine.

When I came to, I was in the local hospital being poked and prodded, a doctor looking very concerned looking at me. 'You're awake,' he announced. 'Can you answer some questions?' My head was exploding, there was no way I could answer anything.

'We think you have food poisoning,' he said. 'Where did you eat last night?' was the last thing I heard before a whirling well of inky black took me away.

When I did gain some semblance of thought, it was scattered, with all the what, where, who and how. Every time I tried to sit up a wave of nausea would hit, the pain tearing at my gut, retching or the bed pan was in order. If I tried to open my eyes for more than five minutes the band of pain around my skull was unbearable. I knew I was wired up for liquids, heart monitor, pulse. All I could do was lie there, I felt like I was dying. The staff nurse asked if she could use my phone. I wanted to say, 'Why?' but all that came out was a groan. I watched through slitted swollen eyes as she took my new phone away. There was nothing I could do, I was immobile. When she came back to return it she said, 'I have found some phone numbers that may help us contact the folk we need to talk to about you. Is there any one you want us to phone in particular?'

'Rae,' I croaked, 'my daughter in Perth,' the drum in my head pounding in time. I could hear Rae's voice over the phone.

'Mum's in Hospital?' She then asked the 'when, where, what happened?' questions. The nurse looked my way offering me the phone. I shook my head, 'I can't,' I whispered, as on top of feeling so ill, I felt like a failure.

Rae was told the circumstances of my hospital stay and was asked for details. She replied in a calm manner, but I could hear that worry underneath asking for, 'regular updates on my condition,' as the conversation ended.

Three days later when I was able to sit up and ring Rae, she said, 'Mum, Jess and I are really worried.'

'I'm fine Rae, really,' I said, my voice now a lot steadier now, 'and I'm being discharged today.'

'Are you sure, Mum? I can come over and stay for a while.'

I had to smile as I could just see us both tucked up in my tiny Mermaid, but I was feeling so much better. 'No thanks honey, but thank you, it was an unfortunate accident. I'm fine now.' She was not happy with my answer, but it's what I wanted.

Discharge now complete, I got a taxi to the caravan park. There she was, my Mermaid waiting for me and our next adventure. I was on medication for the headache that edged around my eyes, so I asked the park owners if I could stay an extra night.

'Of course you can,' they said. 'Did the hospital found out what was wrong?' 'Yes,' I replied. 'Food poisoning, it was written on the discharge papers.'

The manager replied, 'What a shame. You're first trip here and this happens.'

Now I could have sat and wept and said, 'I'm going back to Perth,' or I could shrug and say, 'It happens and carry on,' and that's what I did.

'How far to Kaitaia?' I asked, very determined to do this and hearing hear Margi's voice singing, 'we are women.' *I will do this, one step at a time, Tara.* I had one more night, so I stayed as close to home as possible, the showers and toilets my only walk for the day, Cheryl, the wife of the camp owner, checking up on me each time she walked past.

'How are you feeling now?' She would yell through the fly screen door.

'Good thanks,' I would call out.

The one thing I missed was getting up and making a cup of tea inside as I had to go outside pull out the little gas stove and boil the billy. That is until lying on my bed, I spied the electrical outlet for the toaster, and I groaned at my stupidity. I knew my next purchase would be an electric jug. I slept in, snuggled up in my doona or as New Zealanders say a quilt, waking up at nine am the next day–late for me–my head still quite tender behind the eyes. It was time to move on, I wanted to explore.

Chapter 27

The map I had was fail safe or so the AA assured me. You follow the main road up the east coast and on reaching Paihia I could cross to Russell, then back across the harbour, back onto the main road and carry on to Kaitaia, which would lead me to Cape Reinga the lighthouse, the end of the North Island; my goal.

What I wanted to see was life off the beaten track. I wanted the adventure of being there and saying, 'Oh! You haven't been there yet,' and filling others' ears with my adventure.

The AA said I could cover it all in three to four weeks if I followed their map, plus stopping over at most places advertised on the map.

It actually took four months to cover what I thought was a more sensible route to take, stopping at every little nook and cranny, camping in farmyards more often than not, the farmers were delightful company. The caravan parks were not; more suited for the summer tourists or families on holidays, and I soon found out not that sociable as the weather was a deterrent. It rained, a lot.

I knew I was missing a lot by following a map, so I went and bought myself a GPS. I nicknamed her Victoria as the plush plum accent was pure English. I would often have a one-sided conversation with her, claiming she was wrong as the map stated a different route. Whenever I stopped off, I would ask about farm stays or where to park for two nights so I could see the New Zealand Margi told me about.

The Hikurangi countryside was amazing. Huge slabs of volcanic rock lay everywhere in the fields hundreds of years ago, when New

Zealand was forming mountains, this part of it had been blown to kingdom come, now looking like a Lego set left by giants.

Now sheep and cows roamed around the boulders, munching contentedly on the green grass. There was nowhere to stay not even for a tiny Mermaid. Driving towards Kawakawa, I passed beautiful scenery, white sheep, deep green hills and valleys and the most gorgeous tall flax plants. Nothing was small or scrub; this part of the country was fabulous, rolling hills that led to craggy mountains, reminding me of a holiday in Ireland.

The signpost for Kawakawa came up, so time to pull over and find out more about this little township and if there was a place to stay overnight. Here, the biggest tourist spot was the Hundertwasser designed public toilets.

The most amazing artwork at the entrance to the toilets were tall poles with mosaic pots of all different sizes inserted onto them, truly amazing. Well done, Kawakawa for preserving this monument to Hundertwasser the artist. How it hadn't been vandalised, I have no idea.

My camera worked overtime. Kawakawa advertised a ride on the original steam train, Gabriel, but once at the train station it was out of order. That was the thing all of Northland had in common—most of the cute little places are virtually closed, to have any fun you had to be or know a local. I went to visit the glow worm Kawiti Caves, the narrative given in such a bored way I left early feeling very disappointed, what I had expected to be a learning curve was not that at all. Onwards I went, driving through Moerewa as again, there was nothing touristy to stop for. The most glorious scenery was everywhere; mountainsides abundant, full of fernery and massive trees, waterfalls gushed onto roads or wound amongst the hills, pretty beaches fringed by the famous Pohutukawa trees, a bright red bottle brush flower called the New Zealand Christmas tree.

The forests thick with green life, I would often park on the side of the road just to take it all in, the tiny outlets of beaches vacant, no one seemed to use them. Occasionally I would see a Maori family in dinghies with lines or nets, but nothing like the bustling golden beaches we have in Australia.

They were peaceful scenes, unlike its history which seemed full of war. Tiny inlets and mangroves were dotted all along the coastline, this gave me such a strange sensation of freedom, I was really on my own here and I was 'doin it' as Margi would say.

Signposts to different little townships popped into view. I was tempted to find a spot to rest, but Paihia was only a short distance away. Again, you could not believe the distances the GPS gave you.

Paihia. What a pretty little township, each shop vying for the tourist; hot chips, pies and curios, every sort of beach trinket on offer, but no camping ground. Damn. I was very tired and just wanted to rest up, so I drove up and down searching for a camping place, finally stopping off at the local pub where there was a bikie meeting going on. These sorts of rough and tough looking people have always scared me, but they were quiet and just having a beer. I popped inside the highway pub and into the dim interior where it felt good to sit down with a sigh and order big fat wedges and a cold beer.

As I munched, I took in what I could see; so much hung on the walls, old pit saws, old axes, hundreds of old bottles on shelves, everything the 18th century farmers used to survive.

I read the literature about why I should visit and decided to visit a well-known winery, plus try to find a small caravan park for the night. The headache behind my eyes sat there again, now niggling its way into another migraine.

The publican was not that helpful with any information, but the bikies overheard me ask him.

I was soon given so much advice, the fear of these hard, rough looking men and women soon going, they asked me to sit with them and, 'tell us where you're from.' This was new. It was usually me asking that question, so I stayed drinking icy, mint lemonade with a dash of cranberry, very refreshing, my headache clearing with the help of two painkillers.

I told them about my life in Perth and what a fabulous city it was with its statues, big parks, fountains, especially Kings Park. I was about to continue when the publican yelled, 'Closing time!' I looked at my watch; I had been here three hours! Now it was important I find somewhere to stay and park the Mermaid for the night.

I said my goodbyes, to which this crowd yelled, 'Don't go, Tara. Follow us.' I had no better ideas and was not going to tell Rae about this until after; she would have been horrified at her Mum travelling with a gang of bikies. They weren't drunk or rowdy; I didn't see any drugs taken, although I was pretty sketchy about what to look for in that department. So I followed them onto an old deserted farm road and into what looked like a very ancient farmyard. A relic of an old chimney jutted up out of the black and red bricks fallen down around it. The bikes roared round into what was obviously their spot, my little Mermaid jolted up and over the bumps and holes until one of the bikies stopped me, instructing, 'Park it here, mate,' his deep voice belying his gentle eyes. His name was Jeremy or 'Jeri' and was the toughest looking bikie I had ever seen; the tattoos swirled over his chest, arms and neck, curling tails belonging to scaled fire snorting dragons, their claws sinking into his forearms.

Jeri helped me put bricks at the back of the van, then lead me to the circle that had formed around a huge bonfire. It was dusk and getting cold. I was handed a cold beer, which I declined; pain medication and alcohol don't mix. Then, like children waiting for a bedtime story, they asked me to continue my story about my travels.

I told them about Russ and our life together in the bus travelling the Pilbara. As I talked about us I was handed a tin plate of hot spicy baked beans and thick slices of bread with yellow creamy butter on it. I ate with a spoon, and like the rest of them used the bread to slop up the gravy left on my plate, a mug of sweet hot black tea placed beside me.

I felt very welcome, but it was my bedtime, so I pleaded travel weary. My haven, my little van, said welcome, and I was asleep before my head hit the pillow.

If anyone had tried anything, I would not have had a clue as I was out to it and for some reason I felt safe with these folk.

I presume they must have slept rough; I had no idea where they slept.

When I woke it was to Jeri tapping on my door telling me they were off to the pub for a beer then off back to Auckland, then he removed the heavy chocks from behind the van for me. The previous night, I sensed Jeri was not what he appeared; some of his speech was very American, his accent coming through when unguarded, the gang he was with would hoot and yell, 'How does it go again, Jeri?' when his accent took over.

I said my goodbyes and waved to this close tribe of people. I then took my time warming up a large pan of water and having a wash outside the van, enjoying the privacy, the quietness, magpies and their wonderful call, the smell of pine trees; the only noisy sound was me splashing in my bucket of warm sudsy water, this time a big blue bucket. I washed all over my top half, removing my top and bra, soaping up then splashing off with cold water. Wonderful.

Then I shampooed my now longish hair, the spiky look I was so proud of once–considering myself a little different–now grown into a flat thick crop of silver hair that needed a really good wash.

I shampooed my hair and emptied the bucket over it. It felt so good, and as I towelled off, the fresh air made my body and scalp tingle. This was the medicine it needed, I felt revived. I refilled the bucket realising I would have to refill the Mermaid's small water tank again, then off with jeans and knickers, suds up, rinse and towel off.

Fortunately, I had the towel wrapped around me when I heard a motor bike coming my way, it sounded like only one, but I was not sure, and panic rose in my chest.

My first thought was, here comes trouble. I raced inside the van locking the door and fumbling around for clean clothes, and of course when you panic, nothing goes right.

The bike roared into the yard and stopped opposite the van. Heavy boots crunched over the door shaking the Mermaid a little under the heavy thump it received.

Instantly, I was thinking, oh God, I'm going to be raped and killed, and no one knows where I am. I've been so stupid going along with this bikie crowd, crazy thoughts ran like wildfire through my head; the top I had tried to pull on now partly scrunched up in a tight ball in my hands. Fear crept into my heart my reactions clumsy. 'It's Jeri here, Tara. Saw you were still parked here, is everything alright?'

Pulling on a pair of jeans and my scrunched top, I almost jumped into his arms. 'Oh, it's you, Jeri,' my voice wobbled, giving away I was really scared.

'Hey, easy there,' he said. I stumbled outside and he caught me by the elbow, holding onto my arm.

Jeri stood there with a wide smile trying to juggle a paper cup that smelled of heavenly hot coffee with a fresh bran muffin. 'Want to eat?' Jeri said.

'Do I? I'm starving,' I replied.

Jeri and I sat on an old log devouring the fresh muffin, pulling it apart and enjoying the smell of fresh baking. We shared the coffee, pouring half into one of my cups. Talking was out, both of us enjoying the silence and food.

Then he started talking about himself I discovered my intuition was right, this was no rough tough bikie, he was a Harvard educated man who had fled normal life stumbling into this nomad bikie gang

Metal Mermaid

halfway around the world. It was easier to be tough and free than let his heart twist with hurt over losing his family in the Twin Towers disaster in America.

Jeri told me every detail, every last bit like he had been hanging onto it forever, just waiting for this moment. His breath ragged as he told me about his teenage children and wife that were never found in the rubble. How he, police and volunteers had searched, calling their names for days.

He told me of the guilt he felt at the argument he and his wife had before he went to a business meeting; she wanted him to join them, but there wasn't time to rearrange, so they went their separate ways. He had been at a meeting on the other side of town, his family were visiting friends who worked next door to the Twin Towers.

The worst part was he could still hear their names being called as he went to sleep. The memorial had been horrendous as there was nothing to say goodbye to, only photos that smiled back at him. He felt that one day they would suddenly pop up and say, 'Hi Dad.' As he talked, he looked like a man who really needed a hug.

Between the stops and starts of his story, I made tea with the last of the water in my little tank and we ate a packet of cracker biscuits with the last of the cheese from my small fridge. I put my arms around him.

'Jeri, I recently lost my husband, although nothing as horrific as your story, but grief is still the same, I guess. This trip is my way of working through it.' Then I suggested something that even surprised me.

'Let's find that famous Pacific Ocean and go for a swim. No crocs here, are there?' He burst out laughing.

'That would really put Paihia on the map, but they do skite about their monster eels that eat ducks,' he snorted with laughter.

For the first time in many years I rode pillion on a motorbike. Off we went roaring our way to the ocean where we splashed and dunked each other. Once home, I wanted food. I changed inside and Jeri changed outside and then back to the local pub for slap-up pub grub. I knew Jeri wanted more time with me; he was young and carefree, and I was carefree but had a little bit more age and wisdom on my side and wanted to do my own thing. I was dropped off at my van we hugged for a second, the obligatory keep in touch promises made and we exchanged phone numbers. A quick tidy up inside the Mermaid and off I drove, looking for a store to buy more water and groceries.

Chapter 28

I finally arrived on the outskirts of Waitangi, a beach township that looked promising, and on the way there passed a road sign to an orchard selling produce. I took the directions, drove in and loved what I saw, purchasing more than I should have, and off on the road once again, music blaring and the sudden realisation that Jeri had been attracted to me.

I blushed then giggled at my silly thoughts, so glad I'm on my own, I thought. Rae and Jess would be shocked at my behaviour which jolted me; another thing I had to do, ring my daughter as soon as I was in Waitangi.

The tourist pamphlet promised a fabulous camping ground with golden beaches and blue water. A tourist bus ran through the city, so maybe I would be able to see more than parking in a campground watching the grass grow and trying to find people willing to talk to me. So far, I found the caravan parks nothing like Australian campers; the people friendly enough but there was something missing. Perhaps it was because I was a single woman travelling on my own. Maybe when I spoke to Rae tonight we could work it out together; it rankled me.

In the orchard shed window I had seen an advertisement about a tall ship sailing daily. It was the *R. Thomas Tucker* and departed from Russell, which was a ferry ride from Paihia, I made an instant decision; I wanted to do this trip, so I rang the Paihia tourist office. I had missed today's boat but the one tomorrow left at ten am. I was to be at the Paihia wharf at nine-thirty am the next morning. I booked my passage.

Now to find somewhere to park for two days as the local caravan park was full. I was really disappointed until the owners saw how little my van was–they thought it was really cute–and I was shown a very small space just behind their woodshed and only half the cost. The manager connected my electric plug to the woodshed outlet, and I was, 'Ready to go,' as he put it.

I was completely out of sight from tourists and their families. Good, I thought, peace and quiet. I commented that for such a small town it was teaming with a huge international mix of tourists. The owners nodded in unison, 'Used to be such a nice pretty seaside village. They call this progress.'

He sadly looked down at the overflowing rubbish tins, the rubbish blowing along the streets.

'But look at what you have around you, Pohutukawa tree's bright, fire engine red framed the multi coloured green hills, blue Pacific waters lapped white sandy shores.'

A glazed look came over his face as if he'd heard it all before.

I was disappointed in his attitude, but as I turned towards the ocean, there in the distance I could see what looked like a boat full of Maori warriors coming to shore; my mouth must have been one huge 'Oh' as I gasped, 'Look.'

It was a Maori Waka–a huge canoe being paddled by tourists–a popular business run by a local man called Hone. The name rang a bell. Where had I heard it before?

The excitement watching this magnificent craft glide towards me was catching, the crowd that gathered just about pushing me over the bank into the water.

The Maori chant that went with the dipping of the paddles was hypnotic. You could hear it from the shore, the melodious chant the leader was calling to the people paddling.

My first sane thought was, how do I be part of this? The camp owners gave me contact phone numbers and my fingers actually shook as I tapped the numbers in. It was answered with, 'Kia ora,' the Maori hello. I made a booking; the price made me gasp but I was now on the next Waka going to sea. The late afternoon could not get here soon enough. I headed back to the Mermaid, doused myself in suntan cream, donned a huge floppy hat and sunglasses, grabbed my credit card and keys, and locked everything else in my van.

Excitement was rippling through me as I had never ever done anything like this before.

Soon enough, I was helped into the magnificent Waka. We waited around for a little while for the latecomers, and Hone and his crew looked magnificent in their native costumes. Being a stickler for time and tides, he gave the order in Maori to cast off. I was now part of a team given instructions on how to sweep your oar in the water, so we dipped our large white pointed oars into the deep blue sea and to the beat of a wonderful chant, off we glided.

It was pure magic. You could almost imagine being part of a tribe coming home from a day of discovery. I loved it, every minute detail of the Waka stuck in my mind and couldn't wait to relay it all to Rae tonight.

The lifestyle from the centuries passed was explained as we sped along. This truly was the old adage; sea spray in your face, being so close to the water, the spray foaming as it landed onto hot skin, arm muscles bulged, you could feel your core muscles working. What an experience. I did not want it to end.

Once back on shore, my legs were a bit sea wobbly as I walked back to camp. Once I was inside my home I had a quick wash, and looking in the small mirror, the tanned face and mile wide grin was a tell-tale sign Tara was having fun. What struck me the most, there was no makeup, the hairdo had long gone and in its place was soft white almost curly head of hair that was unruly and windblown. I was looking healthy and tanned and when I changed into a long skirt and singlet they were both very loose on me; I had lost weight as well. I was impressed with me.

For once, I was totally *au naturelle* and felt wonderful. I remembered all the fussing and fluffing about when I was with Russ; putting on the makeup and gel in my hair before we went anywhere, making sure he was pleased with the way I looked. I had changed dramatically, and I liked it. I was responsible for me and me alone, I pleased no-one else but me. I wanted to keep it like that.

Dinner that night was a can of tuna with a light salad, my thoughts a thousand miles away about things I should be doing and should have done. Dusk in Paihia is a little different to dusk in the Pilbara; clammy, damp and cold with the ocean wind blowing straight into the camp. In the Pilbara it can get bitter icy cold at night, but those diamonds in the night sky were still wonderful no matter what country I was in.

As I ate my dinner and leaned back in my camp chair, the peace and solitude were soothing, the other campers obviously gone out somewhere. There was no one around, not even the tinny sound of a TV or radio; the camp was dark. Where I was sitting, all I could hear was the lapping of the ocean onto sandy shore, sea birds and forest birds settling for the night and no snakes in New Zealand so my feet were bare. How nice to be able to have bare feet and not worry about what was going to slide over them. Still, that's my phobia.

By torchlight I flipped through some brochures about this pretty place and all there was to do and see. Now was the time to ring my daughter, and I also thought I would ring Margi in Auckland to say, 'Hi. I'm fine, and this is where I am now.'

Rae was worried and still unenthusiastic about my trip alone. We exchanged pleasantries and what I had done until now and I admit to white washing my story about Jeri somewhat; no need for her to know the exact details.

I told her almost everything, of where I had been and what I had done, and then it was Jess's turn on the phone. He wailed at me

'I miss you, Nana. When are you coming home?'

'When you're Nana is ready to, Jess.'

He was most disgruntled, actually arguing the point with me of my 'duties' to him and his Mum. For a twelve-year old, I thought he was showing all the signs of being a rude, stroppy little man.

Rae took over the conversation saying, 'He really misses you, Mum. We both do.'

I felt like yelling at them both, 'You had your chance, you tossed it all away by your behaviour,' but I kept it peaceful. What they did not know was the more they argued and blamed and contorted the truth to suit them, the less I wanted to go back there; life on my own so far, was great.

I asked about her fiancé and soon to be husband. There was a silence, then she dropped her bomb. 'Mum, because of your behaviour he is having second thoughts about us being a couple.'

That sentence gobsmacked me. 'I beg your pardon?' I said. 'You're blaming *me* for your behaviour?'

'Well who else is there to blame?' she said. 'Because of your actions and not letting us live in your home, it all fell apart.'

Apparently, her wise and brave fiancé had said, 'Look at the mother, see the daughter.' How original, I thought. My heart saying, 'So be it, if that's the way you all feel. Fine. Let's see how this plays out as I don't have to go anywhere but where I am right now.'

I did not mean physically, I meant emotionally. I felt I had changed a little and I liked what I saw internally.

Rae's voice was full of spite, her words hurtful as she accused me, 'This is all your fault, Mum. Maybe once you're home and become responsible for your actions, we can work on our relationship, especially between you and Jono, that's if he wants me.'

I felt like she was saying that once I had done my thing, I would hand them the keys to my life and my home and be a good, quiet, obedient Mum and Nana. They had no idea who I was or what I wanted.

I ended the phone call sooner than I had expected, 'Better go now, Rae. I have places to go, people to see,' Click… conversation ended.

I seethed until I calmed down. I found the small bottle of white wine with a half glass left in it, and sipping slowly, I was now quite happy at the thought I had no-one but me to answer to.

Margi was my next call, answered by one of her children, who then handed me down the line of the family until Margi yelled at them to, 'Give me that bloody phone, or else. Tara!' she yelled down the line. 'Where are you? been thinking of you.'

I told her all the goings on and about Whangarei food poisoning, my hospital stay, then winding my way up here to Paihia, meeting Jeri and going on the Waka trip. She chuckled at my adventures, 'You don't do things by halves, do you girl? Hey, when you're in Keri Keri ring me, I have family there who you can stay with.'

That sounded promising. I said I would, and we said our goodnight to each other with, 'Keep well and safe.'

Bed please, my body said. The problem with my family? I purposely put that away to think about another day, the half glass of white wine working on my nervous system. I packed up, put away dishes, then went off to bed. It was warm inside, so I just lay on top of the bed, and through the small sky light I saw the twinkle of stars. Tomorrow was my day on the tall ship. I felt the thrill of excitement buzz through me as I fell asleep.

I had read somewhere: yesterday is past, today is your present, tomorrow the future, it was right; today was *my* present and today I was off sailing again, this time on a huge tall ship the, *R Thomas Tucker*. I was up early waiting like an eager school kid for nine-thirty to arrive and deciding to go as a passenger on the ferry to meet the ship was not a silly thing, with vehicles of all shapes and sizes literally jammed on. The sailing ship moored at the wharf; the passengers a mix of ages–mostly people of my age, and two families welcomed on board. As we boarded, instructions were given through a loud hailer on what to do and who to obey. We were put into teams, and as I had come on to experience the working vessel I was willing to try most things.

Chapter 29

The first-mate, Lyle, a tall slim, tanned, blond who had a twinkle in his blue eyes, I soon found out was a Kiwi and knew these waters well. He had worked on the *Tucker* for many years, loved the lifestyle, and at forty years of age knew this is what he wanted in his life. As he gave us the spiel on himself I could see his love affair with this boat; it showed in the way he demanded respect for her. He worked the crew and passengers with style, his voice brooked no arguments. 'Do it my way or sit down and shut up.'

Once I'd had my turn at the wheel and rope pulling, I made for the galley for a hot cup of tea with fresh scones, jam and butter. It sounded yummy and was part of the cruise deal they advertised.

I was late so there wasn't much on offer; the families on board had made short work of anything presentable. The galley was a mess; jam and doughy crumbs littered the floor, butter and cream was smeared all over the table, empty orange juice paper cups littered on the bunk seats, and half empty tea mugs were stacked in the small sink. Lyle had descended into the galley just before me and saw my face. It must have shown disappointment, as his did, and he bounded up the stairs. I heard shouting, then two adults came down rather sheepishly to start the cleaning up followed hot on their heels by three teenage kids from the two families on board. I sat to one side as they cleaned, reading an emotional poem about a metal mermaid that was framed on the wall, I was quite surprised that the name of its author was Lyle.

It had a rhythm to it; the words were deep, flowing from his very soul. I had to ask about his poem; soft sad eyes said it was about a small mermaid which had been a landmark in Russell. Made of bronze and forged with passion, a popular Icon for all, her tail twisted like a *Koru*–the heart of the New Zealand national Silver Fern. One night she was stolen. 'If it's not nailed down some bastard will nick it,' he added.

Our trip around the harbour was wonderful. The poem was tucked in my pocket, given to me to keep safe inside my own mermaid. I was thrilled Lyle trusted me with his words.

On the trip back to Paihia I was so tired, glad to be back at the caravan park for an afternoon sleep. Once awake, it was under a hot shower then a wander into town for a takeaway meal. Cape Reinga and the lighthouse, that was my goal. I learned the Maori believe the spirits of their dead leap from this point to end up in the heavens. What a lovely thought.

It was proving quite a ride to find my way there with so many little townships to stop at. I was enjoying it very much; I could feel my spirit stretching and growing with every new experience. It was this one thought that led me to realise I was not making new acquaintances via the camping grounds as we did in Aussie, instead it was going out and introducing myself to new people. It was a way of meeting and greeting I had avoided when I was a married woman; I was used to my safe married cocoon. I was now coming out of my shell and loved it.

My next stop was across to Waitangi where a huge Maori war was fought and a story about a flagpole was to be heard once you were there. I was wrong to think Waitangi was a township; it was more like a part of Paihia, but very interesting all the same. The treaty of Waitangi is now celebrated with a national holiday in recognition of European and Maori people living together as one.

It seemed in some faction of the Maori, all was not well in that field, but I'm not politically minded and was not prepared to argue my case with the orator who was giving his point of view loudly at a local restaurant. I left as soon as possible.

I rang Margi to say I'm on the outskirts of Kerikeri and once again the phone was handed down with every one of them saying hello. 'It's Tara,' I repeated over and over, until I heard Margi's voice greet me with, 'Kia Ora, love. How are things with you?'

'I'm great, thanks,' but before I could go any further she said, 'Tara, I have to go, but have you got pen and paper handy? Here is the phone number of my cousin, they are expecting you. Keep well and safe, love.'

'You too, Margi.'

I was off to meet her family. I rang twice, no answer, so I drove to the address. I found their house–a small, faded blue cottage, roses and impatiens filled the front garden, windows twinkled in the sunset. This is delightful, I thought. I parked on the roadside, then knocked on their open front door.

I had never been so wrong about a 'quiet, retired couple' as I was about to meet so many family members. I was overwhelmed with kindness, offers of food and lodging from the time I walked into their backyard, the innocent, 'Hello? Anyone home?' that I called, to the friendly, 'Out the back,' that was yelled at me from a distance. This was the beginning of a life changing adventure which would be with me for the rest of my life.

Greeted by a woman who mirrored Margi in every way, her name was Pania, her husband, Mathew, and a family that filled the back yard. It was no small garden, as I soon found out. This backyard was a quarter acre block filled with fruit trees, a massive veggie garden, garden pots of all descriptions brimming with herbs, overflowing with an abundance of fresh food. What took my eye was a large mound of dirt with steam rising from it.

All their faces alight with a welcome, 'Come join us.' First, I was expected to give the Maori greeting 'Hongi' to all the adults, then it was the kids who immediately called me Aunty and gave me hugs. Sleepy babies were put into my arms to admire, I felt so welcome.

Names flew around in the air; my one thought, how will I ever remember all of them?

I still find it hard to believe I spent just over three months with that wonderful family. We ate a delicious Hangi that night. The chicken melted in the mouth, as did the pork, the vegetables all home grown were so good, then the pavlova arrived–homemade with eggs fresh that day from a cousin's chook farm. That old rivalry question put to me, 'Well Tara, who made the pavlova first, Kiwis or the Aussies?' It was said with a smile and there was no suggestion of rivalry from the folk who asked it.

I shrugged my shoulders, 'I have no idea.'

That first night I was instructed to park my little mermaid in the back paddock under some orange trees, or wherever there was a space, as this was a family of large proportions; cousins, nephews, aunties, uncles, daughters, sons. One huge family showing the utmost respect for my hosts–the two elders of this family, Mathew and Pania.

Chapter 30

The days sped by, and each day I was involved with what they did. I was taught about food preparation, Pania's slim brown fingers skimming over the food as it was prepared, there was no question of who was coming for tea, it was expected all her family just turned up. Pania's admonishing of her family was quick, honest, to the point and worked; they had five rules in their home, no booze, no smoking, no swearing and respect and love each other.

If you followed the rules you were fine, if not, then the family came down on you like a hornets' nest. I witnessed a couple of times when one teenager tried to be dishonest. This family was a tight no-nonsense one. 'Those are the rules,' I heard one male adult say. 'Break 'em and I'll break you, end of story.'

Pania and Mathew's eight children were all in their thirties and forties with big families of their own. Included in their lifestyle, I willingly joined in. The men did the hunting, fishing, net mending, wood chopping, and running the small farms that surrounded the original homestead; the pale blue, two-bedroom cottage I had first seen.

The women tended to the food preparation, gardening, child rearing, and were the caretakers of the family health, hearth and home. To me, an old-fashioned way of life, but as I watched and listened, it worked for them so why change it. Each one of them healthy and happy, if not, Pania was the first to question why not; she was really in tune with her family and grandchildren, which there were a lot of. I did make her chortle when I said, 'Eight kids in that small little cottage?'

Pania replied, 'Yeah, and each one wanted and loved.'

I was included in their crabbing, fishing forays, their family meals and many celebrations. Mathew took time to talk with me, a shy man but well spoken, he told me of their history in the area and watching his parents struggle with the ownership of the land going to the white man. Mathew used the word 'Pakeha' when he told this story. He said in the past the Maori, 'used this word as an insult to the white man,' but today it was an accepted word to call Caucasians. I learned so much about the way they felt about their country. Mathew had been wise, seeing the future with the two cultures having to live side by side. He bought up a huge acreage around him and used modern machinery along with Maori custom and belief, most of the land now farmed by his sons and their sons or Mukupuna, their grandchildren.

Pania and her daughters taught me how to clean, cut, then weave flax leaves into small flax bags, and kitykits used for anything and everything. I learned to dance a poi dance but first I had to make the poi pois to dance with met with my efforts were met with laughter at my clumsy attempts, often hushed by Pania, but I got there. However, there was no escaping the night when I was encouraged to use my own Poi's. One went flying over the treetops, the other broke apart and hung limply by my side and there was no stopping the eruption of mirth.

There was no way Pania could stop the others from giggling as she herself was doubled up with laughter. I felt a little silly, but the family enjoyed my clumsy attempts at joining in, there was too much laughter not to join in with them. Believe me, when the Maori laugh there is no way you cannot join in; it starts from their gut and jiggles and wriggles around until it spills out.

What entranced me most was when they all sung in harmony. We were all sitting outside and Pania would start singing, Mathew played his guitar then the daughters would take on the tune, their voice's hypnotic, their song entrancing. They sang many songs but the one that grabbed my throat was an old one called 'Pokarikariana'. It was so beautiful, they harmonised so beautifully. Then they sang an old song I had not heard since I was a young bride: 'Irene, good night Irene.' My grandmother's name was Irene, the tears forming as I listened and remembered about my life with her, I always knew I was safe and loved with my nana.

A sadness came over me lasting for days as I worried about Jess, his recent demanding argumentative ways. Pania encouraged me to talk about it.

I told them about the sudden change in my family after Russ's death and she listened, not giving an opinion. At the end of my story it clicked. I did not need to carry my family's anger. I was able to love them from a distance, if that's what I chose to do, and as for Jess, well he knew I loved him.

When I went on day trips. I always had a car full of smiling brown faces that wanted a ride in Aunties' car. Mathew and Pania came with me to Cape Reinga explaining their beliefs and the sacred ground I was about to stand on. I was shocked at the amount of tour busses up there. Tourists tramping all over the place, overflowing rubbish bins with rubbish littering the ground, seagull's screaming, international tourists and their families running amuck, and so many different languages. There was no sanctity or respect shown, yet to my hosts this place was holy ground. I felt embarrassed about the tourists who should have known better.

Two bus drivers stood leaning against their large buses, both smoking. When they finished they stamped the butts out into the ground and Pania's face flinched. I put my arm around her, here was tourism at its worst.

Mathew showed me where to park and walk for a good view. Very few people were on this path as it was a side view of the lighthouse, the very last pinpoint of light in the north. Pointing to the lighthouse he said, 'That is the white man's world. Our belief is this,' flinging his arms wide open. He told me the most beguiling tale that they believed their spirits leave for the heavens by leaping off this majestic point of land where the two seas meet; the clashing waves of the Tasman Sea and Pacific Ocean. Today was a good day, he claimed; it was only a little rough. To me it looked so different; the two seas crashing up against each other delivering their own verdict of might and power. Huge sprays of foamy sea spray towering into the air, our faces wet with sea mist as this force crashed onto the rocks below booming out its discontent then giving away to a rushing, sucking, sigh.

I loved this part of history that had not changed. Mathew had only one thing to say about the scene at the light house, 'Wonder how they would like it if I did the same to them in their country.'

I had to agree, remembering the respect we're asked to show the Australian Aboriginal people and their land.

I too had experienced such disappointment at one particular celebration at the Swan River in Perth. I empathised entirely with Matthew and Pania's emotions.

That night driving back to Paihia through Awanui, we passed many small settlements, through the small fishing village of Hohoura, then into Kaitaia. I told them how the Orewa tourist shop told me about a different road to get to Kaitaia to reach the lighthouse. Mathew grinned. 'You could have done that, instead the spirits bought you to us and our house.'

What a lovely thought. I had to agree it had certainly proved a blessing for me. 'Time for dinner,' I announced as my tum was rumbling, and shouted my two new friends' fish and chips, Mathew sloshing vinegar onto his by the cup full.

'I like them sour and mushy,' he said, Pania adding more salt and tomato sauce to her packet, and all of us enjoying our meal out of newspaper. The pine trees we parked under creaking trees that swayed in the soft wind giving off the most heavenly smell. I could not help but get out and fill my lungs with the smell of pine mixed with fresh night air.

Pania had noticed how deeply I loved nature when I was with her, picking their veggies for our tea or fruit for the table. She offered me the chance to learn some local herbal remedies and I was all for it.

'While you're staying with us, I will teach you.'

How wonderful. I was learning something new every day, these folk had shared so much with me. I offered payment which she declined.

On our way home they showed me the Paua shell house in Kaitaia, a small home with its front and sides covered in huge Paua shells. An artist's dream of beautiful colour glowed when I shone the headlights onto it, it certainly had the wow factor. Pania told me the history of this house; it all started approximately fifty years ago as a small decoration by the front door, the local community had taken an interest and started leaving sacks of clean empty Paua shells on the door step, that's how it grew to what it is now, she explained.

The first occupiers had long ago passed on, but the house was kept like this by all owners since. Now it was tourist attraction.

'There is also a ghost story attached to that house,' she whispered like it was secret. 'They say the very first owner often walks around the house at night re-arranging what he does not like, so you go to bed one night, and the next day, what was once done has now been rearranged'.

Kaitaia had a weird feeling to it. Although the pubs were doing a roaring trade, there was a feeling of loneliness and abandonment to it. I felt it was time to finish our dinner and drive off.

I was invited inside Pania's little pale blue cottage one time. Any other time I had been welcomed to sit outside under the veranda or under the huge plum tree in their back yard where an eclectic mix of chairs of all descriptions gathered like a large group of big bummed friends having a chinwag, baggy seats of old, where much advice had been and was still given out, where Mukupuna's were soothed and tears dried, where flirtation was giggled about and huge belly laughs of humour often erupted.

This communal patch was the heart and soul of Mathew and Pania's home; I considered it an honour to be involved.

Chapter 31

Tonight as I drove into their driveway, I was invited inside the house; the wooden floor was polished to within an inch of its life giving off a golden sheen tempting any dust to land on it if it dared.

Everywhere I looked shone and twinkled with cleanliness. Their home was sparse, yet the driftwood inside was a designers dream with its pale ghostly white colour, it was used for many things; a magazine rack, coffee table and two cleverly made chairs. My mouth gaped open as I looked around me. In Australia we pay huge amounts for furniture to look like this or import it from other countries. Here it was washed up on the beaches to use as they saw fit. What I saw was very expensive haute couture furniture made by Mathew. Pure white curtains hung at the windows, a well-used leather couch was covered with a black and white cow hide and knitted cushions were everywhere. A sepia photo on the wall of their wedding day nearly sixty years ago, both standing in European wedding attire. They were committed to each other from the very beginning. This home and garden was Pania's kingdom; the land was Mathew's domain, and I was no longer a guest, I was one of the family.

The next day, I sat under orange trees adding to my travel diary, the bee's humming over the pretty white buds now forming on a new crop, the day proving to already be a humid one. Margi had arrived in the night; between her and Pania, my morning tea was fresh Maori bread and treacle.

I learned the Maori people love to debate anything and everything.

When I broke my news to them, 'I've decided to leave in one weeks' time,' pandemonium broke out. Every conceivable where, what and why I should not continue my journey was raised, Mathew bringing it to a halt with, 'The woman's got a home to go to.'

I spent the one week writing down herbal remedies, putting photos and notes into my diary and laptop and saying goodbye to many new friends.

Three days before I left, a young teenager came to see me. He was painfully shy, the blush staining his dark skin, his denim shorts tattered around the bottom, the seat of his shorts thread bare. Warik asked if he could, 'Paint a picture on the back of my van.'

I stopped short as I had never thought of that. I had not even written Metal Mermaid II on her tail yet. I must have looked apprehensive as he hung his head and shuffled his feet. A ripped textbook with smudgy pencil sketches was shoved into my hands, and before me I saw art in all its wonder, wonderful Maori designs, page after page. I asked questions about the meanings of the drawings of sea creatures, Tikis, fish, crabs, mystical creatures from Maori fables and pictures of carvings, until one small sketch took my eye–a Mermaids tale with Maori motif all around it. I had found my Metal Mermaid II. This was the one, and I said so.

Warik started painting a day later, his easel Pania's plastic bread board, his paints whatever his dad had in the shed. I thought to myself, 'Oh well, if it doesn't turn out I will have it removed professionally,' fingers crossed. True to his word, Warik worked early until late every day and his work took on meaning to us all; this was a real work of art. His concentration, dedication and ability to transfer his simple drawing onto my van was remarkable. Slowly, a Mermaid's tail appeared, drops of silver water flicking off it as it dived into a pool of pale blue and silver, the tail was a metallic mauve and deep blue and each scale seemed to glow in any light it was in, day or night. Around the picture was a Maori motif in black, it was beautiful.

Warik's chest puffed with pride as he wiped off his brushes rinsing them out in an old jam jar, his lean brown body flecked in the colours of the Metal Mermaid he had just painted. He stood back, 'There ya go, Aunty,' he announced.

'Warik,' I said frowning at him. You could see him visibly pale, his eyes saying *she hates it*, 'you forgot to sign your name.' I gave him a huge hug. This small motif of a mermaid's tail glowed, it fitted and stood out like a true piece of art always does. 'Thank you, Warik. I love it.'

My day to leave had arrived; packed up and ready to go, I was sad to leave these wonderful people, Pania and Margi patting my back this time to comfort themselves more than me. This family was what I had dreamed my family would be like, and when I had spoken to Rae or Jess at night and told them what I had done for my day, it went down like a lead balloon, their only question was when are you coming home? Or, bet that cost a fortune. What was wrong with them? Where was, 'Hey, that sounds great Mum, how exciting,' or, 'I would love to be part of it.' Instead, this big Maori family who I only just met could not do enough with or for me; my family of two in Perth oozed discontent, often spiteful gossip mixed into it. Why was my family so darned rude and demanding? Was it because we, Russ and I, had tried to give them everything they could possibly want?

Rae only had to look at something and Russ and I would try to get it for her and when it came to education nothing was too much trouble. The same with Jess. We, his grandparents, had paid for his private education and were still doing so through a trust we provided until he was twenty.

Apart from that we had literally paid his way as Rae had been a solo Mum. Even then it was not her fault; I will always remember when she told us the news of her pregnancy.

'It's not my fault,' she cried.

'Then who's fault is it?' I asked, being shushed by Russ and told to, 'Leave it alone, dear. It's happened, she needs our support,' so I shut up.

Rae never wanted or needed a thing. She never had to struggle or budget on a solo Mum's pension, which she received regularly, and we paid for everything extra she needed. Whenever she wanted extra food, it was help yourself to our pantry or freezer.

I still remember her face filled with delight when Russ and I revamped our home with new furniture and big telly, pulling up worn carpets and replacing them with big Turkish rugs we had bought and shipped over. We gave Rae the choice of any cast-offs she wanted.

It was a relief to give them away and not have to throw them out. We were happy she wanted it all, and when we learned she had sold her old belongings and replaced it with ours we did not blink, it seemed the logical thing to do, but now I saw the greed.

Recently Rae had asked about Russ's will and when would she be able to read it. I had asked, 'Why? It's all in the lawyer's hands,' to which she grumped and hissed about it being unfair and she needed to know how much she would receive. I could just see her fine black eyebrows shoot up as I quietly said, 'It all goes to me, Rae, Russ's wife and your mother.'

The conversations clipped from then on, it was me that kept in touch; her phone calls to me had stopped. I knew if she even had a hint of what it was all worth, she would ask for large portion of it, so kept it between my lawyer and me.

I certainly wasn't broke, and with the investments Russ had made I was never going to need or want for a dollar. Maybe if I had obeyed my gut instinct at first and been stricter with her. Instead, we had bred a gulping money monster who had blackmailed us with emotions and our love for Jess as his grandparents. To my shame and disappointment, we were to blame just as much as we had never said no, do it yourself. Time for me to teach this young madam a lesson in manners and respect. Spending time with this Maori family had certainly shown me a few things. One of them was, nothing is free, you work for it.

Chapter 32

I was all packed to go, the mermaid all washed, ready and keen to go on more adventures with me at the wheel. On her tail the Mermaid's Moko with Warik's signature entwined into the motif. I hitched up and drove out onto the roadway, sadness inside me. I was not only leaving one small yellow patch of grass in the back paddock I was leaving the most generous of families I had ever met and a heart full of memories. 'Bye,' I called. 'Keep in touch.'

I drove past the pale blue little cottage beeping my horn and waving, the younger members of the family running after me calling, 'Bye Aunty.' I was going to miss this family. Who would have guessed, my meeting Margi at the Auckland Airport would have turned into this adventure?

Haere Ra my good friends, take care, I could have sworn my van wiggled her tail that little bit to show off her new mermaid motif.

Mathew told me about the seaweed pickers at Awanui, so I drove back towards Kaitaia as I wanted to capture this on camera. It took forever to drive there, my back aching from sitting for such a long time.

Finally, I reached Awanui on the West Coast of New Zealand. It seemed silly that within a three hour drive I was across the country looking at a different sea. The beaches here untamed; seaweed, shells, wood, all sorts of flotsam being washed up to shore, and in the distance there were tiny old shacks built from wood of all types.

As I walked closer, some of them were not so tiny and had a permanent feel about them. Pot plants with geraniums on windowsills, canvas verandas erected, some shielded with wooden porches, others with small fences around them, some pristine and tidy, others their back yard was a bomb site. All sorts of paraphernalia had been collected, a hoarder's paradise by the looks of it. The one I was standing in front of sported glass windows of all shapes and sizes, a small porch, and an old rocking chair sat proudly upon it. The house looked like something out of a child's story book or a hobbit house. Very tidy; large logs of wood were dragged up and placed around a small front garden and painted white, marking its territory. From the roof sprouted a small chimney, even that looked like a caricature I had once seen in a Harry Potter movie.

I knocked on the door post where many bits and pieces hung off a large piece of drift wood; black and white seagull feathers entwined into a flax rope that bound it all together, and it clacked in the wind sounding flat and toneless, nothing like a wind chime.

I thought I should ask for permission to photograph this picker's home, but no-one was home, no-one answered when I called out, 'Cooee.' Only silence, yet it looked lived in. My decision to snap a few shots was instant, my camera clicked away. I went to the back of this little wiggly house where mounds of drying seaweed hung on fences of driftwood that stunk. *Pooh!* It made you gag it was so strong.

Walking back towards my car and Mermaid, I spotted a tiny old lady with a sack on her back. She walked towards me and I wondered if this was the owner, so I approached her.

'Go away,' she screeched, waving her walking stick menacingly at me. 'Go on, piss off you nosey bugger!' She was almost charging at me, her old wrinkled face full anger, 'and stay away,' she yelled. I sprinted off and away to the safety of my car and van and took off at a very fast rate of knots.

I was on my way again. I had taken some good photos, was a bit shaken, but still I had to laugh at this little old lady and her

Metal Mermaid

belligerence. Next port of call, Maungatepere–a very small farming town. Finding a spot to park to buy a chocolate milkshake was not a problem, it was deserted. Then onto Dargaville. Nothing much to offer there, obviously a mix of farming and fishing but there wasn't a soul in sight to ask about what went on here. It looked very country, some of the houses olde world and rather cute looking, so where next?.

My map said Helensville. This place was again really pretty, and after buying some teabags at one of the local stores I was told I could camp at a local farmer's field, the store owner ringing the farmer to ask if it was alright, then gave me the directions. It sounded positive but then I was told the price was fifty dollars a night, with a stay for three get the fourth one free deal. I said, 'But it's just a paddock. What is there for me to pay that much?'

The storekeeper looked really embarrassed. 'Better if you carry on Ma'am.'

'Yes, I think so as well,' I said.

Where to from here? Well to get anywhere I wanted to go it was a winding drive through Auckland city and suburbs. Or I could take a bypass through Auckland that would lead me to the Coromandel Peninsula. I pulled over to study my map.

Dry dust was swirling everywhere, old dry corn husks rattled in the soft dusty wind. An old wood mill on my left looked deserted offering the perfect time to snap some photos. The atmosphere was still, a photographer's dream.

My camera lens zoomed up into the upper hatchway where a rusty winch and hook hung down from the opening, it creaked its rusty song as the soft wind played around the old links. The place smelt of decaying wood, a forgotten era, and would be a classic country town photo. I clicked away, quite happy with the results, checking on camera settings and the photo taken each time.

Resting my back against the car, I was quite comfortable in my own little world. Suddenly, in the gateway not six meters away from me stood three men, young, unkempt and beer with bottles in their hands.

'Hey bitch,' one of them called. 'Want a bit of this?' He gyrated his hips and started to unzip his fly.

I fled to the inside of my car and put my foot down, the Mermaid swinging out suddenly behind me. Loud crashes followed me; I knew they were throwing bottles at me and could not go any faster to get the hell out of this town. An hour's drive away I stopped and checked for damage; there was a small dent high up on my van, a shard of brown glass on the jeeps little bumper. I was still shaking from the crude malevolent behaviour. In fact, my last three experiences had not been pleasant at all; chased off, almost fleeced by a farmer, and threatened with abuse. Should I report this to the police, or would I be just another tourist?

I was certainly going to add it to my Facebook page to warn anyone thinking of stopping along the country road to leave as fast as you can. I must admit, the photos I had taken were charming but sadly, the people left a bad taste in my mouth. Time to put my GPS into action, typing in my destination, it took maybe two minutes to configure. There was the highway for me to follow. God Bless the GPS.

A four-hour drive awaited me through Auckland's highways and byways, the GPS not failing me once. I was not stopping off at Margi's. I was on a mission. Papakura, Pokeno and Pipiroa whizzed by, my car making short work of the miles, and by nine pm that night I was finally in the Coromandel. As I drove into the township, I saw a caravan park sign on the outskirts. I headed there praying they had a vacancy for me.

The blinking red sign said 'no vacancies'. I drove up the winding road for a good hour but there was nothing else in sight and as far as I could see no turning point. I was going to have to reverse down the narrow road in the dark as there were no streetlights. My worst nightmare coming true.

I started to reverse feeling confident but the lurch I felt made me slam on all brakes; the van's back wheels had suddenly lost traction and she started tipping to one side, my foot and the brake pedal now glued to each other. I tried to go forward but the wheels just spun around. I got out of the Jeep to find nothing but air under my feet; pitch dark and no solid ground that I could see or feel to get back onto the road. Terror took hold. I wanted to scream with the suffocating fear that gripped my throat and fumbling around for my phone, I found the number of the AA. The phone rang then twice, 'Please leave a message.' Not much bloody use. I threw the phone back onto the passenger seat.

I searched for the torch remembering it was stored in the boot, without light I could not find the road or see where I was? Was I dangling over the side of the road ready to crash down the bank and into the sea? Drowned or missing went through my mind.

I had to fight the nausea that started to roll over me. I had to stay in control–I had–my imagination causing all sorts of horrors to erupt in my head. Crawling across to the passenger side, I tried to open the door to get out on the roadside, but the door would not budge. I sat up all night with my foot on the brake and the handbrake pulled up tight, the sea just below me. I could hear it surging over rocks or sand. I had no idea of my situation. Dawn was taking its time to creep up over the horizon, and every time I fell into a sleep I would jerk awake, the fear I felt was like no other I had ever experienced.

Daylight started as a very faint line, then became a slight glow. I held my breath as the sky brightened; hopefully in ten minutes or so I would be able to see where I was and what had gone wrong. Morning had never felt so welcome in my whole life. To say it felt good is an understatement–I was ecstatic. I sat up to take in where I was. The situation was dire, of that I was sure, and was holding my breath expecting sudden death to swoop in and grab me knowing I was in the most dangerous of situations, and that my holiday–perhaps even my life–was over.

Foolish is not the word I would use when I discovered I was backed into a small ditch on the side of the road next to a paddock. The car and Mermaid both on a slight tilt on the paddock side, not the sea. If I had just reached out with my foot one extra inch or two I would have found sure footing. I got the giggles, my knees sagging with fatigue, my nightmare of driving off a mile-high precipice at sixty kilometres an hour firmly fixed in my head, my over-active imagination overruling common-sense. I then realised the reason why I could not get out on the passenger side was that the door was locked. How stupid am I? Grabbing my phone again, I rang the AA number. A male voice answered, saying, 'It will take me an hour to get there.'

'I'm not going anywhere,' I said with a smile.

Chapter 33

A large brown cow wandered over to see what all the fuss was about, she looked at me then at the fence line the Mermaid had clung to all night. I'm sure she smiled as well; stupid tourist written in her big brown eyes.

Finally the AA car came barrelling down the road to haul me out. An old man driving, he stood there, hands on hips and harrumphed. I wanted to apologise but for some reason I thought, damn it, I'm a paying customer so get stuffed. He towed me out of the overgrown grass and muddy ditch, made sure everything worked, revved the hell out of the engine, presumably blowing out anything struck up the exhaust pipe, and was about to drive off, saying, 'Follow me.'

'Well I would if I could, but I can't turn it around,' I replied. With a groan he said, 'Here, get out, let me.'

I was in a foul mood myself with no sleep and the fear not quite gone. 'I beg your pardon,' I asked. His stare challenged me.

'Look lady, you want this thing of yours turned around or not?' he snarled.

'Well yes, I do, thank you,' I replied through gritted teeth.

He did a pretty good job of turning my little rig around with just a few scraping sounds coming from underneath. He riled me, though, treating me like the village idiot. I felt if I said something to him, he would walk off in an instant leaving me stuck.

I decided mouth shut, get the job done, then I was going to call into this person's workplace and have a word with his manager, or was I being small-minded, tired and childish? Time to think it over once I found a caravan park.

I signed papers and he drove off with a rush, obviously his breakfast was waiting for him. Starting my car, I followed his taillights out, rounding a corner that just blew me away; the sea was grey, flat, calm and beautiful, and there was nothing for miles but the ocean. Between me and the side of the road was a massive drop right into the sea. No fence. No signs of danger. Just huge rocks below that would have killed me outright if I had gone over.

I had driven past this very spot without a hitch late last night not noticing it was there; too busy looking for the kind sign that said 'vacancy.' I shook all the way to Coromandel township.

Two caravan parks later, I finally found one with a vacancy, and as I paid my fee for one week I asked why there was so much activity? The tired, faded women gave me a half-hearted smile shoving a pamphlet towards me. I gave it a cursory glance and spied 'Art Trail'. Tucking it into my purse, off I went to find my patch of grass, back the Mermaid in, make a cup of tea and sink onto my bed, gulping back tears of relief. 'Don't be silly, Tara, you're alive and safe.' The hot tea worked wonders; I slept for three solid hours, and once fully awake saw the colourful pamphlet declaring Art Trail sticking up out of my purse. It looked good to me.

Once I took an interest, I found the Coromandel alive with energy. While there I sourced so much to do and see, not all of them advertised, as once I asked for more information that's exactly what I got from the artists. The Art Trail was fabulous and I got the hands-on treatment with most of the artists. I visited wood-turning studios, and studios with brightly coloured abstract paintings, montage, collage, and pale watercolours. Every studio was different, selling vibrant pieces on canvas, wood, glass and pottery.

One particular artist painted amazing beach scenes; I succumbed and bought a very small one to put inside the Mermaid. There was pottery, my hands loving the feel of clay. In a jewellery studio I made a small pendant from shell and a tiny piece of Greenstone, the New Zealand jade. In another, I watched glass blowing turn into a multi-coloured fish and a blacksmith's studio two doors down formed wrought iron into amazing works of art.

A factory down the road made tri-cornered canvas; a first for me. The week sped by. I asked if I could stay another week, and when confirmed, I paid for it immediately; I was having so much fun. The little tour bus that pulled up every morning in front of the caravan park drove me around the Art Trail, the driver now knew my name. 'Morning Tara,' Pat would call out as I got on. Off we would chug, sometimes the bus was full and sometimes there were only one or two on board.

Pat told me about a train which went to visit the renowned potter Barry Bicknell, who lived on a few hectares up in the hills. It sounded wonderful. Pat arranged a ticket for me on the Creek Railway through a magical Kauri forest, stopping at the top of a mountain called the Eyeful Tower. The view from this point was amazing, the potter was amazing, his work sought and bought internationally. Charmed by his studio and his ability to explain his passion of pottery, how he used different clays, what to mix and not mix, this man was a mine of information. It was an interesting three hours and I thanked Pat profusely for getting me there.

The Nest, another gallery, was a weaving studio. Not like the Maori weaving that Pania and family had tried to teach me, this woman could weave concrete if she wanted to. Words like 'beautiful', 'amazing' and 'gorgeous' in my mind did not give the artist enough credit; I would have called it sublimely delicate, the only words to describe her exhibition. Her hands flew over strings of vibrant colours ending up with a multi-textured wall hanging that took your breath away.

Pat invited me to accompany him to the Coromandel fireworks exhibition. 'Yes, I would love to go,' I replied expecting to go on the bus with others. Pat arrived all swished up and clean shaven, which was uncommon from what I had previously seen; his long grey hair now in a thin ponytail, wearing a clean, rumpled shirt and long baggy beach shorts. It screamed bachelor.

He knocked at my door. I was dressed in a long skirt of silver threaded Bali silk, a pretty blue top and sandals. I had put up my hair in combs, with a little eye makeup and lip gloss. His comment, 'Wow you really scrub up well.'

Our transport was his car, and I felt like a child as I asked, 'Where is the bus and other people?'

He looked mildly surprised, 'In the garage. We are it–you and me,' he said.

Pat had packed a picnic hamper and a chilly bin full of ice. Two champagne bottles were tucked deeply into the ice, his hand on my elbow guiding me into the passenger's seat, he gave me the seat belt to click into place then closed the door. My thoughts racing. *Does he think we are on a date?* I had only agreed as I thought it was a fireworks show with a crowd included on his bus, not on our own.

Too late to change my mind as we drove off. Parking at the communal grounds, we joined many others sitting on picnic blankets as kids ran around screeching and playing tag with each other. I felt quite safe in a crowd. Pat sorted the picnic gear out, spread out a blanket for us to sit on and then opened the champagne. 'To us,' he declared and threw it down his throat. I watched his prominent Adam's apple as it bobbed up and down with eager appreciation of the cold drink. Prickles of apprehension went down my spine. I sipped mine thinking, 'Keep a clear head, Tara. There's something going on here.' Pat chugged his way through the bottle and opened another. 'Come on, Babe,' he slurred. 'Keep up.' So I was 'Babe' now, not Tara.

'Sure thing, Pat,' I agreed, tipping mine out on the grass behind me. The fireworks went off and we all ooh'd and aah'd at the pretty lights blazing their way across the sky. As I looked over to where Pat was sitting, I received the thumbs up sign and a leering wink. 'Want to snuggle up?' he slurred.

'Oh dear God! Why me?' I thought.

Pat stumbled off towards the toilet block, I had seen a taxi rank close by the park, so I walked there and got myself home, locking up the Mermaid tightly. Once inside, I undressed, my head slightly aching, but that night I had a deep sleep with troubled dreams.

There had been nights like this before where I could almost smell Russ and his aftershave. Tonight, as I lay there thinking to myself, 'Why me?' I could again feel Russ there beside me, his clean, male smell with a hint of lemongrass was around me. I wanted to feel his arms around me again, I still missed him incredibly. I wanted to hear his sexy chuckle, listen to his deep, even breathing as he slept. I wanted to lay my head on his chest and listen to his heartbeat strongly and soundly.

'I miss you so much, Russ,' I whispered to the night sky. Will I ever feel affection for another as I did with you? I suddenly realised it would soon be two years since he'd died. Sleep finally arrived. Dreams of a previous life with Russ and Rae as baby, I woke with an aching heart for times now past, shaking myself mentally as this was no time to feel melancholy.

Chapter 34

Whitianga thermal pools offered a spa so I rang, booked, and drove to the address an hour later, feeling relief seep into muscles around my neck and shoulders as they were massaged. The headache behind my eyes that was never too far away from a migraine went away with her touch. I was now ready to go forward on my journey. I headed back to the caravan park. I still had two days to stay and intended to travel the district a little more. The tourist shop told me Thames and Paeroa were worth a visit, but they warned me to leave my van where it was, if it was possible, as the tourist season was unusually high, and accommodation was looking sparse. Well, I had two days so why not just drive there and back?

It was the right decision, as both townships were packed. I opted to pack a small bag and put it in the boot so if I needed to stay over I had all I needed and would sleep in the car, not the comfiest but it would do for one night. Thames and Paeroa ready or not I was coming to see what you had to show me.

As I drove out of the caravan park there was a forlorn looking Pat sitting in his empty bus. I waved and beeped my horn and as I drove past his face looked haggard but I was not stopping to ask why. It was plain to me that too much booze was the culprit. Sorry Pat, I'm busy and I really don't want you for my companion, now or in the near future.

Waihi, the hot water beach, was tempting. I was told by a local, 'It's easy, lady. You dig a hole in the sand and lie in it.' I watched as he did this, hot water spurted up creating a sandy muddy bath. When the tide rushes in you get the ocean mixed with volcanic water. All along the beach you could see people bathing in the hot water, it was supposed to be therapeutic and I take my hat off to those who say so but I was not one of them. In fact, it looked like a day at Brighton in England, with tourists wandering around with hankies tied in all four corners on their heads, turning pink to red in the sun. I could not understand that culture and couldn't understand this one.

It was time to up and move on. There were folk passing by covered in thick, slimy sand; no not for me. I was off to tackle the Karangahapie Gorge. Warned this gorge was very twisting and turned in tight little corners, I had to be very careful and keep the speed down. They were not wrong; it was a nightmare of a twisting, turning road that I almost squealed with fear at many times, especially when I met oncoming traffic. There was no way on this good earth I was going to do this at night, so wanted to get back to the Mermaid. There was one parking bay where it looked worth stopping, the views amazing, so I was busy taking photos. I remembered the Maori fable about a mystical dragon-like creature in the gorge beneath me. They called it a 'Taniwha', and fingers crossed it was a fable, I could not have handled a Taniwha as well.

The one beautiful attraction in Waihi was a church I passed by; it was so pretty. Stopping to take a photo, one of the parishioners invited me inside. The Maori motifs where incredible, what really took my eye was the huge stained-glass window of the Virgin Mary and Christ cloaked in Maori costume. Paeroa was amazing. Driving around looking for some sort of tourist billboard, it was Sunday, and like Perth, everything was closed. It was by sheer fluke I saw some teenagers walking along in the street dressed in Scottish kilts, so I stopped and asked why. They were helpful, inviting me to attend a rehearsal of the Paeroa Highland Games and Tattoo. Marching teams covered the fields in formations and it was so much fun with the noise, laughing, clapping and cheering other teams on. I was thrilled I saw something few tourists got to see and this time I videoed it with my phone. What a kaleidoscope of music and colour, the tight formations were amazing. How they knew what foot to put where would have confused me, but these folk were smart; the steps were perfect. No-one was being stupid or silly, it was all serious while they were practising, after that there was a clan barbeque. I left them to it even though I was made welcome and the smell of cooking sausages was heaven to my nostrils.

I slept in my car that night, the seat set right back and with my pillow was quite comfy. I was really tired so bought myself a meat pie and a lemonade from the dairy across the road. Mrs Mac's pies were also famous here and tasted just as bad as they did back home. The thought of driving through those winding hills back to the Mermaid was a deterrent for even a brave driver. A public toilet was a five-minute drive away, so I quickly walked there and back, the cold-water tap a blessing as I felt sticky from travel and dinner.

Tauranga was my next place to visit but first I had to tackle that horrendous gorge again and pick up the Mermaid. I was fast asleep, having parked under a streetlight for safety, when clunking on the window woke me, the local police asking me to move on. I explained my situation to the officer, and they allowed to me park in the police carpark for the night with strong warnings that this area was not safe at night, especially for a woman on her own. I thanked them for their kindness and feeling a lot more secure than on the roadside, I slept deeply, waking up to a glorious day. Again, off to the public toilets, a quick wash and buying myself an orange and banana at the corner shop. On my return I discovered a deep scratch down the side of my car. While I had been washing my face and buying fruit someone had vandalised my vehicle. I drove off feeling very pissed off with Paeroa.

A three-hour drive back to pick up the Mermaid, hitch her up and go where? I was tired, scratchy and annoyed that some miserable little sod could happily ruin another's car like that.

I again asked if I could stay for an extra night at Coromandel. The answer was, 'No sorry.' My space was booked to someone else.

I was so tired I felt like the ground kept shifting from under me, I really needed a good meal and a good night's sleep. Staying here was not an option, so I wearily hitched the Mermaid to the car, started the engine and drove away from the camping ground.

Chapter 35

Pulling out onto the main freeway, I decided to drive straight through to Tauranga; it was a city and appeared to have many caravan parks. I plucked one from the Google directory on my phone and rang ahead. 'Yes, welcome.' I booked in for one week. All I had to do was get there in one piece over that awful mountain gorge again, so time to stay alert and awake. It was breakfast time and I had to get some energy.

Pulling over at small café not noticing a certain tourist bus was parked further down the road, I walked in and ordered. 'Eggs, bacon, baked beans on toast, with a pot of hot tea on the strong side. please.'

I sat down to read the paper and wait for my order when I heard, 'Hi Tara. How are you? Where are you going?' I did not want to have any conversation, so I buried my face into the paper. There was loud throat clearing then the paper was rattled in my hands.

'Hi Tara.'

My temper snapped and I threw the paper down, 'I know what you bloody said, and if I wanted you to know I would tell you, now go away.'

Pat scurried out of the shop, the café cook looking amazed at my outburst.

'Sorry,' I said. 'He's been annoying me lately.'

'That's our Pat, scaring off the tourists,' the waitress said. I did not add to it as I would only be insulting. I did, however, enjoy my meal immensely, slurped back the hot tea, and off I drove replete, happy to be off on another adventure.

Tauranga is a large city and after finding my caravan park and settling in, setting up my little camp for the first time, other campers came over and greeted me. An older couple, Connor and Bridie–both Irish–were touring New Zealand and working their way around.

'But don't tell the tax man,' Connor laughed. What a delightful couple. Their van was their home and had been for the past year, and they had been in this caravan park for nearly a month, picking fruit around the countryside. If Connor found work on a farm, Bridie would find work in the township somewhere. Their life was simple, and I was delighted to have found like-minded people. Bridie loved to cook, and when I had come home from my tours I would be yoo-hooed to pop over for a hot cuppa and a biscuit or two. I knew she really craved another woman to natter to and I enjoyed her company.

Tauranga was a tourist's Mecca, every little knick-knack or Kiwiana was there in every shop I ventured into. I had to buy some new clothes, as my own were now way too big for me, opting for the Salvation army shop, 'the Salvos' as we call them back home, then it was on to a hair salon. My biggest issue was, do I get it cut short again or simply tie it back and grow it? I also fancied just shopping for the hell of it, and if I felt like it, maybe the movies.

Tauranga is a large bustling city in the Bay of Plenty, and when you want to find something to do there are so many choices. As for me, I found the picture theatre and enjoyed watching 'Avatar'. It was a re-run from the previous year and I had taken Jess to see it, both of us loving it. The movie was worthwhile seeing again, so here I was on my own, in the dark, munching on a choc-bomb ice-cream and enjoying it. After the movie I planned a little therapy shopping, with the thought not to buy too much as I lived in a very small space; a little grocery shopping for my tiny kitchen, some meat and veggies for dinner, plus a nice cake to share with Connor and his 'bride', as he called Bridie.

All was going to plan. I did all I had to do and arriving back at the park I could see the Mermaid from the gate where I got out, the Mermaid drawing on her round bum had become a welcome beacon to me. *My home* it seemed to say.

Bridie yoo-hooed and waved; she was at the clothesline hanging her washing out. Unpacking all my goodies, I put the jug on and set out my small picnic table. Bridie smiled as she wandered up. 'What have you been up to all day?' I invited her to sit and I would divulge all.

'And while I'm at it,' I asked, 'would you like a cup of tea and a piece of chocolate cake?'

'I'd love that. Can I ask Con to join us?'

'Con!' she yelled. She could have won a hog calling competition, the poor man banging his head as he came rushing around their van. 'God, woman, you wail like a banshee.'

Con always made me laugh with his comments. 'Want a cuppa and a piece of cake?' I asked.

'Does a bear crap in the woods?' he replied.

For some reason that struck me as super funny and laughter ripped out of me. I had to sit down on the ground, I couldn't stand up I was laughing so hard.

Afternoon tea with these two was good medicine.

Four days rushed by and, as well as touring, I helped Bridie make jams and chutneys to sell at the local farmer's market that weekend. It was a flurry of activity, but we succeeded between us. There on her kitchen bench by Friday night were fifteen jars of onion jam and twelve jars of lemon and persimmon jam, which smelt and tasted divine. I hadn't tasted this delight before and I was hooked. Plus, fifteen jars of a mixed berry jam she had labelled 'Berry Exotica' and fifteen jars of courgette chutney for the markets on Saturday and Sunday.

We had cooked from dawn until dusk from Friday noon and it looked amazing.

I offered to help them set up their stall. It was fun, almost selling out of their produce, and I was given a jar of each for payment but the Sunday ended on a sad note as Monday morning I was leaving Tauranga.

I had not seen all the sights but had made some wonderful mates. I said goodnight, promising I would call in tomorrow to say goodbye. As I fell asleep that night I felt sad I had to leave, but a little excited that I was on my way again to drive around the coast to Gisborne, my GPS all set up to guide me, my van all packed up and secure.

I recently read about the tale of the Maori Mermaid and this I had to see for myself, deciding I was going to go to Napier to actually see a Metal Mermaid. First, I had some necessary groceries to buy and not from the camp shop–they were too overpriced. I was supposed to be out of there by eleven am but the time was twelve-thirty as I drove up. I saw my little home attached to a tractor obviously to be towed away, the new resident waiting just inside the campgrounds. The other thing I saw was Con on the tractor being carefully guided backwards by Bridie. I was greeted with, 'Thank Holy Mother Mary and all the saints you're back! They were going to toss you out, so we offered to park the Mermaid alongside us.'

I could see they had taken down their canvas annex and clothesline to accommodate me. Now that's good friends for you, I thought. Bridie's fair complexion now beet red in the afternoon heat, Con for once silent, he was fuming, not because I was a little late but because the camp owners had no empathy.

I had some smoothing over to do, so asked Con to park my little van out in the parking lot, of course with the camp manager's permission. I did some greasing up to them and thanking them for the extra week and consideration. Then once I had made sure they were fine with me parking there for approximately, 'An hour and no more,'

I went over to my friend's van and helped them reassemble their awning and clothesline. Con brooded, 'Pure insulting,' he muttered. Bridie fussed, talked incessantly and made no sense at all.

Giving them both a hug, I thanked them for their friendship and consideration, said I would be their camp neighbour anytime, told them where I was heading to, and gave them my phone number and a big box of locally made chocolates.

I drove to Ohope beach for my first stay that night. A two-hour drive, we purred along, my van, the car and I all feeling great. I settled into a free camp site offered by the community for one night. It had a cold water tap and public toilets across the field, a bit of a dash but the day was warm, and I was really very relaxed. I snuggled into my bed for the night, slept peacefully, woke up in the morning, made myself a cup of tea, poured milk on my Weet-Bix for breakfast, cleared away my dishes, tidied my clothes, then wandered over to the public toilets. I spoke to the janitor, asking, 'What is there to see around here?' Marty, the janitor, who wore a huge name tag on her overalls, told me a story of Oppo the dolphin that used to swim here and was very famous until it was shot.

'But that happened nearly forty years ago,' she said. 'Since then, no more dolphins have made themselves known to any one of us who live here.'

How sad, I thought. Humans and their fear of the unknown. By then I was busting to go inside and complete my morning ablutions, a big sigh as the hot water from the shower hit my body. I could hear the sea washing up onto the sand, birds calling, wind in the treetops and I could also hear a distinct, 'Yoo-hoo Tara, where are you?'

Chapter 36

I could not believe it. Hitching my beach towel up around me, I fumbled outside and saw my friends' van pulling up next to mine, it was Bridie and Connor. What the heck? 'Missed you,' they cried in unison. 'What, why?' I was a little fazed by it all. 'Why are you here? What are you doing?' I asked. Bridie was the first out of their old truck and tried to speak but she was gurgling nonsense, Connor than came to the rescue, 'Mind if we become your neighbour just for a month or two?' he asked.

I was so confused. 'I'm moving on guys. I'm not staying here.' Bridie was just about on her knees with the giggles, tears running down her ever-rosy cheeks. 'Your face is a picture,' she gurgled. Con's smile was infectious as well. I could feel bubbles of laughter building up inside me and soon all three of us were giggling like naughty school kids. I took a big breath and said, 'Stop. What's going on?' the towel I had around me becoming cold.

Connor explained, his Irish brogue breaking in and out of the English language. 'We tought that was a little unfair of themselves to chuck you out, we did.' Then Bridie took over, their arms now around each other.

'Look Tara, we have another four months here in New Zealand picking fruit and going to the country markets selling our produce. We know you are trying to see as much as you can as well, so why not join up as a team? You like us, we like you, we would welcome your company and help that's if you want to.'

Then she stood back, hands on broad hips and said, 'How's that!'

Well that gave me something to think about, it was the least likely situation I had thought of and I will admit I was dubious about this adventure together. I had planned on doing it on my own, owing no-one anything, time or money, and I must admit I enjoyed being on my own, a lot.

The look on their faces when I said, 'I need some time to think about this,' was not good, concerned frowns replacing the smiles.

I went inside my van, closed the door, removed the damp towel, changing into jeans and t-shirt, pushed a brush through my hair, all the time considering my options. Making myself some tea, I thought some more. This is not what I had planned but it may be heaven sent as I could see the real New Zealand instead of touristy stuff all the time. This could be my chance to travel onto the unknown roads and meet the locals, what I had intended to do. I had struck it lucky with Pania and Mathew, but so far I had to really dig deep to see the real Kiwi. I know they're rare and uncommon but that's what I came to see, the real Kiwi, and I did not mean the bird variety.

I could hear Connor and Bridie puttering around outside their van, filling water bottles and doing what caravaners do; checking everything is in place and ship shape, their voices murmuring as they worked.

I grabbed the rest of the chocolate cake I had bought the day before, opened my van door and yelled, 'Put the jug on, I'm coming over.' My decision was made. It was yes as far as Napier, then I was going on my own. They agreed to this, and suddenly I was of part a team.

We planned our next stop, the Tanetua country fair, held the next weekend. Our next question was where to find a camp site so we could preserve the produce and bottle it up. Con wanted to find work on a farm as he adored horses, and Bridie and I wanted to pick fruit for jam and buy the veggies for chutneys. I was having fun; I loved the markets, plus making jams and chutneys. Who would have thought at this stage in life I would have a new career as an entrepreneurial jam and chutney maker plus label writer?

It was community camping where we were and for one to two nights only, any thoughts of staying here, soon dismissed by the tractor that chugged over, the caretaker holding out his hand for the ten dollars per night. His look deterring any requests to stay longer muttering, 'Bloody camp gypsies,' under his breath. I looked up at Con. He shook his head, and I could not help myself saying, 'Excuse me, did you say something?' This awful unkempt, unshaven person smelling of stale sweat, his fingers and teeth stained from smoking had the cheek to call me a camp gypsy! He must have seen the anger on my face as he said, 'Nope lady. Just here to collect what's owed.'

The difference between us and him was outstanding; we all looked clean and healthy and smiling. This person stank, his unshaven face yellow and he called us names. I wanted to physically punch him one. How dare he assume we were anything like him just because we preferred to caravan around New Zealand. What a rude shmuck!

Both of us pulled out of that place, heading off towards our destination hoping we would find a place to stay more permanently as this was problem number one. My van was so small I could park almost anywhere, but their van was big and so was the tow vehicle. Con and Bridie needed space, so fingers crossed, we needed a caravan park genie to help us.

We pulled into a small country township that was aflutter with flags advertising the Bucking Bronco competitions and country fair. I stopped at the local dairy to ask about parking our vans, the owner said, 'Sure thing, love. Round the back, you're the first to arrive.'

I could not believe our luck as round the back was a huge grass patch, ablution block that was so clean and fresh with plastic flowers adorning the wash rooms, showers that sparkled, unisex toilets, and for the men it was an open shower under the pine trees.

Rangi was the owner's name, and what a fabulous greeting. The price, ten dollars a night with the use of all amenities. Rangi made a fuss of us making sure we had soap for the piping hot shower, all of us very grateful for her kindness. Next question was how long can we stay, Rangi? She was so laid back. 'Long as you like, sweetie,' she replied. 'Love the company.'

Bridie explained that we intended to make jams and chutneys and sell them at the coming fair and weekend markets. 'Hey, help yourself,' Rangi said. 'Need any information of where to go and get stuff, just ask.'

My last thought that night as I went to sleep was how safe I felt here and how much fun I was going to have if Rangi was what the true-blue Kiwi was like. I could not wait. When I woke up in the morning, I had another neighbour–a horse float with the most gorgeous chestnut mare inside. I'm not a horse person but this horse lived up to her name 'Beauty'. I loved the way she smelt and nuzzled me as I fed her carrots and apples. 'Not too many,' Carole the horse owner warned me. 'She'll get fat. She's here to ride in the competitions.'

Later that same day, Con arrived back to their van a little worse for wear. He'd been down, 'To the pub, darlin',' he slurred. I had noticed his absence and had decided not to ask any questions as it was none of my business.

My tum hit rock bottom. I hated drunks with a vengeance. Was this who he really was–a sly grogger? Bridie read me well as over our combined dinner she whispered, 'He's fine Tara. Himself is celebrating his new job.' Con was now fully employed and had decided to join the boys to celebrate.

He was helping build the stalls for the country fair, now Con the roustabout and very proud of his new position in life.

Bridie and I were told fruit pickers were wanted for a day. We left early in the morning driving there in my car. An hour down the road was a fruit farm; my arms, legs and head ached by the end of the day and all I wanted was a hot cup of anything and a lie down, which I got thanks to Rangi. We were allowed to keep any windblown or fallen bruised fruit, Bridie and I both delighted at the boot full of promising jam. As for chutneys or pickles, there was nothing, although we searched high and low for what we wanted.

Rangi tried to help us, ringing her family and mates, nothing available was the answer. As Bridie diced, spliced and cored all sorts of fruit, I washed the Agee jars in an old copper Rangi had in her back yard; the smell of boiling water bringing back memories of my childhood when my mum boiled the copper to wash the blankets. It triggered a desire to ring Rae and Jess; I had become quite hesitant, as all I got was snide comments or demands to come home.

Today was no different as I said, 'Hi honey, its Mum. How are you both?'

'There are three of us here, Mum.'

I could sense the animosity immediately. 'I'm just checking in to say hi. I'm fine, staying at a place called Tanetua. Say hi to Jono as well.'

'Mum, I need to seriously talk to you, and I can't do it now,' Rae demanded. 'I will ring you tonight, and Mum–this is serious, we need to talk as soon as possible, so please answer your phone. I will ring you five pm Perth time, is that alright with you?'

'Yes it is. Talk then. Bye Rae, love to all.'

'Yeah right,' she said and put the phone down.

It played on my mind how easily I let Rae pop my happy balloon, and it was noticed during the dinner shared with Rangi, myself, Carole, Bridie and Con–a communal get together–all sharing where we were from, what we did as a living. I let them talk, only answering when asked a question, excusing myself as soon as possible to go inside my little home and await the phone call from Rae. Bridie followed me giving me a big warm hug, 'If we can help, tell us,' she said. I must have looked mournful as I nodded and went inside.

True to her word, Rae rang. 'Mum,' she said before I got my hello out, 'I need to ask you what you are doing with the house, it's an overgrown mess. Jono and I want to move in as soon as possible, someone has to act responsible. I also want to know where and when my share of Dad's money is coming to me. We want to start a life together, but you are holding us all back with your disappearing act and refusal to contact me.'

I was stunned, speechless and all I could say was, 'What are you talking about Rae? I have hired a gardener that regularly mows my lawns, trims gardens and hedges. As for money? Well, you already know I am the only recipient of Russ's will, plus in sole charge of Jess's education trust.'

'Yes, I know all that,' she interrupted, 'but we all think it's totally unfair, plus Jono wants to home school Jess and use any money left for a home for us.'

What a bloody cheek this young woman had! I had to think about this. 'Tell you what, Rae, I will ring you back tomorrow at lunchtime. Let me sleep on it.'

'Well I hope you do or I'm going to have to get a lawyer involved with this mess you have left us with.'

Again, the phone clicked off in my ear. What mess had I left? I was confused by her nasty attitude and accusations and now emotional blackmail. What was wrong with her? The light was still on in Rangi's kitchen and I needed someone to talk to. In fact, I need Russ to talk to. I was so angry I felt there was steam exploding out of my ears.

At the table coring apples and peeling fruit sat Carole, Con and Bridie, Rangi making tea and pikelets/ I saw them all look up and the dam full of tears burst. Eventually, when I had calmed down enough, I told them about Russ, Rae and Jess, about how we were close as a family and now it was awful. I could not blame Jono; Rae was a free agent and could make up her own mind.

I told them how Rae accused me of being a lesbian because of my friendship with Gilly, then I told them about Gilly; how I was sucked in, only to be told to, 'F–off,' at the airport.

Bridie's face looked worn and sad, Carole looked indignant, Con was angry and Rangi tut-tutted while she bustled about preparing our supper.

I was amongst good friends here as they wrangled with my problem and what I should say and what to do. It was Carole who came up with, 'Do you have a friend or neighbour that can take photos of your home and grounds, have them sent them to you via the internet?'

What a great idea, we all agreed. 'I'm sure I can find someone,' I said.

Carole continued, 'Now the big question is–can your daughter contest the will?'

I told them I had been in contact with the lawyer's firm about six months ago as they had emailed me with advice and requested I leave all the money in superannuation and live off the accrued interest. I had agreed to this and signed the papers he had faxed through to me. No, Rae cannot contest the will. Russ and I had a trust fund set up for Jess until he was twenty-five. The house, contents and bank balance were Rae's once I died.

I went to bed very stressed, my night full of Rae's demands, the morning bringing no relief as I could not eat or drink until I had sorted this mess out. I rang my best friend, Jo, who was very surprised to hear from me other than through our weekly emails to each other; our way of our catching up.

She was shocked at my news about Rae's demands, 'Cheeky little bitch,' she declared. She offered to do the photo thing and came up with a brilliant idea. 'Tara, I have my cousin from the UK coming here to visit for a while, why not rent your home to her and her husband, just for the next few months? I will vouch for her. In fact, I will pay the deposit to you for them. I know they would love this opportunity.'

'Rent my home out fully furnished?' I asked.

'Why not?' she replied, 'what are you doing with it?'

I did not have the time to think about it as Rae was on the war path. 'Okay, if you vouch for them, let's do it,' I said.

One huge problem solved, I would ring my lawyer and ask them to fax Jo a rental agreement with a minimal amount for full upkeep of the house and grounds. And she was sending me photos of the grounds, front and back gardens and any comments of neglect, wear and tear that I needed to hear about.

Mr Rounding, my lawyer, was next. I asked what he though and it came out as a wail. 'What am I going to do?' 'Nothing,' he replied. 'It's as you said, the house and all contents are all yours to do with as you will, and as for the superannuation–she can't touch it.' We discussed the education money, it made my stomach turn when he said, 'She can contest that. In fact, we had a discussion with your daughter yesterday.'

Somehow, I was not surprised. Mr Rounding continued, 'I was going to phone you to discuss this sudden turn of events.'

'How much is Jess's fund now?' I queried.

'Just over twelve thousand dollars,' he replied.

'How do I go about giving her this?'

He must have heard the despair in my voice and said, 'Tara, I can write to Rae stating that you concede to releasing Jess's education fund, but if she contests Russ's will or enters your home without your consent, you would have no hesitation in taking matters further.'

Chapter 37

Phew, I was emotionally exhausted. This was too big for me to handle. I promised I would ring Rae, so I pushed in her number on quick dial. She answered, 'Yes, what?'

'Rae, I've been in contact with Mr Rounding. He is writing to you releasing the education money for Jess. He will have a cheque ready for you soon.'

Her voice brightened, 'I thought you would see sense, Mum.'

'That's not all, Rae,' I continued, and could hear her breath catch as I told her, 'I have rented the house out from today, so it's no to you moving into my home.'

'You bloody, nasty, spiteful old cow,' ground out from my daughter's mouth. 'You want to see us fail, don't you! You would be happy to see me single all of my life. Well believe me, you'll pay for this,' and the line went dead.

I collapsed in a heap. I had done what I could, given her what I could, and this was what she thought of me. Bridie found me sobbing into a pile of wet tissues.

'I wonder what her Da thinks of her, God rest his soul,' she said crossing herself. 'Come on now, don't waste your breath on that daughter of yours, you have a life to live and fruit to boil,' she joked. She cleaned my face with a soft wet towel, her voice soothing me as a mother would. 'I'll make the tea while you blow your nose.' Thank you, Lord, for the panacea, hot tea and someone's shoulder to cry on.

The next day I received the photos of my home and grounds. They were lovely, not overgrown and looked fabulous. It made me a little homesick. I also received a large deposit for the rental on my home. I emailed my replied in huge red font, 'Thanks. All under control and have decided to keep gardener on while your family stays there.' I included the phone number of my lawyer telling them all the rental papers were ready at his office. Hopefully, the heaviness would lift from my heart.

The next day, Rangi's wisdom and kindness was what worked on my heart as one huge arm went around my waist. 'I have a challenge for you, young lady; we were both in our early sixties.). Come with me.'

She led me out the back to her garden. 'I hear you're still having trouble finding veggies for your pickles.'

'Yes, there seems to be a shortage of zucchini and tomatoes, that's what I want to make relish.' We walked around her veggie garden, it was not a huge one but enough to feed her and the Whanau when they came back home, or on occasions like this when she had paying guests, as she called us.

Growing on the trellis by her small garage was a bright green leafy vine. It covered the side of an old shed, trailing onto the ground. 'This here is known as a "choko". It's a vegetable you can cook. To me its tasteless, but some people stuff it full of chicken or meat and herbs and eat it like that. I prefer it as a filler for pickles or jams.'

There was also the last of the season's corn that was drying up, some parsley and spring onions, and half a dozen full grown tomatoes.

I had never seen or heard of choko before; shaped like a large egg or a pear and almost the size of an ostrich egg, it had light lime green skin with pointy prickles all over it. When you cut open the weird looking veggie, the flesh was translucent, small seeds clung to a fibrous stem that was the core. It didn't have a smell and was very juicy tasting like sour water with a slight yellow tinge to it. 'What a strange looking plant, are you sure you can eat it?'

Rangi had a large tum that shook up and down when she laughed, this time she chortled at my hesitant face. 'Well, I've eaten these for years, as I said I don't actually like them but a good filler for days when you think there is not enough to go around.'

This was a new idea for me, experimenting with a veggie I knew nothing about.

She was right. I was intrigued. While Bridie was humming away, busy over a large pan of some sort of jelly she was making, I set to with the chokos. To compliment them as a filler I experimented with different herbs and other small amounts of veggies from Rangi's now depleted garden. First, I made small amounts as I did not have a kitchen to cut and dice the veggies. Rangi offered me a hot plate and a large wooden bench in her shed saying, 'You can do as you wish.' I stayed for hours experimenting.

I felt like a scientist writing down all the ingredients, cooking, mixing all sorts to make them tasty. I trashed a few failures first, one of the two pots I had purchased for my own use also trashed because the base was badly burnt.

Rangi to the rescue once more, giving me a huge cooking urn, then back to the drawing board. By the end of the week, I found a recipe that worked made with 10% corn and parsley, 25% garden tomatoes, large brown raisins, sugar, spices, salt, black peppercorns and chilli flakes plus 50% chokos. Time to experiment on the gang I was living with.

Con took a small spoonful of my chutney with the roast pork that Rangi and Carole had cooked that night, it was not so much his face but that he took two helpings, one after another. 'Yum, Tara, that's so good.'

We all took a teaspoon of the chutney and yes, it tasted like tomatoes in butter with a sweet tang to it as it left the tongue. It was very nice.

'I think you have a winner here,' Carole said. Bridie just smiled as she patted my arm. 'It's really good.'

Rangi glowed, her work done. I was feeling so much happier than a week ago, I had let go in more ways than one with her encouragement and ability to let me mull it over and keep my hands busy. They all ate more and talked about tomorrow; Con concerned that the job he had taken on would not be finished in time.

Another job I fell in love with was grooming Beauty. One day, Carole had been very busy training another horse and complained her body was tired, so I offered to brush Beauty down for her while she had a shower and made herself some dinner. I found Beauty loved me back; her rubbery lips would nibble on my sleeve or she would blow out huge puffs of sweet horsy air and almost sounded indignant on my behalf when I told her about my daughter. By the time I had finished brushing her down and making sure she had enough water, I was smiling. Beauty listened to all my worries and shook them off, her magnificent brown eyes telling me she understood perfectly.

Carole was an enigma. Not adding a lot to the dinner time conversations in the communal kitchen, she loved horses that was obvious, she was a friend of Rangi, again that was obvious by the easy banter with each other, but with the three of us she was guarded and I would often find her staring at one of us as we ate, most of the time at Con. We all tried to make her feel welcome, Bridie and I trying to draw her into our conversation or ask about her day. Con tried as well, at times successful. She would beam at him; her smile transformed her face from pretty to animated.

Carole would chatter to Beauty while grooming her, and Rangi if they were on their own, shutting up once any one of us walked in. Rangi took it upon herself to inform us it was not a personal slight or dislike for us; she had been molested. Carole had been a child of ten when Rangi became her foster Mother. My heart went out to Carole, it made me sad to think of all we had given Rae in her life, how fortunate she was, while this poor woman still suffered from memories of her family's abuse. Disappointment and lack of trust were her companions now. There's not a lot anyone can do; accept it for what it was and be patient and kind. Understanding was the key to Carole.

My chutneys were a success. There they sat all in a row, twenty jars of bright red tomato and choko chutney. Bridie had made her specialty home-made onion jam, ten jars of a fruit salad jam, plus ten jars of orange and pear jelly you could use on ice cream as a sauce or on your bread and butter. I swear this woman could make anything from nothing.

Off we went to the markets, Bridie so determined that it would all sell, she proclaimed, 'I've asked the jam and chutney leprechauns to make sure it all goes within the next two days.' As she spoke she nodded her head, agreeing with herself.

Our stall that Con had a hand in building was right on the corner of the fairground. To one side of us was a cake stall, on the other was a stall for knitted clothes, opposite us was a candy floss machine that proved very popular all day long, and to the side of Mr Candy Floss was a pretzel stall. The first two hours were so slow; nobody passed us by except to buy candy floss. My spirits flagged until two very well-dressed ladies walked up to us asking for a taste test before buying.

Bridie was the one who came to the rescue. She had bought tiny paper cups and miniature wooden spatulas just for this purpose, giving a very professional spiel about our produce. Ten minutes into their taste session they had bought two jars of each product. From that moment on, we sold to anyone that passed by, and by three pm we decided to pack up and leave as she was almost out of stock. When I checked my stock, I had sold out.

Bridie punched the air with a, 'Yahoo, we did it.' I was equally as happy for us both. As we drove home, I knew this really was not why I was here. It had been huge amounts of fun, but I did not need the money or work, but friendship and travel, yes. I had enjoyed making up new recipes, the packing, selling but giving a spiel about how good it all was not my thing.

Chapter 38

Time to be honest, Tara. Over dinner that night I told them of my intentions to move on and why. Bridie looked heartbroken, her reaction a little over the top, I thought. Con looked at me and shrugged his shoulders. I had not had a lot to do with Con lately, he was a working man and over our dinner at night we would talk and laugh but by the time I woke up he had gone to work and I had noticed a difference in him; he swaggered with self-confidence these days.

Carole's input was, 'You do what you think best.' Rangi offered no advice but looked thoughtful.

My little van looked so inviting as I had left the light on inside and it glowed its special welcome. Tonight, I just wanted to crawl inside and sleep, although feeling very guilty at upsetting my new friends. I just wanted to be on my own tonight, and once I lay down on my bed I fell into a deep sleep. My phone rang at two am the next morning, sleep a heavy blanket over me. I whispered, 'Hi,' expecting Rae or Jess, but I was wrong–it was Rangi. I could hear crying in the background, my alert button immediately on go, I said, 'What's up Rangi?'

I was sitting upright in bed as she whispered, 'Can you come over, Tara?'

Rangi was waiting for me on her front porch, a small flicker of torch light her give away.

'We need to sort something out, Tara. I could do with your help.'

Sitting in a chair on the front porch was Bridie, her face swollen with tears. Kneeling, I put my arms around her, her body heaving with grief for some reason. 'What's happened?'

'It's him, the dirty bastard,' she wobbled at me, her finger pointing at the shadow in the corner of the porch. I had totally missed it when I had walked over to see what the trouble was. 'Con, is that you?'

'Tis me love,' he said.

'What on earth is wrong with the two of you?'

Rangi took my hand. It was warm and she smelt of face cream and toothpaste. The news was devastating when they finally got it together to tell me. Con had been seeing Carole and had been doing so for over a week. 'Why?' was the first thing to pop out.

'Don't be naïve, Tara,' said Rangi. 'He's been sleeping with her.'

It did not make any sense, wasn't Carole the battered child? Wasn't Con married to Bridie? Good heavens! Again, I wanted to yell why me? Instead we all sat on Rangi's front porch with hot drinks and tissues while Bridie told us of her misgiving's but had hidden them from us.

'This is not the first time that friggin' Irishman has wandered,' she cried.

I looked up at Con, his face haggard. I thought he was about to say, 'I'm sorry,' to Bridie and swear his undying love. I was prepared for Bridie to smile, have hugs all round, and we could all go back to bed. What Con said floored me.

'Bridie it's over. No more wandering for me, I want to stay here settle down and become part of this community.'

Bridie howled like a hurt dog. 'It's her, isn't it? Her and her bloody horse.' Con was a spent man, his pride in tatters as he bent beside her, kissing her hands and said, 'It is Bridie. I don't expect you to understand but she needs my shoulder to cry on, my hand to hold hers, my love to keep her safe.'

Bridie's sobs seemed to throb through me as Con continued, 'You want a different life to me, Bridie. You don't want to settle anywhere, and I do. I have found a real purpose right here and I want to be part of it.'

His confession lay like a huge cavern between them. My own heart hurt at his raw honesty. He walked off the porch saying to Rangi and me, 'Look after her will you please. I will be back tomorrow to sort things out.'

I felt like someone had pricked my party balloon. Where had all the fun and laughter gone?

The morning wrote its arrival with a pale orange streak across the dark blue sky and we all went to bed in our own vans and homes. Sleep hunkered down in the corners but would not come near me, my brain trying to understand what could happen in ten days, my heart giving thanks to Russ for his faithfulness and belief in us as a couple.

If he ever did stray, I never knew about it or even a hint of it. Russ was and always would be my man. I hugged my pillow to me. I wanted to help but also wanted to run away; I did not need this in my life. My thought's jumping all over the place, my head aching at the problems people can cause when they don't think out the consequences of their actions, and where was Carole amongst all of this?

'What to do aye Tara?' Rangi asked while we ate marmalade on toast at the breakfast table, Rangi's eyebrows drawn in a worried frown. Bridie was not to be seen. I made her a sweet tea and toast with cheese, the rest of the chutney on it. Knocking lightly on her door I called out, 'Come on Bridie, got to get something down.' There was no answer. I knew if that had been me, I would have been exhausted, so I went back inside the house. Leaving my choko recipe for Bridie with Rangi, on the envelope I wrote, 'Hope we met up again. I enjoyed spending time with you.' I said my goodbye to Rangi, she helped me hitch up the mermaid to the car, hugging me as she said, 'Harerai Tara. Safe trip.'

The Rotorua signposts came into view. I pulled over to call a caravan park as I wanted to settle for a day or two. This was more like it–on my own and looking forward to the day. My request for a caravan site met with, 'Yes, we can offer you a site.' It was late in the day when Rangi phoned me, she wanted me to know Bridie had committed suicide and Con had taken off.

What do you say to that news? My head reeled; my heart hurt for these four lovely people who had been nothing but kind to me. Then the doubts and thoughts of *what if* set in, knowing at the end of the day there was nothing I could have done. They had chosen this path and only they could deal with the consequences. I left a message on Rangi's phone asking when the funeral was. I would not return but I would send flowers.

Time for Tara to do as she declared over six months ago–travel New Zealand. I was not sorry I had met Bridie, Con, Rangi, or even Carole. We had met and enjoyed each other's company, had many laughs and so much fun. The women I had met had helped me over a huge hurdle with my own family and for that I was grateful. I would miss them all; never sorry I had met them as they were now part of my life's tapestry. I offered up a prayer for my wonderful friend Bridie. *God guide you and keep you safe.*

I emptied my small kitchen cupboard at the back of my Mermaid and the small one inside. Anything which looked like it was Bridie's– a jar of jam, pickle, knife, tea towel–I threw out. The Maori were not the only superstitious people around, I had my own beliefs. I was still dealing with Russ's death in many ways. I was disappointed in Bridie's choice of a way out; it was too easy. The struggle comes when we choose to deal with the emotional hurts and start forgiving and healing within ourselves.

Chapter 39

Rotorua is a beautiful place; gorgeous gardens and an overload of Maori cultural information, but for now I'd had enough of the culture.

Margi was wonderful when we spoke on the phone. Her advice was, 'Keep going, love. Keep seeing and doing what you came here for, you will know when you have had enough. You're here for a reason and you will know when you want to go back home.' She also told me of her nephew, Warik, who painted the Mermaid on the van; he was accepted into an arts course. My enthusiasm encouraged him to enrol and he had bought himself a laptop. 'First one of us to have one of them things or even work one of them blinkin' things.'

I had booked for a week at the Rainbow Trout Caravan Park. It was really pretty and, true to their adverts, you could see the Rainbow Trout swim upstream. I visited a sheep shearing demonstration and saw some rams stand to attention all in a row and 'baa' on command, but all the fun of watching, seeing and doing had just gone for me, Bridie's death often haunting my thoughts. Time to move on, I thought. I'm restless.

Rotorua stunk of sulphur, the hot pools at the camp were quaint but I had no inclination to soak in them. I also noticed I was getting slight headaches again; nothing too serious just an ache behind the eyes that seemed to go after a good sleep.

After four days of touring and many sad thoughts, I decided to move on, and hitched my van and drove away without a backward glance. My GPS had Gisborne keyed into it. I was on the road again, sick of the constant damp drizzle while in Rotorua, hopefully Gisborne would be better. It was going to be a long drive, a good five hours or more. It looked promising, even the name I could pronounce properly. I guess it's me, I thought. Maybe I expect too much from others.

I only made two stops, one to refuel and one to eat and use the bathroom. While at the roadhouse I asked if they knew of any caravan parks I could book into and they gave me an address and phone number. I drove on, putting my phone on loudspeaker and booked my site, telling them my whereabouts. They said, 'See you in about two hours.'

I arrived at a pretty foreshore, stunning trees silhouetted in the sunset, my faithful Mermaid now tucked into her resting place for a week. I curled up inside after securing the car for the night. A hot Milo and sleep were all I wanted.

When I showered in the morning, I noticed my face. I looked haggard; I was too skinny, my hair now long and in a plait, straggly, dry, wispy bits stuck out at the sides, my head ached, I felt tired and generally rundown. I recognised the symptoms of stress.

What I need, I thought, was a good clean up physically and emotionally. My cure was to rest up, eat well, read, sleep and feel better about what had happened with Con and Bridie. Then I needed to sort out clothing to be washed, ironed and put away, tidy up the little pantry and fridge and have a good sweep out. Then to clean the car; I hosed it and wiped it with a soft sponge wiping all the dust away. By two pm I was out to it, my body so tired, my head painful again as a migraine thumped behind my eyes, painkillers and a hot water bottle my only remedy. I lay there with no-one knocking or calling, ringing, ordering me to attend, asking advice, no jam and chutney making, no laughing, no noise, nothing but peace; all I could hear was the wind in the trees. The nausea built up in waves and I knew I was going to throw up, a towel and small bowl by my bed, I snoozed on and off. I had many of these damned headaches throughout my life, so I was not that worried. The concern came later when my vision was badly affected.

I was in bed for a few days until it had gone, at least that was normal for these episodes if I did not deal with the pain as soon as I recognised the symptoms. I had not taken any notice, preferring to clean the car and van. I admonished myself for thinking it could have waited. I'm not good at being sick and even worse at nursing, my daughter once calling me 'Nurse Not.'

I opened a packet of ginger biscuits thinking they were Rae's favourites, made myself a very hot tea and lay down, prepared to sit it out for as long as it took. The painkillers hadn't worked on this mother of a headache yet, so time to lie still and relax if possible. I felt safe here tucked away under a group of tall willow trees, the entire park surrounded a lake, the view would be fabulous when the hazy vision cleared.

Sleep, they say, is the best healer and I tend to agree. Whenever I woke I would drink a big glass of water, wander out to use the bathrooms, shower, make a hot tea, nibble a biscuit for the ginger in it mainly, then back to sleep. No-one bothered me, not one little peep. Wonderful.

The fourth day, I woke up with a clear head. I was ravenous, full of energy and wanted to get out, air my little van out and air all the bedding out. I did all this within the hour, that's the beauty of having such a small home. My washing popped into the washing machine and then hung on the communal clothesline; the camp laundry was a lovely clean place. I had paid four dollars to fill two washing machines with hot water and now my bed linen and clothes looked and smelt fresh and clean. The day looked like it was going to be a fabulous one–sun and light winds, perfect.

Chapter 40

Now time for me. Time for Tara to comb her hair, brush her teeth and go out. I found the number and rang a hairdresser who offered a package–shampoo, cut, massage and manicure. I booked and paid for it by credit card.

The manicurist commented, 'Have you been chopping wood?' and I felt like it. My shoulder muscles still ached, my hands stained and calloused with all the picking of fruit, pickling, sterilising the jars in boiling water. My feet were in a worse condition, according to the beauty therapist, so I had a pedicure.

Then the unruly mop was washed and trimmed. I was told by Lucy, the hairdresser, having a soft body perm was so much easier than all the combs and clip I was using. Her huge blue eyes taking in all my split ends and generally untidy hairdo. I took her advice and at the end of three hours my hair looked stunning; soft curls pulled back by two large tortoiseshell combs. I now sported a soft feathery fringe, my skin looked amazing, my head and shoulders felt great, so now it was off to a second-hand shop for some clothing, clothes that would not make me look like I was ill as the weight loss was now considerable. Lucy told me about a second's boutique only two roads away, much better than the clothing at Vinnie's, her dainty tiny nose wrinkled as she said it. I was pointed in the right direction. Lucy was right, it was an Aladdin's cave and not too bad on prices. Taking a few items into the changing room the shop assistant said, 'I was buying the wrong size for me.'

'What do you think I am?'

'Let's see… ' She whipped out her tape measure. 'I'd be going with a size twelve,' she announced.

'No!' I cried 'I'm big, a fourteen or sixteen.'

'Well not anymore,' she quipped. 'Good for you, here try these on.' She gave me at least six garments; three quarter pants, tops, plus two pair of light jeans. She was right, size twelve fitted beautifully.

'I'll take them all.'

If she was quite surprised, I was in shock. I had not been a size twelve since I married Russ. When I'd arrived in Auckland, I was a size sixteen.

My thoughts strayed to Rae, Con and Rangi but I forced them away; I'm not going there today. Walking back to the car, my arms full of parcels, I saw a coffee shop. It sold fresh baguettes with smoked ham and cheese. My mouth watered and to my delight it also sold books of every description. Time to stop and refresh myself and have a read. I felt starved for some great novels and was sick of quick reads like magazines and newspapers. I ordered a huge green salad with my fresh baguette.

I left the café with another fresh bread roll, the salad which I couldn't finish now in a plastic container, and three new books. Great. Bedtime reading here I come. The fresh food giving me energy, I could feel it in my veins. There was one more place I needed to find, an information kiosk to find out what I could do here. It really reminded me of home, Perth.

The lady behind the counter gave me a list of what I could do in four days. I chose the wine tour for tomorrow, the aquaculture tour for the following day plus a Farman helicopter tour for the same afternoon. A wiggle of excitement was in my chest as that was one thing I had never ever done before. On the third day, a sunrise tour to Mount Hikurangi, the tour operator to confirm that one, as sometimes it was closed due to being on private land. I was really excited about my plans; I was finally about to do things on my own. It felt right, like I was wearing no-one else's coat but my own.

Once back at my site I bundled my purchases through the door and retrieved my fresh laundry from the clothesline to make my bed; it smelt divine, of fresh air and sunshine, even my bath towels were fluffy and looked brighter. Then I sorted out my clothes; my new ones placed into the drawers under the bed, deciding my old clothes were too big to keep, I bundled them up taking them over to the office to ask if there was a clothing bin close by, the manager telling me, 'In the laundry is a table we allow campers to leave unwanted items. Put them there. If they don't go, we put them in the Vinnie's bin in three days.'

Fair enough. I did as he suggested, and as I passed by an hour or two later not one item had remained. Enjoy them, I thought.

My trip to the wineries was great. I tippled, sipped, judged and lunched with other tourists, none of us were professionals at the wine business, so our opinion was just that, an opinion. I enjoyed myself very much; a little fuzzy in the head as I wasn't used to all the wine, the apple cider definitely a favourite with me. I slept like a baby as soon as I lay down, not waking until midnight and feeling slightly confused as to where the day had gone.

Day two was going to be even more exciting. I was up early, showered and dressed in my new jeans and warm top as the wind was a little chilly in the early mornings. Eastland Aquaculture was amazing, again picked up at the park's gate, driven out to the Paua shell farm and shown the process of Paua shell farming; it was fascinating. I had seen almost the same technique of oyster farming in Bali except the pacific waters are cold, so the system of growing these beautiful sea creatures is almost mathematical. I defy anyone to leave this place without buying something made from the beautiful Paua or 'Abalone' as we in Australia call them. I bought drop earrings and a dainty heart-shaped necklace, then it was time to go. I was the only tourist left to drop off at the end, so the driver dropped me at

Farman Helicopters.

I was so excited, my stomach quivering in anticipation. First, a short introduction to the pilot, a young Asian chap in his late thirty's called Cho. Strapped in, earphones on, I was told I could converse freely with the pilot. The rotary blades clattered to a start then up we went, lift off. Straight up in the sky and around in a twirl, no time to feel anything but a tad scared. Cho saved the day by making conversation about our destination. He also gave me instructions on where the sick bag was, he did this with a smile, only I knew how close I was to having to use it. We followed the Motu River, which was shallow in places, white pebbles glowing up from the banks, and where it was deeper it glowed an eerie green. We flew over Lake Waikaremoana, its colours changing from deep blue to deep turquoise as the cloud passed over, our shadow a small dot on its surface. My camera was busy clicking away. I was looking down not noticing the thick white cloud we were headed for. Cho's voice in my ears now changed from light to a more serious tone, saying, 'This is White Island, Tara, an active and dangerous volcano.'

My stomach did a huge flip as his words hit home 'an active volcano,' We flew around the perimeter, white clouds covered our vision, my knuckles now white from clutching the seat under me. I was finding it hard to breathe, then I saw a deep crimson glow amongst the clouds.

'Cho, I don't like it here,' I cried.

He took one look at me. 'Okay, home we go Tara,' and we whirred our way back to Gisborne. Once landed, the relief started to set in. I had never felt like that before–ever. It felt like we were going to fall into the hole of red hell fire. Cho offered to drive me home and I gratefully accepted as I was still a bit wobbly after that experience.

I wobbled past the office waving to the manager. 'You look like you've seen a ghost,' he commented.

'I feel like it,' I said, and told him about my flight over White

Island.

'God, you're brave. I won't even think about going there.'

I loved the helicopter ride and everything else. What a way to fly, hovering over scenes of nature that cannot be replayed, but White Island held nothing but a gut-wrenching experience for me. One more day to go before I leave and carry onto Napier to actually see a Metal Mermaid; this I was really looking forward to.

Today I was to watch the dawn come up on Mount Hikurangi, apparently a photographer's dream, and even if I do say so myself, I'm not too bad behind the lens; at least I don't cut off the heads of people and then play the guessing game of who it is.

Before I took off for the day I replayed the previous day's photo session in the helicopter. It started off with Cho smiling and waving to me, shots of rivers and lakes beautiful in their colour and size, but I had stopped filming at White island. I guess fear and photography don't go together.

Mt Hikurangi was open, so the tour was on. The amazing sunrise we witnessed left you gasping in awe. A moment of silent respect, then the Maori elder greeted Rah the Sun. Within quarter of an hour of his welcoming prayer, from a tiny line of rosé blush, it exploded into glorious colour only the heavens can make. My neighbour said, 'How can you not believe in God when you see the magic of his creation.'

I agreed wholeheartedly. My heart was full of the immense pleasure of being part of this ritual which was powerfully healing, reinstating your belief in the universe, that all was meant to be as it was, or as my mum would often say, 'God is in his heavens and all is well in your heart.'

I had captured it all. It's not simply a photo of a beautiful sunrise, it's not until you are part of it when a glow creeps over your hands, face, then deep into your heart. Covering us all in a molten, orange glow you realise you are in the presence of something extraordinary, that there is nothing that can match its majesty and power. There isn't a word to describe the feeling.

It was hard to leave this sacred place, as that's how it felt to me. No-one chattered or laughed; a silent line of people descended the slope into the tour bus, all of us touched by the glory we had just witnessed.

To say, 'I simply snapped a few shots and carried on my journey would sound quite shallow,' as I felt like I had just been on the journey of a lifetime. The sunrise I witnessed was powerful, spiritual, a personal blessing, an experience I for one would never forget.

Napier was a four-hour drive away, the Mermaid and I started off once again. The DVD played 'Red Sails in the Sunset,' a favourite of mine, I hummed along as I drove, not a care in the world with the windows wide open, my new hairdo tucked up in combs, and wearing a pair of old brown shorts and a brown cotton singlet. I felt good as well. The nourishing food I had been consuming was a great health tonic. It all seemed to be working. I was still getting tired spells, my body claiming sleep whenever I rested but had decided my body knew best and I would rest when needed, not when I thought it was time. The mobile phone beeped, an envelope appearing on the screen. Pulling over, I saw it was from Rae. Maybe she has seen sense, I thought. It was a text message, 'Received education money, my family deciding no more contact with you, Mrs Jono Taylor.'

I stared at the screen, my light heart sinking. Why does it keep happening to me? went around in my head. I wanted to be sick, just when I felt great and healthy, strong and capable I get dumped on. I texted back, 'Very happy for you both. Big hugs and congratulations. Glad you have the money. Time to buy a home and settle down. Love to you all, Mum.'

I was determined to keep it loving and friendly. 'Keep the door open,' as Russ would say, hopefully when they all grew up or saw sense they would again be a loving family to me but for now it was time out for all of us. The way things were going though, chances looked slim. So, my daughter was married, Jess had a dad. I sent up a prayer that Jono would be a good father figure for my grandson, that Rae would have a true man in her life not the domineering sly user he had shown himself to be.

Still, this was her life. She had to learn to live it, warts and all, and the same with me. 'I was living the life,' as Margi would say.

Chapter 41

I heard the weather forecast for rain, and rain it did. The heavens opened up, and after the initial hour's deluge it drizzled nonstop. I felt chilled.

I wound my way through water burdened green hills, the rain was making the roads quite slippery, muddy shallow waterfalls now splashing across them. I was having to watch my way very carefully, signs up all over the place warning, 'be careful rockslides,' the picture showing huge rocks tumbling down the hillside. A hazy rain-sodden view of Napier came into view with grey beaches, rolling grey waves, and streetlights giving it a watery sad look. It had rained since I sent the message back to Rae. I took it as a personal sign from above that things were not too happy in Perth, or with me, and I was a million miles away.

'Stuff it!' I shouted and slammed the wheel with my hand. 'I'm bloody sick and tired of that bloody girl ruining my life with her tantrums. I don't care if I don't go back, I just want to be happy and peaceful.'

Russ's voice in my head said, 'Calm down, Tara,' but my loud reaction continued, 'and you can stuff off as well.'

God give me strength. I am so over other people's problems. Everywhere I went I was handed a problem of sorts as if I had a magic wand. Well here's the news–I haven't, and I don't want one. I came here for an adventure, not a world crisis meeting.

I found a small caravan park almost immediately. They gave me the site number as they might not be available when I arrive. The lady on the phone advised, 'Just go there, we will catch up soon enough.' I followed her instructions and found my way without too much trouble, the rain soaking me as I unhitched the Mermaid, parking the car alongside her. I grabbed a towel from the van and ran to the shower block only to find you had to put two dollars in the meter to have a hot shower. 'Bugger!' I shouted.

A lady popped her head around the door. 'Problem dearie?' I watched as her teeth took a millisecond to click together.

I wanted to yell, 'Please don't "dearie" me,' instead taking a big breath I replied, 'Yes, I ran over here without my purse.'

'Oh, never mind,' she said and wandered off, which frustrated me even more. Could she not have lent me a two-dollar coin?

'Breathe deeply, Tara,' I told myself. Take a big breath and calm yourself; you have let Rae rattle your cage again. I was concerned I now had an anger problem; it seemed to sit just under my ribcage nonstop, grumbling with discontent. I would dry off inside my cosy home, wrap up in my quilt and wait to get warm again.

Walking back to my van, I noticed there were many small vans in the campground and not many big ones at all. Some of them had bunting or colourful little flags all around, others had coloured lights glinting on and off as the rain and wind made them jump around. Must be permanents, I thought. It was a big thing over in Aussie, so why not here? Flinging my wet clothes into a bucket, I got into a pair of winter pyjamas then made a steaming cup of beef broth. I curled up on my bed with the doona wrapped around me and read the first of the books I had bought. The 'Russian Concubine' was an excellent read, the very first sentence hooking you into the story. I read until dusk when my tum said, *Oi! Feed me.* What to have? I thought. There wasn't a lot; two packets of crackers, some hard cheese, two ripe bananas, half a tub of butter, stale bread and a tin of tuna. Time to do some shopping and soon if I wanted to keep well. Tuna and a cup of instant rice, tomatoes, carrots and spring onions in the tiny cupboard.

Voila! One home-made tasty meal. I ate, read, and made another hot drink, the rain still misty and damp, rivulets running down the outside windows, steamy on the inside. I continued reading until my eyes closed.

I woke with my van being moved around. What the hell is going on? It was still grey and watery but daylight as I checked my watch–seven am in the morning. I leapt up, flung open the door, roaring, 'What the hell!' at two stunned men, each had one end of my Mermaid.

'Oops… sorry–wrong van,' they said. I have never moved so fast in all my life. 'Get your friggin' hands off my property or else I'm phoning the cops.' I waved my phone at them, and both men put their hands up in surrender in front of them.

'Sorry missus,' they whined. 'We got the wrong one,' the older of the two said. 'We were told to repo this van in this park by ten am today.'

'What the hell is "repo"?' I snorted.

'Repossess,' he answered.

My temper blew. I was sick and tired of others preconceived ideas about me or my belongings. They must have recognised pure rage as they took off, skidding and slipping in the mud. The rain had not stopped, I was soaked in my PJ's and did not care. I marched over to the camp manager's office, muddy water squelching between my toes, banging open the door, the overhead bell clanging loudly. The manager stared at me as I verbally attacked the poor women, my choice of words not genteel or nice. I demanded, 'What the hell was going on, was no-one safe in their beds?' I ranted and raved about security and safety, even mentioned suing them for breach of contract, 'the one I had signed to stay here for one week in bloody safety,' I yelled.

I deflated like a lead balloon when her chin wobbled. Oh no, now

I've done it. I thought this has been building up inside me for some time, and this poor woman was the recipient of my short fuse and bad language.

Suddenly, she smiled, and a small giggle escaped. 'If you could see yourself,' she giggled, her teeth doing their own thing again. Well, that did it for me, the past six months of struggling to stay on top of everything, trying so hard to enjoy it all as a tourist suddenly popped.

I sat down and laughed until my sides hurt. 'I'm Beryl,' she said amongst the laughter.

'I'm so sorry Beryl, it's not your fault.'

She wrapped a clean towel around my shoulders. I told her about my recent visitors, adding nasty, crusty looking old bums that manhandled my van. What if they came back, what if they decided I was not that scary, or I went out and my Mermaid disappeared?

I walked back to my home. I had left the door swinging open in my anger. Muddy footprints inside showed me instantly I was robbed, burgled, whatever you want to call it. My laptop and camcorder had gone along with the jug and toaster, and to beat it all, my bedding. To add insult to injury even further, they had nicked my new book as well. Shit. And no-one had seen it happen or surely they would have stopped it. My purse and camera were locked in the car, thank God. I had my phone on me when I had rushed over to the office, to report the theft.

Written across the bedside table in mud was, 'Thanks.' The bastards had been back, Beryl and her husband following, quickly dialling on his mobile. 'He's phoning the police now, dearie,' she said. 'Grab what you can and lock up the van, you're coming back with us until they arrive.'

I felt ashamed at my previous behaviour; I had been so rude to her.

The police duly arrived, took my statement, said, 'No use looking for fingerprints as it was raining,' and off they went, tucking their notebooks away in their top pockets, looking to me like bookends that nodded and shook their heads in unison. Had they not seen the word 'Thanks' written by someone's hand?

Beryl's husband introduced himself. 'I'm Trev. I'm really sorry, Tara,' he said. 'That's not normal for us. Do you have insurance?' he asked.

"Yes, I do. What do I have to do over here to start the ball rolling?' I asked.

How simple it all was; one phone call then one day later an inspection by the Napier AA branch. I had a call the next afternoon that a cheque was ready to pick up and I could purchase all I needed once again. In the meantime, Beryl and Trev had been so generous to me, lending me all the gear I needed, they even invited me to share their meal that night. I was so ashamed of my outburst I bought Beryl flowers and Trev a bottle of wine. I offered to shout them a meal, which they accepted with delight suggesting a favourite haunt of theirs, the Greek Taverna. We arranged to meet at the office at seven pm that night and go together. I was spending the day shopping and doing some sight-seeing and to view the Metal Mermaid: 'Pania of the Reef.' Beryl told the Maori Folk tale about a Wahine Mermaid who feel in love with Karitoke, the handsome son of a Maori chief. He asked her to become human, but frightened, she ran away to return to the sea people. All I could grumble was, 'Bloody men.'

It was a bit of a shock when told the latest news: Pania, the Metal Mermaid, had been stolen. What! Stolen when? Oh, some time ago, the tour guide said. She was found, though badly damaged and an investigation is being made. Her picture was stunning. I was told it had been sculptured from a real person, taken overseas to make a mould, then cast here in Napier.

What is it with Metal Mermaids and thieves? What's the draw card? Bloody sticky fingered plonkers. Why can't they just leave them alone.

The tour continued to the seahorse farm, and that was brilliant. So peaceful the way they cling and sway to whatever their tails curl around, completely harmless and yet again an endangered species made so by us humans. The curator adding, 'Can't leave a good thing alone,' which did not make me feel better. I was still feeling very disgruntled by all the thieving that was going on. Then I walked back to my car parked in the city outside a huge store called Farmers, the new possessions I had bought today locked safely in the boot with the retractable boot cover pulled tight over them so no-one could see in.

I drove back to the camp and unloaded my things, unwrapping all the new gear making it feel like Christmas again with wrapping paper and cardboard tumbling onto the floor and out the door. I plugged in my laptop and did all the things I had to do to set it up, putting in code words, etc.

A soft tapping on my van door startled me. When I opened it, a small parcel lay on my doorstep. Wrapped in an old damp tea towel was my book, 'The Russian Concubine'. Someone had a guilty conscience by the looks of it. Whoever it was, *thank you*, my butterfly bookmark still in place where I had stopped reading.

It was time to meet the camp owners for the dinner this was my shout.

Chapter 42

Trev looked very smart in an open-neck white shirt, long tailored black pants, his hair oiled down with a little curl over the forehead, John Travolta had favoured this in the movie 'Grease'. The heavy aftershave made you want to breathe out the side of your mouth and he looked like a bodgie from way back.

Beryl was in a matching outfit except she had on long slim white pants, a black cowl neck top and so much gold it's a wonder she could stand upright. Her stiletto high heels fashionably super high–a weapon if needed–the makeup so thick the eyelashes globbed with heavy mascara.

'My Trev likes to spoil me,' she said, her arm jangling with all the gold bracelets, her hair teased into a stiff upright bouffant with copious amounts of spray applied, daring the wind to make it untidy.

I was the one out of place. I had on a pair of casual jeans, a light brown top, the Paua shell jewellery I had bought, a little lipstick and a smidge of perfume. The one extravagance was my hair up in combs I had newly acquired that day–small diamante butterflies, nothing to daring and I had loved the way they twinkled in the shop light.

Beryl nudged Trev, her head pointing my way. On queue he said, 'You look nice, Tara.' He only had eyes for his truly remarkable wife; to actually walk on those heels with all the weight of the jewellery you would have needed acrobat training. I offered to drive their car not being a drinker I thought I would be the safe driver for the night. We arrived with soft Greek music playing in the background. Trev was gallant, fetching us soft drinks from the bar. I had insisted on paying the bill for the night, so Trev ran a tab at the bar. We ordered an entrée of grape leaves soaked in grape oil stuffed with chickpeas and nuts. Not being a huge or fast eater at the best of times, I preferred to eat small amounts and often. I invited them to order what they wanted; I was quite happy dawdling with my entrée. They made me smile; they bickered, made up and made love to each other with their eyes, lots of intimate touching, not caring if they had an audience or not.

The music had built up with a swing, both of them hauling me to my feet. We danced until midnight, and if I did not dance with Trev or Beryl then they would ask another friend to dance with me until I begged for some time out.

The amount of Ouzo those two swallowed was amazing. They sang and danced the night away, Beryl's large white teeth clicking away like insane castanets.

When the taverna closed at one am, I paid the bar and food tab, my eyes wide with surprise when the barman gave me the bill for just over two hundred dollars. I tried to check it over before I paid; the two I had shouted here for dinner now very drunk, yelling out, 'Teeee rara Boom De Ay!' Beryl shrieked out loud saying, 'That's so funny,' repeating it over and over. Trev waving his hands in the air like a conductor yelled, 'One more time,' which she obeyed, shrilling into the cold, drizzly night air.

I was so over this night; I would check the bill tomorrow. On the drive home both had become deathly quiet having fallen asleep slumped over each other like a pair of old tired rag dolls. Getting them inside was a different matter, I did not have the strength. I left them in the car parked outside their cottage, wound a window down and walked home feeling really tired.

The moon was full and deep yellow that night and sitting on the Mermaids step I pondered my life, the moon and I keeping each other company, the silence broken only by the soft call of an owl. Was I not having the adventure I craved? Why do I keep getting involved so much with others? Had I made the wrong decision travelling on my own? Why were Rae and Jess so upset with me? It seemed I attracted emotionally crippled or immature people like bees to honey. Did no-one even think I was learning about myself? It was not about Mother, Nana, wife, friend or lover; this was about discovering who I was, so why was I having regrets about my life?

So many *why's* danced inside my head which was now heavy with lack of sleep. Wishing on the moon to keep me safe through the night, I locked up securely and slept the night away, the feeling of being unsafe invading my dreams, jumping awake two or three times as I swore I felt the Mermaid move.

The hot air balloon ride was cancelled due to constant rain, the message only delivered to me as I was dressing to be picked up. It was time for a hot drink. I opened the van door to once again sit on the step to sip my drink and was stunned by the activity around me.

The camp was alive with people. It looked like someone had painted the camp with bright colours on canvas as it breathed, it moved, the once unsettling deadness of the camp now vibrant. There were people everywhere, lots of people doing all sorts of things, some sitting outside their vans, some talking to others, some busy sweeping windswept debris from their doors and others cleaning out annexes and windows. Suddenly it had a life that pulsed, and I had no idea why.

Beryl greeted me as I entered the office, 'Hey Tara, we enjoyed dinner.'

'Great,' I replied. 'How's the head?'

Beryl beamed, 'Well, we woke up a tad confused but all good now.'

I could not help myself and I had to ask her, 'Where have all these people come from?'

'Oh them,' she replied. 'Family, dearie.'

'What, all these people are your family?'

'Well sort of,' she said with a smile, her big white teeth snapping together and biting off the words as they were spoken. 'We are the last of a circus troupe, some of us now do private work but most of us have retired and *here* is where we live.'

It took a while and a cup of tea to realise I was camping with circus retirees and this is where the old, injured, fed up and brassed off with the circus life came to live out their lives. That explained the bunting, old lights, and old adverts on canvas I had seen when I had first arrived.

A song by the Eagles, 'Welcome to the Hotel California' went through my head; it felt like I had stepped back into a time warp.

It felt a little creepy. Where had these folk been when I arrived? Beryl answered that unasked question as well. 'We all often go on trips to see shows in Wellington. This time it was the opening of a new Wellington museum, Te papa.'

My brain giving off signals, okay none of your business, Tara, don't ask questions. Keep out of it, walk away, it is what it is.

I must admit it felt really safe to be in camp that night with a lot of other folk around; the bathrooms steamy and hot through constant use and smelling of lavender talc and shampoo. It was a pleasure to go over there and be greeted by others. They came in all sizes: the ex-circus folk mostly my age or older, some bent and weary, others bright and cheerful, their injuries, if any, covered by happy smiles. They were a community.

I sat in my van feeling a little lost for words. It was surreal. Trev rang me, 'It's Trev here, Tara. Why don't you join us for dinner? We are having the gang over tonight.'

Why not? I thought, and 'gang' it certainly was–almost fifty people, and more arriving by the minute, to join them in a welcome home party.

I had agreed to pop in for a little while, there was no way my body could take more dancing, or should I say heaving drunken people around the dance floor. As I walked in, Trev grabbed me, his arm encircling my waist yelling out, 'Here she is, people,' whirling me around in a circle. There was silence then a thundering waterfall of words pored over at me until he yelled, 'Quiet! Enough! Give Tara some air.'

A seat was pushed under me, a glass of warm beer pushed into my hand, then it was question and answer time. They were overwhelming; wanting to know how come I ended up here in their camp site, how come I was robbed, why I was travelling on my own, did I have any family, and was I enjoying myself?

I was grilled front and back and sideways. It was all too much, their attitude almost belligerent like I was an unwelcome addition or an intruder into a private circus world gang. If this was their way of making you feel welcome, it certainly did not feel like it. I left, pushing my way through the crowd, Beryl and co calling out, 'Tara– come back.' They followed me out the door, but no thanks, I was not interested and settled down in my haven. I was still awake and still upset at one am. They had all gone to bed and the whole camp was peaceful, and I was bathed in the full bright yellow moon, it was so close I could see the little bumps and hollows on it.

Opening my van door, I sat there wishing that somewhere, somehow, I would find my path; find out why, how and what I was here for? It was so thrilling to travel, yet I missed my home incredibly. I could feel my body relaxing as I practised my form of meditation which is to sit under the moon and commune with nature and my heart.

It was while I was in this peaceful state I heard the tiniest tinkle of bells and the faint beat of a drum. I knew that music, I know I did. I remembered my belly dance days, nothing fantastic just a three-month course, 'To loosen those tight western hips, girls,' my instructor had said and the three-month learners course turned into a year. I had fun dancing like never before, Rae and Russ both thinking I was silly prancing around with a pink scarf tied around my hips and practising hip shimmy's. They both complained the music was really bad.

'Mournful muck,' Russ called it.

Rae called it, 'Snake charmer's stuff.'

When I had announced I was to be in a floor show, Russ had yelled, 'Not while I'm alive,' so I had stopped–anything for a peaceful life–it had never really been an issue with me. I guess you could say then I was obedient; if it unsettled my loved ones then why continue. Now I could just hear the beat, it faintly whispered to me on the sigh of the wind, a catchy tune that made me feel good inside. It was one-thirty am, bed for me. At ten am I was woken by Trev ringing me, 'Hey there, you leaving today?'

'Yes, I am,' I replied. 'Why?'

'Because you're in the middle of a big brown lake. I don't think you're going anywhere today.'

He was right. When I opened the door, I was in the middle of a huge shallow brown puddle. 'Not again!' I swore, stamped, kicked the bed. Ouch! My foot complained and throbbed in answer. I was stuck.

I rang Trev back. 'What have you got to pull me out of here?' I asked.

'Nothing I'm afraid. There is a storm on its way, best you stay put for a while, Tara.'

I ignored him and rang the AA asking for help. 'I'm sorry Ma'am, all our drivers are attending motor accidents. We will be there to assist you as soon as possible.'

Not good enough, I thought, so I rang them back to complain, hearing a recorded message saying in velvet tones, 'Hello, you are in tenth in line. Your call will be answered soon.'

'I give up, I bloody give up!' I yelled. 'Alright, we will do it your way,' I shouted at the Mermaids ceiling. I was over it.

I'm selling up and going home, I decided, then put the doona over me and tried to go back to sleep, my mind racing ahead of what I had to do and who I could contact to sell up and move back to Perth. I felt really good once I had made up my mind, it felt settled but for now it was bathroom time, time to feel that cold slimy mud all over my bare feet and there was no way out of it. I had left the blue bucket outside draining, now it was bobbing around in the brown water like an exotic water bird.

I hate oozing mud, let alone the sharp stones that got stuck in my feet. As I crossed the wet, yucky, sodden grass to the bathroom, memories of Russ's laughter at me in Albany came to mind, wrapping around my shoulders, escorting me to the shower block. I hate the cold damp weather and always will.

I was very proud of the Mermaid. She took to it like a duck to water; nothing was leaking or damp, the water just covering half of her wheels. As I came out of the toilets, I heard laughter and splashing, and again peals of laughter and more splashing. I peered around the corner.

A woman was stamping in the deep puddles around her van like a two-year old, her long dark hair whipping around her face as she jumped with unbridled glee. Mud spattered up her mauve dress that she had tucked the bottom of it up into her knickers, her laughter infectious. I felt myself grin. She looked up and I saw the most attractive dark-skinned women smiling at me.

'Come on in, it's awful!' she yelled.

I shook my head. 'I hate muddy water,' I called back.

She threw back her head and laughed at my discomfort. 'You either like it or you let it get to you. Come on, have some fun.'

Why I joined her, I have no idea. I was drawn to her laughter in the cold drizzle and mud, her sheer defiance of this crappy weather, her ocean blue eyes dancing with joy at being a child. I soon learned who I was puddle jumping with. This was Venus and she was the belly dancer I had heard last night.

The name suited her as she looked svelte. She pointed out her van; silver and mauve with delicate purple flowers on a green vine etched all around the windowsills, flower boxes of red and white impatiens tumbling over each other, bright, fresh and enjoying the nonstop drizzle.

Her invite to join her inside for a hot drink was irresistible for a nosey person like me and her caravan was done out in true gypsy style. In the built-up hard annex fur rugs covered a large floor space, wind chimes made from bronze and silver hung from every corner and not the usual bamboo or tinny chimes you find in the garden– these were works of art; great ornamental clusters that spoke of mysticism. One large bookcase was full of glass balls, carved wands, bells, cymbals and books. Her thick accent I learned was Romanian. She took my hand and led me inside, both of us soaked to the skin.

'Here,' she said, her voice low and husky. 'Undress. You can use this blanket to warm up.' My clothes were wet and filthy, a warm blanket gratefully received. Venus went into the van itself, shutting the inside door. I could hear her busy pottering around my teeth had stopped chattering by the time she emerged in a black velvet track suit, two steaming coffees in hand. 'It has whisky in it, good for the heart,' she purred. 'Sit down, please.' Two large leopard skin bean bags were the furniture in her cosy annex, the heater radiated warmth, making my toes now toasty warm. Sipping my hot toddy, I felt relaxed, my body now warm, my eyes heavy.

Chapter 42

I woke up hours later, Venus curled up like a large black cat next to me, her eyes looking straight into mine, her eyelashes sooty black and thick, her eyebrows shaped like black crow's wings. 'You are not happy? She purred.

She leaned close to me, stroking the furrow between my eyebrows, her breath smelt of ginger and limes; I felt the invitation flicker between us. Rae's accusation of being a lesbian thundered into my brain. I sat bolt upright, panic racing through me, time to leave this camp, it was unnerving. I bolted for her door; her blanket clutched protectively around my body

I pleaded with the heavens for it to stop raining; unfortunately, the puddle around my van was now darker and deeper, the blue bucket enjoying its freedom floating away in the shallow stream that now ran through the campgrounds. Food was limited. I waded to the little camp shop for frozen meals, milk, bread and coins to shower, long hot soapy showers that made me feel better. Four days I sat and waited while the rain pelted down, read or tried to read, snoozed and started a journal on my thoughts and reactions. Toilet breaks were my only outings for each day; I was at screaming point. Finally, a break in the clouds, *hurray*! I went to the laundry and washed and dried Venus's blanket.

I knocked at her door calling out, 'Venus, it's me, Tara.'

Her beaded curtains twitched to one side. 'Come in,' she said, the purring now sharpened with anger towards me. 'Venus, I'm sorry I reacted like that… you scared me,' I apologised, offering her the clean blanket back.

She took my hand pulling me inside but I resisted. 'Come, please come in, I will not harm you,' she laughed, a warm honey sound banishing prickles of fear inside me; *I am an adult* sped through my head. How this ends up? I am an adult, my choices my own.

Venus demanded me to sit. 'Now hold out your hand,' she ordered. She then sprinkled a white talcum over my hand. 'I'll read you're palm but first you cross mine with coin, for the luck.'

She was in luck; I still had my two-dollar shower money in my pocket. I'd never had this done before; I had my cards read at a party once but that had been many years ago. Her long silver painted nail on her index finger trailed over my right palm; it left a tickling sensation behind. My idiot sense of humour came into my head as I thought of that baby rhyme, 'round and round the duck pond, went the teddy bear.'

She concentrated on my palm. 'I see,' and, 'Oh!' popped out and, 'hmm… that's good.' She was bent over my hand and I realised I was just as intent at staring at my palm as she was. What on earth did she see there? All I could see were swirly lines. She must have been looking for a good half hour then she did my left hand; on with the talc, once again the silver nail and the tickling sensation then, 'I see,' and the, 'oh's.' She examined my wrists flexing my hand back and forth, 'to see the lines better,' she said.

Almost an hour had gone by when she dropped both my hands and said, 'if it stops raining tonight I will celebrate the full moon with dance, will you come?'

'If it's not raining I would love to. Now what did you see in my palms?' I asked. As she told me I found it hard not to be a sceptic, was this not a seaside attraction for the broken or lovelorn? My hands tingled as I left but once inside my own home I was blown away by her accuracy and her predictions. She had been correct with the past but did that mean she was correct with my future? She told me, 'Your past love was the love of your life, your soul mate, he waited for you. There is another to meet, not with passion but with mind.' She continued, 'You have had a long road of being shut down by family and friends. You have been given a chance to discover who you are but remember, just because you do not see it, it does not mean it is not there. You need to trust more, learn to accept the fact you are evolving, an elder with honour is your future, you will record your path and past in words and colour.'

The rain finally stopped about mid-day. The puddle was disappearing around me. I rang the AA, connected immediately, and yes, they would be there by tomorrow afternoon to pull me out, thank god.

The sound of wood being chopped took my mind off my own issues. Looking out my window I saw Trev chopping up a large fallen tree. It was old, bleached white, its tall spindly branches held up in surrender of its death. The campground was drying out at a fast pace and in a paddock next to Venus was a fast-growing pile of wood.

Dusk settled into the sky, the bonfire crackled a warm welcome with chairs placed around it, the wind whipped up bright sparks which cheerfully rose, dancing to their own death into the sky. I had put on my winter clothes then wrapped a large bath towel around my shoulders for extra warmth; it felt like more rain. The phone rang as I stepped out of my van, the hot air balloon people were refunding my money. Another storm predicted soon I was really over this dam weather. Hopefully, I would be rescued and out of here tomorrow.

Trev and Beryl did some form or other of a Greek dance–I think the ouzo was dancing for them as there was a lot of hoopla's and knee smacking and two or three jiggy parts to it. Both finally running out of breath, they sat down with a *flump*, both faces beetroot red with exertion. Then two little dogs many years old did a little trick or two, jumping through hoops and standing on hind legs to attention, the older one just sitting to attention as he had arthritis in his hips. Both dogs were decked out in clown hats, very cute.

An aged magician was helped up to do a magic hanky trick or two, everyone clapping like delirious seals. Beryl leaned over to me whispering, 'We like to let them know they still have it,' her teeth clicking in my ear. I applauded even harder for them.

Trev stood announcing supper time. I kept searching the crowd for Venus, her van lights were softly glowing, so she was here somewhere. I asked Beryl of her whereabouts. 'Oh, not Venus tonight dearie. Dancing tonight is Teardrop.'

'Who's that?' I asked.

'It's Venus,' she whispered, 'but when she dances she uses her stage name. They say she could make a blind man weep with her dancing.'

Hot tea, coffee and milo were offered for the ladies, an even hotter beverage was being passed around the men folk, Beryl warning, 'Not for you, dearie,' as the flask was passed to me. I took her advice and declined.

Then more logs on the fire, the flames danced high as it sizzled, crackling gleefully, its power casting shadows of snakes and dragons when you looked into the flames. The tinkle of a Tambourine was the only sign Venus–or should I say Teardrop–was there amongst us. The drum started to beat, and I witnessed the glory of a magical belly dance, hypnotic as she swayed, ecstatic as the beat quickened; her hips and breasts shimmied slowly, then her figure became completely still. The music picked up its tempo, her figure blurred with her movements; her jewelled belt sparked rainbows of light, her skin glowed, her long hair cascading around her golden shoulders, those beautiful eyes flashed in the firelight.

Teardrop raised her arms towards the dark sky, now totally black as no stars or moon glowed. The music slowed to a single drum beat that was erotic and I was mesmerised by her slow sinuous movements. Beryl leaned closer to me, 'She tried to kiss you yet?'

That broke the spell; the look on my face must have told her the truth. 'How did you know?' I asked. She bent over laughing, her big bright teeth clamped together, the laugh became a gurgle and when she finally drew breath she chuckled, 'Tries it with everyone, dearie. Even me.'

I wanted to rush off and brush my teeth; the magic had gone from these people in caked, cracked makeup and tattered old worn out costumes, all begging for one more time on centre stage; it gave me the heebie-jeebies.

I said my goodnights and thank you to all and went to bed. I knew I had seen enough to last me a lifetime. If the palm reading was true it was a warning to get busy, live this life I was given. To tour or not to tour? That was the question.

True to the AA's word, their tow wagon arrived mid-day. I had packed up and made the Mermaid ship shape, everything stowed in its proper place in the jeep. Without a hitch the Mermaid gave up a burpy slurp out of her muddy patch, the AA hitched me up to my Jeep and off they went to their next cry for help. Time to pay at the office, thank them for their hospitality and friendship. Trev and Beryl both asked when I would drive back this way? 'Please call in all and say hello.' All the gestures of good hosts and I showed the manners expected of a good guest, saying, 'If I'm back this way, I certainly will,' all of us knowing we would never see each other again. Once out of the gates I felt like the lone survivor of a very bad thriller movie.

A blanket of grey had lifted from my head and shoulders; for some reason I had decided to carry on. Perth was not going anywhere, so if I wanted to be a wanderer now was the time. One week at a time. Who knows why I was put on that path? Life is no accident, this I knew. We are all here to experience life on this planet. Maybe I was meant to meet Venus and her tribe. Maybe learn to have more faith in myself and the future, so for now I was on the road again.

I was heading, as I had planned, to Taupo for five days; the caravan park–a real tourist one–all booked and paid for early this morning. I was off to see the sights including the Waitomo caves famous for its famous glow worms and was excited just to be driving again and away from circus people and their distractions.

Taupo was sunny and warm, very different from Napier, the atmosphere told of adventure to be had here. The caravan park was just that, a fair dinkum caravan park with plots all in a row for vans, power connections and concrete pads, and as I entered two vans pulled out. To enter there was a security gate that needed a special card to swipe before the boom was raised, then you could drive in. Security roamed the grounds at night with dogs on leashes; this camp was policed tightly for their client's protection. I liked that idea, no noise after ten pm and the boom gate was locked at one am.

My first trip out was to find a grocery store to fill my pantry. Small it may be, but if I was careful I could get three days of canned food in there; it was more like a box with a lid. I had powdered milk in there as I had discovered how to make milk powder and milo milkshakes. If I put it all together with a good splash of water in a sealed container before I started off on any trip, I would reach my destination and have one very frothy yummy milkshake. I also discovered if I put warm water with liquid soap in a large bucket, pop in the days washing, made sure the lid was tightly clipped on, then put it in to the back of the Jeep, by the time I pulled over for the day, my washing was done. All I had to do was rinse and hang up.

As my big blue night bucket had gone missing, I had to buy another. Otherwise I mentally applauded myself on what I had learned. If I shared my clothing with a spare pot, glass and cutlery in the drawer under the bed, it gave me a little more room in the pantry cupboard, and if I laid my clothes under the mattress they were pressed when I wanted to change into fresh gear. I was getting good at this small caravanning business.

Chapter 43

The Taupo camp was what I was looking for, the managers not at all interested if I was painted blue and covered in red dots. They took my money for the five days, gave me an A4 manila envelope containing the camp rules and a few brochures on tourist spots with things to do and see.

Their attitude was pleasant, no nonsense, quite the opposite from the last two camps I stayed in. They warned me showering was not advised any later than ten pm, that was when the cleaners were in. I was given a key to both shower and toilets, a polite thank you, a small map to show me the road and site I was booked in, and off I went. This was what I was looking for, some privacy, peace and order.

Off to the shops with a list of items; there is something about having order that breeds order. For the first time in the last two months I felt I was orderly, just like this camp in Taupo was run to order. I liked this feeling.

I shopped for my groceries, mainly buying fruit, and in the mall I noticed a hot roast shop that smelt divine, so ordered my lunch: a mix of roast veggies, kumara, the Kiwi sweet potato, pumpkin, peas, corn, carrots and a large piece of roast beef smothered in thick brown gravy. And I had a double-shot cappuccino with cream and chocolate sprinkles on top. My body sighed *thank you*. While I watched people pass by, I ate, digesting the first real meal in six days.

As I walked slowly back to my car, I saw a movie advertised: 'The Lady and the Tramp' in 3D, so took myself to the movies. Relaxed, I ate some popcorn and smiled all the way through. Once home, it was a snooze followed by a dinner of hot beef broth drink, then snuggling up with my book with the push up hatch above the bed wide open; it was so peaceful. I switched off the bedside light at about ten pm and slept the night away safe as a bug in a rug. Days like these, I felt I could carry on and see the rest of New Zealand.

The day dawned. I was up and off to the ablution blocks early, washed, teeth cleaned and back to my little home to put the day together. I rang a tour bus company that promised to show me Taupo and, 'You won't be disappointed.' Picked up one hour later, the bus was half full of Japanese tourists who nodded politely as I got on. I found my seat. *Great!* I was up the back on my own and again I was thankful; I did not want to chit chat to anyone.

We were off to the Huka Falls, the biggest waterfalls in New Zealand; you could hear them long before you saw them. Once you got out of the bus, the ground shook under your feet, a fine mist was high in the air but you still couldn't see the falls. Rounding a corner, we were all shocked into standing still and I could now see what all the fuss was about; the falls were magnificent. They roared, reared up in boiling demonic anger as massive amounts of river water crashed down, ending hundreds of feet down in frothy deep pools of green, the huge sharp boulders that littered the bank spoke of danger below. It was 'awesome' as the Kiwis say.

Then after many photos it was back onto the bus and a tour of the lake, the biggest in New Zealand at 610 feet at its deepest point. I was introduced to the pumice stone, a volcanic rock that littered the shores of Lake Taupo, and one of the female tourists started filling up her handbag. The driver stopped her, 'No madam, it is not allowed.'

She pulled her bag out of his hands and yelled at him, pointing to the light grey rough stone littering the shore and then her bag, her voice loud and demanding, there was going to be an argument here.

Her husband barked an order and she complied. See, order works, I thought.

We visited two studios that did Maori carving, one in wood and one in stone. Then a drive back to the camp and it was time for my dinner. As I undressed into more casual gear, I pulled a chip of pumice stone out of my coat pocket, I had put there when everyone else was watching the Japanese debacle on the shore.

It fascinated me as well. I'm sure the Maori Gods would not mind a minute piece was missing; I could take it home with me as a reminder of the mighty Lake Taupo. Then the brain set in, did I need any more problems? Was I asking for trouble by upsetting the universe? The answer was no, so I gave it back to the soil, digging a small hole in the camp garden by the ablution blocks, the relief I felt settled around me.

Day two of my stay was a cleaning day for me; washing, tidying, dusting, cleaning the jeep out then washing the Mermaid and jeep on the outside. Both shed their skin of mud, now sparkling as I washed and polished, rubbing them both down like sleek horses, the only comment made to me was, 'Nice rig, lady,' from a young boy, I guess he was ten.

'Thank you, yes it is,' and that was it the only person I spoke to that day. My lunch and dinner were cold corned beef, pickle and crackers with a hot cup of tea and lots of bottled water. I showered then put on my PJs and lay on my bed reading until I fell asleep.

Waking early morning for another drink of water, then sleep. Even my dreams were ordered. I slept, dreamed, woke up, and the day proceeded.

Day three. Time to plan where I was going and what to see; a trip to the Waitomo caves was on order today. I could drive there or could ring a tour company. I gave the tour company I used before a phone call. 'Yes, we're planning a tour the next day,' they told me. It would be an early start and late return as Waitomo was a four-hour drive with a stop off for lunch.

'Good, I'll book with you. See you at seven in the morning.' Today I would drive myself around to see Taupo.

Still enjoying my solitude, I locked up the Mermaid and drove out of the camp gate, and following the maps instructions, I visited the Taupo community gardens, the Maori Museum, the library that had gorgeous carvings in it, and took photos of a Waka in a large communal garden. I had an English afternoon tea of hot crumpets, the butter melting into them, raspberry jam blobbed on their tops and a big mug of hot chocolate. I wrote in my journal and read the things to do and see in Taupo from the tourism blurb I had received in my envelope.

I was enjoying my day so much. The wind was light but breezy, playfully sticking its cold fingers down my neck, goose bumps broke out, so it was back to the car for a jacket. When the phone rang it shook me out of my reverie. 'Mum, it's Rae.' She sounded urgent.

'Rae, what's wrong?' I asked.

'Mum, can we talk?' The thrill of *she's talking to me* overcoming the little jolt of *what now?*

When she dropped her bomb, my heart sank for her as she sobbed, 'Mum, he took all of it.'

'What are you saying, Rae?' I asked.

'Jono has taken all of Jess's education money and gone. I have no idea where he is.'

My heart squeezed to hear the misery in her voice. She told me they'd planned to buy a home with their saved money and along with the first home buyer government grant had a substantial deposit. Jono had said he would take their cheque to the home builder's office. That was over twenty-four hours ago; he never came back. She had waited for one day before finally contacting the police. Apparently, it was all quite legal. She couldn't charge him with theft as she was married to the cockroach and willingly gave him the money. No extortion charges could be made either.

'Oh Rae, I'm so sorry. How is Jess taking this?'

'We miss you so much,' she cried, then dropped a bigger bomb, 'Mum... I'm eight weeks pregnant.'

'How wonderful, Rae. I'm going to be a Nana again?' Pure joy flooding through me.

The feeling that something was not right stopped me from blurting, 'I'm coming home, Rae.' Instead I said, 'I'm going to ring my lawyer to see what I can do from here. I will ring you tomorrow. I will help you as much as I can.'

'Okay,' she hiccupped. 'Love you, Mum.'

Hmm... funny, when my heart was breaking and I wanted to hear that more than anything else in the world, she snatched it away from me. I shook off those thoughts, but they were determined to hang on in there. I couldn't figure out if I was being bloody minded and selfish or was I being conned yet again. Tara, time to use your wisdom, I thought as I walked to the car; this time I'm not rushing into anything. I would let my lawyer sort this one out if he could. I love this modern technology; all it takes is one phone call and you can solve a crisis without being present.

Rae was completely right; I had signed the amount over to Rae under her married name and she had put it into their account. The education cheque, with interest, was over thirteen thousand dollars. She had banked it into their combined bank account the day after they were married, so it was now his money as well and how he chose to spend it, although unfair on Rae, was none of my business. There were a few things we could try like suing him.

First, they would have to find him. If he stayed in the country it meant hiring a private detective. My lawyer advised, 'It's all going to cost a large amount of your capital, so think about it if you are willing to spend that to get it back.'

Honestly, no!

I felt like I'd been under threat from my daughter for a while now and it had ramped up to a high degree once she met Jono. I rang Jo, asking her to visit Rae and Jess just to make sure she was okay. She was fine with it and promised to go over the next day asking if I had received her latest email. 'My family would like to stay in your home for another two months if it's possible?'

'Jo, anything is possible. I have found that out the hard way.' There was a puzzled silence from her end. I added, 'I will explain it in an email. Love to you and yours, but I'm having a ball.' To which she replied, 'Is there a man involved?' Jo was my incurable romantic mate. 'Nope, just me.'

I walked out of the gardens smiling. Why not say yes to her request of her family staying longer, I was enjoying my freedom.

As night fell and I was snug in my van, I rang Rae to tell her the news about the money. 'Best to let it go, honey. It's going to cost me double that to find Jono.'

Of course, she made all sorts of promises to pay me back. 'You will be on a solo Mum's pension, Rae, be sensible.'

She sobbed and pleaded, 'Could you just lend me anther ten thousand to buy into the home we had wanted?' I felt really bad at her pleading but, 'The answer is no, not while you're still married to Jono.'

As I went to sleep I no longer berated myself with the 'should of could of' scenario I usually put myself through; it was goodnight world, see you tomorrow and off I went to sleep.

I woke with a huge stretch, yawning like a big cat, my usually tight jaw clicking itself into place, my shoulders completely relaxed. The Waitomo caves visit was on today and my body felt wonderful, no aches and pains today. I was walking to the gates for the tour bus a little early and just as well, the bus was already there, the hissing of air brakes always makes me think of a big muscle-bound guy announcing, 'I'm here and I mean business.'

Greeted with Kia Ora by a charming female tour guide, I was shown to my seat and off we went. It was worth every penny I spent. The Waitomo Glowworm Caves are truly beautiful, a fairy land of lights that actually twinkled and we were asked not to speak as they might go out. None of us spoke, but then came the loudest sneeze I've ever heard followed by a mumbled apology, then he blew his nose like a mad trumpeter, not once–that was not good enough, the next nose blow included snorts and throat clearing. The little lights dimmed then flickered on again. What do you say to that?

The guide asked him to, 'Perhaps step outside, sir, until the sneezing has stopped.'

His American twang said, 'But lady?'

'Now sir, if you please,' her brow creased with concern for her native glow worms and their reaction. Thankfully they still glowed, and we then settled ourselves into small inflatable boats called rubber ducks.

Groups of four to a boat including two guides, I noticed the American stayed outside and off we glided into deep velvet black silent darkness, illuminated by small specks of a worm's tail. How magical; a child's fairy land coming true with the wonderful show of lights these little creatures put on for us. Ornate cave patterns were shown to us by torchlight as we glided towards centuries of natural history. Shawl-like limestone formations, crystal tapestries, stalactites, stalagmites and flow stones, words I had never used now flowed as I repeated softly what the guide was saying. In the distance was the roar of subterranean waterfalls that thundered in warning to anyone that came too close. To soon the tour was over.

On our way home, we stopped off at a large roadhouse that served the Kiwi favourite: scones and cream with jam and a hot cup of tea.

Metal Mermaid

The cups were huge and if not careful you could have suffered a severe wrist sprain. I had to hold my cup with two hands. I was not complaining though, I had a brilliant day, my co-tourists all agreeing, even the American, who's rather scarlet bulbous nose told everyone he had a cold. Rudolph reindeer eat your heart out, you have competition.

Chapter 44

Back at camp and with everything in order, I opened my emails to see what Jo had written; she had been to Rae's home, taken her a box of groceries as I requested and was happy to report all was calm. Jess, busy with his Xbox game, seemed fine.

No dramas she wrote, a very pleasant visit and everything was very nice; Rae was her normal charming self to Aunty Jo. Relax and enjoy yourself, she advised. She had given Rae her mobile number if she needed to talk over a coffee at any time. How wonderful to have an aunty that cared. I wondered if Rae would ever appreciate the fact she had a friend who cared about us all and included us in her family.

The next tourist attraction I was very interested in was the fixed wing flight over the National Park. It was one day's drive away, a good six hours according to my calculations and I also wanted to visit New Plymouth. To do this, I would have to drive to the National Park through Turangi to see the three volcanoes and lakes that are either in them or surround them, then cut across to New Plymouth. The most popular flight was open seven days a week, so once home from Waitomo I rang the tour operator's number while my dinner of ham and pea soup with crusty toast cooked. Yes, the weather was good and yes, I could book in for a flight. I asked if there was a caravan park nearby and was told if I had a small rig I could leave it at the airfield until I got back from the flight; it would be safe there.

Leaving the Taupo caravan park early the next morning I tooted, waved at the office lady, the boom gate sprang up and I was off again on another adventure. The road was bare, brush and scrub dotted the sandy loam, a little like Australia except without red dirt.

I pulled over for breakfast, wandered round my Mermaid and gave her moko a pat, telling her, 'You are land-locked now, honey.'

The wind was so cold; the mountainous volcanoes loomed ahead in the haze. I drove until it one pm on one long road that had occasional signs saying the army was doing missile practise in an area close by. Finally, I reached the airfield. They must have seen me coming as I pulled up and a young man walked out and guided me to a small park beside a shed. He shook my hand introduced himself as Daniel. Making sure everything was locked up, he ushered me to a four-seater fixed-wing plane. He made sure I was all buckled up, ran back to the office for a sheaf of papers, and soon we were taxiing down the runway at a great speed.

'Take off,' he yelled as the nose of the plane took a great leap into the sky.

We climbed to ten-thousand feet above all three volcanoes, including Mt Ruapehu–the live volcano that steamed away in the distance. The pilot explained this was where the Peter Jackson films, the 'Lord of the Rings' trilogy, were made. This piqued my interest as Jess and I both loved those movies. We flew over lakes so blue it took your breath away and I saw a land of tussocks, mountains and desert. What an unusual place New Zealand was, so much water and smack in the middle a desert and volcanoes that were still alive. We circled around the tallest one, a deep lake of steam-filled water in its middle. Each side of this country was so green, thick luscious plants and vegetation completely surrounded by sea, even driving over and through gorges there were freshwater falls gushing everywhere. I must admit, in this small plane there was no fear like I had experienced flying in the helicopter over White Island.

I loved it; the sky-blue lakes that steamed in the afternoon sun, white fluffy clouds playing peek-a-boo with the plane and my camera. As we came in for landing, small dots of sheep became visible, the pilot telling me there were red deer and wild horses almost like the Aussie brumby living in large herds around the desert road; it was truly an amazing place. I felt privileged to be able to see it by plane, down we came like a large silver eagle and taxied to the big red stop sign by the side of the runway, which amused me greatly. I was on my own once again.

Daniel greeting and meeting more tourists while I stored my camcorder in the Mermaid, I drove off; it was dusk, and I needed to find a camp spot. I knew it was illegal to camp on the side of the desert road as there are all sorts of army manoeuvres going on at night. I was a good half hour away when the Mountain Air office rang asking me to return. 'It was very important,' they said.

I did a U-turn and drove back, no idea why I was called back, the office had been evasive but they did sound very serious. Perhaps I had left something behind but what was it? I thought I had everything with me.

I arrived at the little airport, its building well lit up, the young Maori woman behind the desk looked very unhappy as I walked in. 'I'm Tara. What's up?' She told me abruptly that I couldn't go in that direction as army tanks had blocked off the road for manoeuvres. 'Damn, what do I do now?' I asked.

'Well you could stay here for the night or follow me home; you can park in our driveway until the morning. Even though the army would be all around me, I felt really uncomfortable staying in the unlit car park for the night, especially since my experience of the police carpark south of Auckland, so I conceded to her front yard, thank you very much.

She putted off in her Fiat Bambina; I had not seen one of those cars since I was in my thirties, her headlights giving off a mellow light into the black night, her little red taillights beacons that I followed. We arrived at her little cottage about three quarters of an hour away. She drove up her driveway and dogs started to whine, then a cacophony of yelping and barking; I sincerely hoped they were chained up. Switching off my lights, getting out of my car and smiling, I held out my hand to say thank you. Turning her back on me, her footsteps receded on the gravel path. How bloody rude! To add insult to injury, once inside she switched off all the lights leaving me standing there in the dark with my hand extended, the noise of dogs barking sounded like they were aiming to have me for supper.

I fumbled in the glove box for the torch and flicked it on in relief only to find right beside me was the biggest, hairiest dog I have ever seen. My heart was in my throat as I said, 'Nice doggy,' and inched past it. The dog growled, baring its teeth, exploding into a rage of barking at me. A light flicked on in the house, 'Ned, shut you're friggin noise up or I'll cut ya bloody throat,' a man yelled out.

Silence settled. Ned sulked, going back into his doghouse and I scrambled quickly into the Mermaid. Early the next morning I was woken with loud knocking on my door, 'Hey lady, back up, I want to go to work.'

Stumbling out, very sleepy in my coat and PJs, shoving my feet into sneakers, I backed my van back down the driveway and parked. The young Maori man pulled up alongside me winding his window down, the frosty air making soft white hazy pillows of his breath, 'No use driving back there, we are all off now.' Anger at me radiated from this young man, why?

'And good morning to you too,' I said as he screeched off.

Driving off at this hour into the unknown without being able to have a morning pee or a cuppa was not on. I was not dressed and was now in a foul mood, my bladder groaning for release. Pulling off the road I made for a bush hoping the army wasn't too close with their manoeuvres. At least I had no worries about snakes here. Back in the van I threw on jeans and a top, brushed my hair, which by now badly needed a wash; in fact, all of me cried out for a shower. I drove across to Stratford where I parked on the city outskirts and made some breakfast and had a cold-water wash in the basin using the last of my cold-water supply. It still rattled me that some people like those this morning can be so rude.

My head was aching, and I was feeling nauseous, scratching around for pain killers in the early morning with a half cold cuppa is not fun. Again, thoughts spinning of why am I doing this? This was not an adventure; this was sheer hard work. A little voice saying, your choice, you're an adult. There was only one way to go—forwards.

Stratford is a pretty town with large elm trees along the main road, their leaves turning gold, and cute little wooden cottages. I was later told they were the original railway houses for the workers and their families, most of them had fretwork around them, shutters on the windows and painted pretty colours. Stratford had the most amazing flower display and it seemed everyone grew something that blossomed into fabulous flowers; sweet peas ran riot over old stone fences, rocks from old volcanoes dotted lawns, not small rocks but huge monuments of an era now past. Everlasting daisies swayed with the wind, their annual life nearly over. The grass forever green, smothered in lawn daisies, gardens a riot with forget-me-knots, tiger lilies, naked lady lilies, an amazing assortment of colour and texture in the gardens. Obviously, people took pride in their homes.

What I needed right now was a campground, a lie down and to not move for a while. I guess if you wish hard enough it will come to you, and I came across a sign saying 500 metres to your left, Stratford Caravan Park. Hopefully at this time of year there are plenty of vacancies. I must have looked drunk or hungover as there was a distinct pause when the campground manager welcomed me, her eyes measuring me up, a no formed on her lips. I managed to say I have a migraine, and her eyes changed again, this time to empathy. 'Site thirty, love,' she said.

I drove in, found my number, parked, un-hitched my Mermaid–all done in robot fashion; my head felt like I had a huge drum crashing inside my skull. Boil the jug, more pain killers, a hotty around the neck then try to sleep for the day. The earth could have opened and swallowed me I was so out to it. The question of why am I doing this when I could be home in my comfy bed with no worries about a little van and a car, rolled around in my head.

Sleep did not help. I woke five hours later and immediately threw up. I needed to rehydrate as soon as possible, my kidneys on fire with the two lots of pain killers I had taken. Thank God the small plastic basin I had used for washing was still on the bench. I continued to throw up my head pounding, my eyesight blurry. This was one doozey of a migraine, it had been a while since I had been this sick with one but recognised the symptoms, so fear was not a factor; I knew either tonight or tomorrow I would wake up almost pain free.

I was almost right, it cleared by late afternoon; I felt the muscles in my neck release. Very slowly, the change in the pain was sufficient enough for me to get up and make a very hot cup of tea and scrounge around for the rest of the ginger nut biscuits I had left over. A-ha! I spied three of them tucked away in a plastic container, they were really stale by now but to me at that moment they were manna from heaven. I felt guilt free scoffing all three bikkies in one go and with two mugs of hot tea and a very warm hot water bottle around my neck I was improving.

The camp manager knocked on my door that night. 'I hate to ask as I know you're not well, but how long are you staying?' she queried. Her name was Madge according to her name badge. I looked at my Mermaid, her insides musty and messy, my doona and sheets wrinkled and sweaty. 'Is it possible I can stay for the week?'

'No worries, Darl,' she replied.

'You're an Aussie,' I almost swept her off her feet in a hug. 'You're the second one I've met since I've been here.'

'Yeah, that's cause all the Kiwis live in Aussie now,' a great bubble of laughter rolled out of her, 'and your next question is what are you doing here, right?'

'Right,' I replied. I felt like I had met a dear old friend who understood me. Madge was a small, tired, faded, dyed, permed frizzy blonde woman with a face full of lines and wrinkles.

'From Silverton, mate. I was an extra on the *Mad Max* movie being filmed there.' Her handshake more like a miner's grip as she pumped my hand up and down. I flinched, 'Oww.' I was still tender around the neck muscles. Madge must have seen me flinch; she was suddenly all business. 'Okay, Darl… one week booked it is. Pay us tomorrow, I'm about to close for the day.'

Off she stomped, bandy as a monkey on a barrel, she rolled from side to side once her speed was up. She reminded me of a sand toy that went from side to side frantically if you hit it. I used to love those toys, whacking them then watching them wobble in all directions. Jess and I had played with one for hours when he was a baby.

Madge was strict, no nonsense and full of love for those she deemed needed it whether it was human or animals, her grating smokers voice once announced, 'Rather look after the stray animals love, than some of the bloody humans I've met.' To this I had to agree.

Madge lived in a caravan out the back of the office. The grounds were immaculate, if a leaf or feather dare blow onto the pathway or the rock garden she was out there with her broom sweeping anything up and into the rubbish. Her small office–an old donga–was surrounded by another rock garden. So many plants thrived there, so many bright coloured roses and geraniums of pink, white, red and orange climbed over fences and up an old lamppost. A fishpond with pretty goldfish was beside the office where ferns of all descriptions grew all around.

As I signed the register I asked, 'Why did you move here? It's always raining and cold.' Madge smiled; her chipped tobacco stained teeth glowed in the lamplight. 'Why not, Darl? I had a rotten marriage, two rotten kids that don't like me and I don't like them, my brother owned this and the bastard died leaving it to me, so here I am and I'm as happy as a sand boy. What about you?'

To Madge it was all clear cut. 'No emotional crap,' as she called it got in her way. She looked the world in the face and told it to, 'Bugger off, I'm busy.' Go Madge, this little lady had guts.

Madge was a real trouper and always ready to help. 'Darl, sleep off your headache and then clean yourself up, you look bloody awful.' I knew tact was not in her vocabulary.

A large PRIVATE sign hung on the gate to her front door, you could not miss it or mistake her intention of privacy. The lawns a vivid green that dandelions sprouted on and so many daisies. I remembered the days when I made daisy chain crowns and did the same with my daughter, my heart giving a little squeeze for those happy days.

I rented the camp vacuum and bucket and then set to work once again with the ritual of cleaning. I couldn't believe how grubby the Mermaid was.

If I looked up at any time I would see the curtain twitch in the office, Madge keeping an eye on me, I guess, making sure I did not run off down the road, waving her vacuum in the air like a mad women. When I returned it she said, 'You've emptied it and cleaned the bucket and vacuum cleaner?'

'I have,' I said. Still she examined each one for any details of dirt I might have left behind. She ran her hand around each bowl then looked at her fingers, blue beady eyes scrutinised every nook and cranny. She gave one curt abrupt nod and stored it all away under the counter, giving me my deposit back, less five dollars for the electricity I used.

That afternoon I was off to do some food shopping, stopping off at the office to ask for directions. On Madge's lap laid the mangiest cat I have ever seen. His fur was all tangled, one eye was missing, his purr so loud it was like sitting inside the jeep with the motor on. Madge's face was pure glowing love for this little cat, her blue veined work-worn hands carefully cleaned him down, her voice almost like his purring endearments to him as she rubbed a soft cloth over his eyes and head.

'Poor old Tom. Not wanted, just like me aye Tom. Never mind old boy, I love you.' Madge never saw me at the door but Tom the cat did. As I backed out of the doorway I swear I saw a smirk on old Tom's face as I left.

Chapter 45

I drove into town thinking over my list; what I needed and what I wanted. My first stop was a café for a hot coffee and something nice to eat–a ham salad, plus I saw a large chocolate lamington inside the glass dome. It looked so fresh and yummy, I gave into my craving and bought one. Shopping done, tummy fed and replete, I found a hairdresser and had my hair trimmed, my perm still doing a great job of keeping it neat and tidy as I travelled. Back at the caravan park business as usual, unpacking, storing; my chocolate lamington sat on the bedside table, this was my supper tonight. Then off to the office to pay my dues. Marge did the sums, she used a calculator, the price was not too bad. I paid with my Visa card and we both got on with our busy days. Me touring a city that had little to show except for a museum, library and hospital, I was hedging my bets to see if I could find a local that was willing to talk to me. I would have found a lot more to see and do but sadly my days at the park were at an end. I had seen very little and Madge had closed up like a clam once I had paid up. I had certainly made myself at home at the café down the street since being here and must have tried everything all homemade and rich with custard, eggs, or crème; the sponge cake was heaven.

The café owner was from South Africa, a new recruit to this area, so not much help there. He was sorry to see his cash cow go but it was time I was on the road again before I regained those fourteen kilos I had shed.

Driving up to the office after I hitched the van on, I beeped and waved to Madge who was out weeding her already weedless garden, her bandy legs covered in light brown tights made a perfect O that old Tom wound in and out of. 'Bye Madge, lovely to have met you, take care,' I called out.

Standing up, her blue eyes watery, she waved back, 'You too, Darl. Drive safe.'

Woo hoo! I was on the road once again.

New Plymouth was my next port of call. I had already phoned ahead and found a caravan park, booking a site for two days. I keyed the name of the camp and the road into the GPS. One large red ribbon appeared on screen and Victoria, my GPS voice, said in her very sexy Oxford English voice, 'Take the first turn to your right.' I did and there was a sign board that said New Plymouth this way, stating kilometres, road conditions and the weather. It was winter in New Zealand; the wind had now become quite cold and bitter, chilling the bones.

After a four-hour drive with only one toilet stop, I reached the campgrounds, Victoria announcing, 'You have reached your destination.' My answer to the obvious was, 'No shit, Sherlock.'

My camp site number was 53. I was an expert on backing the Mermaid in by now but the manager, Rick, insisted he walk me to the site and practically bellowed orders at me.

'Turn right, a little to the left, stop, come forward a little,' as according to camp rules my van had to be exactly five-hundred millimetres off the road. From his hip pocket he unfurled a measuring stick, looked at my tow ball, nodded and gave me the thumbs up. With the ruler clamped under his right arm pit, he strutted back to his domain like he had won a war, stomping and bellowing his way back to the camp.

I could see other campers scurrying about cleaning up their site as Rick stomped back to the office. Two senior citizens came over to me, 'Hello, I'm Thelma and this is Kerry. Don't let him scare you off, dear,' she said. 'He's profoundly deaf having been in the army in Vietnam, you know, the bombs and all that stuff.' It all fell into place; the military frog march and the bellow he had on him. I guess army days are hard to forget.

Her hubby mutely agreeing, he looked so tiny next to this woman and she was only knee high to a duck herself. Rick's heart was in the right place, she assured me, Kerry nodding enthusiastically but not one syllable left this little man's mouth.

Thelma nudged Kerry in the ribs. 'You take no notice of him, dear. He's shy.' He stumbled to the side a little and my arm shot out to save him from falling, but she pulled him away from me saying to him, 'Have you finished those dishes? They won't dry themselves you know.' Poor Kerry. He looked every part the hen-pecked hubby; meek, mild, subservient.

I was not going to get involved, even though Thelma did her best to tell me the titbits of the camp and all its goings on; apparently it was nearly full of retired permanents, most of them single men. Her eyebrows rose up and wiggled at me. What the hell was that supposed to mean?

I did the usual search in the township looking for a tourist shop. It was not too hard, a big blue **I**, for information, stood out in the middle of the city.

Once inside the overheated building I collected an armful of brochures and just wanted to sit somewhere quiet and soak up all I had done and seen. Brochures on the South Island were tempting though, the staff warning me I'd freeze in my small van in the snow. I could see the headlines now: 'Frozen Aussie found in snow bound caravan.' Now the brain was going into overdrive.

I read all about the 'what to do as a tourist' information. Flyover? Done that. River cruise? Done that. Kayaking? Done that. Tour bus to lots of Maori culture displays plus a Maori greeting with a lunch provided? No, I've done that as well. There was bungy-jumping, golf and movies but all I wanted to do was sit, perhaps drive around, take snaps of what I thought interesting and add to my journal on the laptop, so that's exactly what I did.

In the early afternoon I wandered back to the camp, putting my nose into another book and read for an hour. I made a light lunch, snoozed, my neck still tender from the muscle spasm the previous week, put the latest snaps onto the laptop and wrote on my blog page, but I was restless.

I will go and have a nice long hot shower, give my neck a massage at the same time I thought. Thelma, looking out her van window, must have seen my door open and she invited me to a bingo game that night at the camp. I puffed out my cheeks and rocked on my heels undecided; I really did not want to get mixed up with the camp goings on.

'Okay Thelma,' I agreed.

'Oh goody.' She clapped her small many ringed hands together. That was the first thing I had noticed about Thelma, the rings on her hands. How the hell did she do anything? Even lifting them up to clap looked highly dangerous to me.

'I will pop over at seven pm and pick you up,' she gushed. I had this feeling I was being set up, but what do you say to a little old lady that looks like the grandma in the big bad wolf story?

I muttered, 'Alright Thelma, see you then.'

Now I'm not one to down us seniors, or say, 'Old people rock.' I consider it crude, but this crowd did. Rick bellowed the numbers and the rhymes that went with them, 'Number 7 legs eleven, number 44 out the door.'

Thelma won a couple of times but I had lost interest by nine pm. I was under the impression retirees were supposed to be genteel, but these old boys were into the booze and ribald jokes about women and their purpose (at the bench, barefoot etc.) wafted around the room.

The older ladies were well into their boozy cups, giggling and giving them the eye and by ten pm there was a fair bit of touchy feely going on. I definitely heard Thelma giggle and say, 'You're such a naughty boy.'

I looked down at a bald pink head, he was so bent over with age, a huge pipe clamped between puckered lips which he removed when he saw fresh meat… me.

'Allo Sweetie,' he croaked, then flashed his baby pink gums at me. Now I know I'm lonely but come on! Do I have a sign that says 'oh please pick me' on my forehead? His gnarled blue veined hand shot out and pinched my leg.

'Ow!' I cried, 'that hurt,' frowning at this little man that annoyed me. He did it again, so I slapped his hand away saying loudly, 'Stop that now.'

Thelma was now screeching, 'Leave my friend alone, you nasty old man', the hall now resounding with name calling and opinions. What I did glean from this passionate verbal exchange was this was the camp Romeo! You've got to be kidding me, was my last thought. It appears Romeo was not too short of abusive language himself, calling Thelma a very dirty name and a, 'Dried up old tart.'

I saw it coming. Thelma threw a right hook at Romeo but I was in the way. *Ouch!* Bright lights, then darkness. When I came to I was in Rick's arms being carried into his office. 'Ice pack and a shot of the malt will fix her,' he roared into my right ear, his voice reverberating through my body.

'Carry on as normal,' he ordered. The party continued with a slow cheek to cheek dance with Zimmer frames, playing cards, bingo and booze.

Rick let me down gently on his couch, finding me an ice pack for my now swollen jaw and a tot of whiskey to clear my head. I refused the drink, but the ice was so good on my face.

'You're going to be badly bruised,' he roared. 'Stay here until you feel better; I have to make sure no one steals the bingo money.'

Out he stomped. *What?* It felt like I was in an insane asylum. It took me a fuzzy while to do up my coat and find the latch to his office door, then I was out of there. Running was not an option, the pain was awful but I found my way to my van and locked myself in.

I then rang Margi and told her what had happened, my swelling jaw making it hard to pronounce some words. There was a silence then, 'Oh Tara.' She erupted into huge gales of laughter with big whooping noises in between as she took a breath and by the time she had finished, I to was giggling insanely at what had just happened.

I couldn't open my mouth, my jaw was so swollen, so my giggling sounded like water sloshing in a blocked pipe, spit ran down my chin and tears bubbled over to join it. I was on my bed doubled up, cackling like a crone.

'Let me make a couple of calls,' she said. 'Get some sleep. I will ring you in the morning.'

'Shokay,' I giggled through clenched jaw and hysteria, this insane camp was catching, I felt lightheaded and quite woozy. What I had witnessed was not normal I was sure, or was it? I had no idea. I was not going to enquire. I was going to leave asap. Sleep came very easy that night.

The morning dawned pearly blue, white fluffy clouds blending into each other. A perfect autumn morning, the air sweet and clean, except for the pain in my jaw; it felt very swollen. I looked in my hand mirror, *oh dear Lord*. I was black and blue with one nasty deep scratch down the side of my face, the pillow slip mottled in spit and blood. That little lady packed a mean punch.

I wandered over to the showers meeting up with Thelma in the ablution block. 'Goodness me, what happened?' she declared. 'Did you fall over?'

'You could call it that,' I gurgled. 'You hit me,' I said.

'I did no such thing!' Each indignant word spaced, her voice now raised and echoing in the large brick building.

'Don't you remember?' I questioned her.

'I most certainly do not. If I hit someone, I would know about it,' her large diamond rings glinting at me, the deep scratch no longer a mystery.

Thelma gave me a withering look and like a big duck waggled her large haunches out the door, trotting off and tutting about my accusation.

'What a rude woman,' she said, 'blaming me, for being clumsy.'

I guess by now she was telling the camp residents. But when I overheard the answer to Thelma's complaint I was livid

'She was most likely rotten drunk. Those Aussie women have no manners, drink like fish and sound like parrots.' They had the audacity to call me rude. So now I was the one being called names. Dear God, why me?

Eating was out; I prepared an ice milk shake made with milo, slurping with joy at the numbness it caused to the inside of my mouth. My phone trilled and it was Margi.

'Morning. How are you today, Tara?' she asked.

'A little worse for wear,' I gobbled, as my jaw would not work properly.

'You sound like a turkey.'

'Feel a bit like one today, Margi.'

'Okay, pen and paper ready Tara, here is the name and address of a good mate of mine, lives at Opunake beach. She has invited you to stay with them for a long as you like. I have given them your phone number and they will ring and give you the details of how to get there.

Text me when you arrive, will you? And please, take care of yourself Tara.'

I had no sooner put my phone down when Margi's friend rang me, her accent slight but hard to pick whether it was Russian or Swedish. She understood I found it hard to talk as Margi had told her what had happened and introduced herself as Petra. 'Well, you are most welcome here to join us.'

Chapter 46

I decided then and there to up-camp and go no matter how sick or injured I was. Everything I had put out the day before I stored away, pulled my hair up into small ponytail, patted aloe vera cream on the big black and yellow bruise now fully blossomed on my jaw. The deep scratch on my cheek went up to my nostril, it looked red and felt tight and sore.

I was emptying out the jug and putting my little kitchen into place when Kerry arrived. He helped me pack up my one camp chair and table stowing them under the Mermaid. I shook his hand and he patted me on my shoulder, 'Sorry love,' he whispered, 'she's a right little sod with a few in her.'

Kerry waited around until I was in the car backing up to my van, helping me hitch the van onto it. He scurried back inside his van, as we both spotted Thelma galloping down the road at great knots, her eyes bulging, her mouth already working with some sort of awful abuse for Kerry. Before she could accost me, I was in the car driving up to the office, Rick bellowing at me, 'Leaving are we?'

I nodded, mumbling, 'I want a refund please.' He looked like he was on the verge of saying, 'Get stuffed,' but instead he nodded his head. I flinched as his voice blasted the air with spittle in my direction, 'Don't blame you, love.' I was so happy to leave this campground.

Opunake is really small but the ocean and beaches on the way are amazing. It did not have the gold or white sands of home, this was coarse black sand, driftwood built up in huge piles on the beach. Huge fat brown kelp bundled themselves into mangled knots on the sand and in the water they looked quite evil; heavy swollen brown kelpy hands that would drag you down.

The air smelt of salt and the sea. Waves far out heaved and rolled, the weight of water proving too much as they charged up onto shore, then spent they changed to foam with lacy tops whispering of its adventure onto the sand. Seagulls rode these rolling waves like experienced surf boarders. One lone seagull flew past me squawking his welcome. The hills and forests had a wind worn look, but still lush; native flax grew everywhere, bell birds, tuis and sparrows sitting amongst of the long stamens of flax flowers, their mixed song a delight.

The scenery, as I drove along the west Coast of New Zealand through to Opunake–known for its wild weather and raw beauty, was breathtaking. I must have stopped ten times to take photos. I loved it.

Petra, true to her word, was waiting at their gate. I drove up beside her, she smiled and waved, got in the car and up we went to their home. Unbeknownst to me, a life changing experience was about to take place.

Paradise was the name they had given their land and I soon realised why. I had to agree, it was amazing; wonderful and peaceful, here was the real New Zealand literally untouched.

Petra was stunned by the gorgeous bloom of colours now on my face. 'Wow, that was some punch,' her hand tilting my chin so she could see it better. Ronan, her husband, was coming out their door with welcome drinks, his eyes widened as he saw my face, 'Holy shit,' he exclaimed. 'Get the number of the bus?'

I wanted to laugh but it was too sore. The cut now raised and looking quite nasty.

'I think you need help,' he said, and help he gave as Ronan was a retired doctor. While Petra made up some sort of cold poultice with herbs from their garden, Ronan examined me. 'Nothing broken, and I think you have a little bit of whip lash,' as his long fingers pressed muscles at the back of my head and shoulders.

'Now,' they both declared, 'from what we have heard you're very determined to do your own thing, but this is a working farm so while you're here why not stay in our cabin out the back and heal up. You need soft food and warm drinks, plus some physio to your neck and jaw.'

These two people were wonderful, opening their home, arms and hearts to me, a stranger. I gratefully accepted. I needed to stretch my body out, feel the sea air, and take some time out from driving. I took up their offer, offering my thanks. Petra put her index finger to her mouth, 'Give it a rest,' she said.

I then did the one thing I thought would never happen while I toured; I moved out of the Mermaid into their beach batch. On calm sunny days I sat and watched Ronan carve mythical creatures from driftwood. Petra was an amateur jeweller, her figure often bent over her work bench creating works of *fabulous art* as she called them.

On cold days, the strong sea wind buffeted my little home, whipping around the corners, rain splashed against the window. I hunkered down inside, warm and cosy, a small pot belly stove in the corner of my one room giving off a comfy heat, it puffed out the occasional cloud of tea tree smoke that smelt wonderful.

I spent those wet days reading books from model ship building to the history of dinosaurs in New Zealand. I emailed Rae apologising for my tardiness in phoning her, explaining I had 'fallen' and had a badly bruise my jaw so talking was difficult. As the week passed we emailed some more. I told her about the beauty of the West Coast of New Zealand. I told her of my many experiences and who I had met on the way, once again leaving out my time with Beryl and Venus.

I now had time to email my close friends in Perth, taking great joy in writing again, adding how much I enjoyed being here at Paradise and finally about Petra and Ronan and their wonderful generosity. It was the truth; I only had to sneeze and one of them would be there to ask if I needed something.

They were so naturally beautiful inside and out. My face soon mended with the tea tree poultice Petra applied to my face morning and night. I healed with barely a scar on my cheek.

Ronan massaged my upper body and did physiotherapy until I could turn properly. The food they cooked for me was mashed or blended, and on the day I put a small piece of fish in my mouth and chewed, they applauded.

Petra practised Kiwi bush and flower healing; I had seen this up North with Pania's family. The careful extraction of the precious healing oils and herbs added to a base oil then added to a small flame steamer which lit up Petra's office in a deep yellow glow. The entry to her workshop had two massive poles as the lintels, both carved by Ronan with Nordic gods sitting proudly, part of Petra's heritage. Fish, crabs, shells and mermaids adorned the top lintel running across the ceiling and looking down at me was the king of the sea. His beard and tail curled around and around a pole, his trident held proudly erect, it was sensual. I learned the timber had come from an old shipwreck that run aground in the early 1900s. They were stained and gauged, huge iron bolts still studded the wood in some places, yet it seemed to fit with Ronan's loving touch.

Petra's jewellery astounded me; there lay intricate designs of shells cast in silver and gold, a bronze necklace so dainty, made with bronze wire and periwinkles or 'cat's eyes' she called them. 'Where do you find all this stuff?' I asked.

'After a storm, Tara, the sea gods of wind and sand deliver it up to our doorstep. You wait and see, once we have a huge storm I will take you fossicking.' It sounded very exciting I had to agree, my head made other suggestions though. I felt my time here was coming to a close. Making noises that I must see this and that; don't want to be a nuisance. I finally told them of my decision to move on to see the rest of the country. Wellington was maybe a day away.

'And then what?' Petra asked. 'South Island where it is snowing and very cold?'

Ronan agreed. 'Stay a little longer, Tara. If you feel you could be of help, then tomorrow you can work with me.'

Work? I had not thought of it as work. I had been helping around their home, cleaning and cooking as it was, I thought of it as doing my share.

'What on earth do you mean?'

'You will see,' he said, his index finger tapping alongside his nose. Petra looked skywards.

'Heaven help us,' she murmured. They would not say any more and changed the subject, the phone ringing, breaking up our dinner party. Ronan came back to the table smiling. 'No-one goes anywhere tomorrow. That was the metrological service warning us to buckle up and head down for a day or two. There is a big storm on its way.'

Petra said, 'Well you asked, Tara. Now here is your answer; we will need help to close up all the sheds and workshops, close the chook pen, put your Mermaid into the big shed and park your car around the back.'

Petra barked orders that I and Ronan followed exactly. She brooked no back chat and took over the safety of their Paradise, and like good soldiers we carried them out. I shooed the chooks into their pen, closed off the aviary with steel shutters, Ronan's prized breeds looking at me disdainfully as if to say, 'Just who do you think you are?'

I put the Mermaid inside the big shed, closing the big shutter steel doors and parking the car around the back of the shed under an open sided shelter where once firewood was stacked. I was so busy doing what I'd been told I hadn't noticed the dark purple clouds forming over the ocean, the waves now rolling in fast, getting louder and louder as they hit the shore. Gone was the light foam playing with the soft wind I had seen on my arrival. I saw destruction and anger as the sea hurled itself on to the shore and road. My first cyclone in New Zealand.

The next thing I tied down was the beach batch, closed all the windows, shut all doors and switched off any electrical items I had running. By the time I had done all of that I was getting damp with sea spray and the fog that rolled in very suddenly. Petra ordered me to sleep in the lounge until the storm was over. 'Rather have you safe and sound with us,' she instructed. I knew she was worried and could be abrupt, so no offence taken.

Steel roller doors now adorned the lounge front windows; a cosy tea-tree fire was lit. I felt very safe and comfortable with Petra and Ronan and we spent the night talking about their home. They found this small block of land on their honeymoon ten years ago, fell in love with it and bought it.

The cyclone threw whatever it could at us. It was wild, terrifying, exhilarating, breathtaking and there would be a second of silence then away it would scream again; it shook the house, rattled roller doors, sucked out the smoke from the chimney, the fire roared its delight. Once, when it turned quiet, I stood in the shelter of the doorway watching the waves grow and charge the beach. From far out they would build up until they were mini green rolling mountains careening towards us then dump themselves onto the sand, the boom of thunder a warning that Mother Nature was once again doing some housekeeping. Petra stood beside me rubbing her hands together. 'Great fossicking when nature has finished showing us her might.'

Living in Australia, I had been in cyclones that tore bricks from buildings, sucked the very air out of your lungs, exploding hailstorms. Once I had nearly been struck by lightning, my skin and hair fizzing as it jolted into the ground five metres from where I stood.

When I had lived with Russ in Cloncurry, Northern Queensland, we had experienced massive rainstorms, the rain drops as big as light bulbs. On one occasion, the immense flooding tore down a steel bridge and tossed it onto nearby boulders. Chinaman's Dam, the local lookout, had flooded the water a deep chocolate colour, huge trees thrashed about in the turmoil, the floods also delivered three big saltwater crocodiles to a favourite summer swimming hole. Thunder would shake the house and would growl and prowl around the skies for ages. The fork lightning was scary; when it hit the ground you knew it, a crack then a boom as it delivered its electric punch into the earth. Old silver gums would burst into flames like a tree sentry with a torch, the very air became alive.

However, this storm was nothing like that; it was oily, greasy, almost like a sneer at humanity as Neptune's green waves rose up into peaks and thundered loudly smashing into the sand. Hopefully we're safe in Paradise. As we sat waiting for the fury to calm down stories were told; Ronan had built the house himself, Petra also worked at home to bring in more money, on the days she was free she drove up to the seaside town running workshops in jewellery making and homeopathic remedies. Roping in anyone and everyone, especially tourists who wanted a bush adventure.

She and Ronan had the community to thank for their welcome. Friendships were built while building this paradise. Everyone that turned up was asked to trample straw into mud and at times twenty people were there stomping and talking and singing, making mud and straw bricks to build the walls of their house. Yes, there was some bad publicity by some who shunned them, calling them raving, rude hippies and greenies but they ignored it and kept on.

Ronan had gathered huge tree trunks from either the forest or the ocean to build the door frames and lintels; the entire house was built from recycled rubbish, 'Things people did not want,' as Ronan put it, 'but we did.' Until the house was built, they lived in the beach batch I was living in and slowly a homestead emerged with a very

Scandinavian touch to it. The outbuildings were old sheds no one wanted any more. People would ring Ronan and helped collect them, even the aviary had been a recent prize from a neighbour who was throwing it out. Ronan said, 'My eyeballs almost shot out my head when I drove past and saw the notice on the fence gate: "One large aviary, free" so instead of the milk and butter I was supposed to buy, I came home with that instead.'

Petra smiled at him. 'He's a collector, you might call him a hoarder, but we use everything he brings home.' Inside their home, apart from the pole carvings, there was also Ronan's Kiwi past, the Koru and Tiki were there as well, beautifully crafted. The large kitchen bench was made from swamp Kauri the colour of butter. A huge slab took up one side of the kitchen, in small pockets in the bench Petra had displayed seashells, all sorts of tiny fossils, a small nugget of gold and a small garnet, even a petrified bush Weta. Ronan then sealed it with a varnish, they both spent many hours varnishing the Kauri slab, the little memory treasures now embedded forever.

The circular bathroom was pure artistry, rainwater warmed by the sun and the fireplace ran through old brass pipes that had a moss-green tinge to them. Ronan forged the massive shower head, seven-foot high at least, its template an old steel bucket, it felt like standing under a tepid waterfall, the bath had claw feet and had been professionally re-enamelled inside. On the outside Petra had painted amazing scenery of the snow-capped mountains amongst the clouds, a tribute to her heritage.

The floor was polished concrete, small seashells had been set into it, the wall facing the bush made of green bottles, they glowed an eerie green in daylight. The hand basin Ronan carved from swamp Kauri wood was set into a concrete oval, the taps were new, given to them by a friendly plumber who had laid all the pipes.

The toilet was in a separate room away from the house; it was a green toilet–no flushing, you did what you had to do, sprinkled a mix of sawdust and pot ash over it all, close the lid and off you go. The door posts to the toilet were a work of art, you could sit there for a day and discover so much; bottles of wine and grapes carved into the wood with the leering, fat lipped, boggled eyed God, Bacchus. The tinted window you faced gave a different meaning to watching the world go by.

There was one bedroom and to me that said it all; lambskin rugs of every colour scattered everywhere, two huge, old, massive pieces of timber from the sea cross-braced against the walls, the roof was domed with three large mulled windows all angled at a large four-poster bed inherited by Petra adding, 'My parents pride and joy. My father had built it, I was conceived and born in it, so I am part of it,' she concluded.

Ronan had done wonders with all sorts of timber making a small dressing room screen weaving driftwood, flax and wire together and from this Petra hung seashells.

All the knick-knacks, the pretty little collectables, the uneven tallboy with straw baskets instead of drawers made it a treasure trove. The splendid intricacy of the large room took your attention and then you saw it, the magic of this bedroom: two huge stained-glass church windows, ten feet tall and set into the wall. It was magnificent; angels and saints, the heavens, stars and moons filled your eyes and took your breath away.

Ronan saved this from destruction.

'Wow,' was all I could say. 'You two have really made this your paradise.'

They stood with their arms around each other, nodding with pleasure at my reaction; contentment and love for each other shone in their faces. My heart squeezed. That night I missed Russ's strong, loving arms wrapped around me.

The storm roared for three days; we were house bound. If you dared go outside, which I did because my middle name is stupid, you were whipped by branches that cracked off forest trees or blown down into a shallow muddy puddle, both Petra and Ronan giggling at my dilemma as I dripped onto the porch crying, 'Help!' Mud puddles and I seem attracted to each other but then New Zealand always seemed to be muddy and wet.

Chapter 47

On the second night, Ronan served dinner–Paua soup with fresh crusty bread. Petra had made an herb salad and baked tomatoes with a goat's cheese stuffing on top. Served with a cranberry juice, garden mint and slices of lemon in soda water, it was a meal fit for a king. All three of us tucked in, making 'mmm' noises as we ate, the conversation wandering from one thing to another; what Petra had to do with her jewellery intending to go to local markets and further if that's what it took, she was busy booking stalls and a gallery had shown interest as well.

Petra and her lack of marketing skills were her downfall, so she hired a professional whom she was meeting in three weeks at a Wellington gallery. It all sounded well organised to me. Ronan was sorting out a carving he had been commissioned–five totem poles for the local council. He had designed them in sections of three pieces per pole and you could turn each separate section around, his aim was to encourage interaction with the kiddies.

Again, I felt it was time for me to move on. I told them over our dinner that night, 'Well, when the storm is over, I will be on my way. I have a lot to do and see.'

'Thought you might say that Tara,' Petra replied. 'Would you consider another option that Ronan and I have already discussed?'

'What are you two up to?' I asked.

Petra and Ronan now looked serious. 'Well,' they chorused, 'we've been thinking about you moving on and seeing the rest of New Zealand.'

'Oh,' I thought, here it comes. I'm being asked to move sooner than I anticipated or when the storm abates. I was so wrong.

Petra pulled out a huge map of the North Island. Ronan cleared the table and they unfolded their plans to me, asking me if I would care to be part of it.

While the storm raged to a crazed peak outside, inside we calmly discussed all possibilities. They suggested two opportunities. Number one, Petra was going on a fossicking trip. Her goal was to find gemstones, she'd been told the far South Island beaches abounded with garnets, tiger-eyes and moonstones, the occasional sapphire and many different shells. This was her destination but first to Wellington to speak to her marketing manager. She also wanted to attend small country markets on her way there to sell her jewellery plus mix and mingle with other artists, picking up ideas.

They planned a dinner in Wanganui to meet other artists of the same creative expression as Petra. Then Ronan continued, 'I intend to travel to Wellington with Petra.' He was collecting a consignment of five fifteen-foot tree trunks recently milled in Fielding and arrange for their transport to Opunake ready for work. His one fear was the milling company was big on using preservatives to age the wood and he disliked preservatives in any form, acknowledging in this day and age at times it was necessary, but he still was adamant about it not being used on wood before he carved it. 'Bloody stuff is toxic and dammed dangerous,' he claimed.

'No arguments there,' I replied.

Then they outlined what they were asking of me. 'We both know you want to travel a lot more and acknowledge it's your path not ours. What we would love to happen is for you to accompany us to Wellington as there are so many small townships on the way we know about that you will never see again if you miss them. After Wellington, we would like you to accompany Petra to the South Island as I will be returning home to set to work.'

'I thought there were two options on the table?' I asked.

'Yes, there is. Please do not feel obliged to agree to anything, it is a question only.' Petra replied, 'If you choose not to accompany us, would you think about being the caretaker of Paradise while we are away?'

'How long will you be away for?' I asked.

'Approximately three months for me,' said Petra.

'And four weeks for me,' Ronan added.

Questions formed in my head, the two of them sitting quietly waiting for my barrage of thoughts to pour out, there were too many to consider. 'Let me sleep on it, guys. I will write down my questions for tomorrow at dinner time.'

It was amazing and I felt honoured they asked of me, but did it fit in with what I wanted to accomplish?

Normally, sleep is instantaneous for me by the sea but tonight my head buzzed with questions. The storm was now down a notch, just a strong breeze. Mother Nature had run out of puff for a while. I tossed and turned for an hour or so, then as quietly as possible I let myself out the back door, patting the face of a small carved owl. I had seen the others do it as they went in and out and asked them why? It was Ronan's totem which protected them.

I made my way to the Mermaid, patting the totem on her rear. I let myself in the door and realised if I thought they were quaint to have a wooden owl as a totem, then what would they think seeing me patting my caravan, smiling like an idiot and murmuring endearments to it, but I felt it was more than a part of my life in New Zealand.

Okay, the scales had tipped with two opportunities; what do I do? I wrapped a blanket around myself, fetched my faithful notebook and trusty pen and started writing. There are times when I've written a problem down and the answer becomes pretty clear. Other times it just sits there, squiggly black letters on paper. I wrote down the opportunities and the questions I would like to ask. Was I more concerned about the path I wanted to follow and where I would end up at the end of my trip to New Zealand?

What I wrote, though, was how much I enjoyed Petra and Ronan's company. How special their home was. I felt alive with creativity, my paints and sketch paper now sketching the Opunake shoreline or sitting in the backyard where I was again in tune with nature, the amazing green mountains and fields surrounding me. These two people had never offended me or worried me in any way; they went about their business every day making sure I was healing to the best of our combined ability. The fact that Petra worshipped the moon, or her favourite Scandinavian Gods did not faze me as it would have at the start of my journey. Watching them touch Ronan's owl totem was part of their life's celebration. Listening to the soft thunk of Ronan's chisel as he carved into a fallen tree or offered up a prayer of thankfulness to the universe for this bounty. I joined in their pre-dinner prayer of gratefulness for the opportunity of experiencing and sharing our life on earth.

I now realised as I wrote about them, I enjoyed every minute of their company, relishing our night-time debates and discussions. In fact, it was what I had been missing, decent deep conversation with intelligent people. I appreciated their intense concentration at their work benches while I journaled my thoughts, sketched and healed.

They had respect for other human beings, either speaking on the phone or having guests, and if any of their guests made disparaging remarks they would politely but firmly ignore them or ask that person to leave their Paradise.

The debate that flowed around the evening fire was not at all about hierarchy or 'I'm the boss'; no ego or attitude was encouraged. We discussed philosophy and the why we were here. There were bible scriptures, Koran verses, the Catholic Douai version, even the Crier from the salvation army, each was discussed. What I soon learned was values change all the time, but principles don't; they are yours for life.

Petra would sit there amused at my half-hearted belief of a God she could not even imagine. One of terror and anger ready to destroy humanity at the touch of a finger, loving only those who obeyed him and only him.

'But each religion is different,' she claimed. 'Take the American Mormons, they believe in many wives, but Christians say one only wife. When I hear your man-made conclusions, it confuses me. What does this strange, angry God of yours want? All I see is this old man judging me, and if I'm found guilty, then tortured with fire and brimstone. Then on the flipside, this God promises undying love for all humanity. It smacks of hypocrisy.' Her logic was spot on.

She added, 'Don't you think your God might be more upset about wars and the huge global melt down we are causing this planet? After all, it is part of the creation of the universe or do you think he has you and only you in his eye non-stop? We are part of a huge spiritual plan; maybe we come to this planet as teachers? Or maybe we come here to experience what God cannot; the unfathomable nature of mankind?' Petra was now fired up about religion.

She explained her theory; when we as spirits incarnate on earth we come with a pre-signed contract, so to speak, to teach what we contracted ourselves to do in a higher realm. I had to agree. They had shown me not to be afraid of something so alien. I could accept their worship of the universe, Gaia, Mother Earth and did not have to follow or believe. I had my own path to follow, my own beliefs and my own theory. These two accepted that and got on with their life, non-judgmental and happy to let me be part of it all. Their life was almost stress free; they knew no matter where they travelled they would be provided for. It was their faith and trust in the universe and each other they asked me to share with them.

As I scribbled down my pros and cons of the two opportunities, part of me wanted to stay in Paradise and spend more time with

Ronan. He was great to talk to, his opinion valid, he listened to my theories on different topics and I found that an unusual combination in a man. The larger part of me wanted more travel but so far, travelling with the company I had chosen was emotionally cumbersome. I had been here nearly three weeks and enjoyed their company and appreciated their home.

What to do? I curled up on my bed which smelt of lavender perfume, it was comforting. The weakening storm still caused the tin and wood to creak and groan and my last waking thought was, 'I'll think about this in the morning.'

Chapter 48

I was woken by Petra shaking me awake her voice worried, 'So there you are? Why are you out here?'

The cobwebs of sleep soon wiped away as I saw the concern in her eyes. 'Petra, oh sorry, I came out here to write down my thoughts.'

'Well the storm is over, come and see for yourself,' she said. It had stripped the surrounding trees almost bare, the sea still boomed, its roll still greasy and huge, the beach littered with everything imaginable.

Ronan came to the van door saying, 'Time to go, Tara. You're going to have your first lesson in what we call work.'

'Not without a drink first,' Petra cried, rushing inside, her joy and happiness at the fossicking excursion was obvious. The warm lemon and elderberry juice a wake-up drink and very yummy, a great tonic for the liver. Ronan drove their Pajero out, attached a trailer onto it and we were off to join many other locals also doing some collecting.

First we hauled kelp on board. 'Beautiful for the garden,' they said in unison. This was not some little job, the pieces were massive some as long as the trailer, we also found a smashed dingy that, with much grunting and heaving, got put on board the trailer. We also discovered four huge plastic fishing floats.

Ronan said, 'I'm off back to Paradise.'

Petra got two large straw baskets from the back of the Pajero before he took off. Our morning was spent digging through piles of sand or stones for any treasure the sea had given up just for us. We were not the only ones on the beach, this was the locals favourite beach, a carnival feeling was there and we were met with open arms, hello's, hug's, introductions, some treasures were swapped, others given; some a repayment for favours in the past.

Whatever it was, I loved it. As the wind whipped our hair blowing the sea foam onto us, I truly felt part of the universe, that I had made the right choice. I would tell them my decision once we were all back in their home. By the time we got home I felt exhausted, the wind and sea air certainly took it out of you. Ronan had the jug on the boil. I still loved my cup of tea, he admitted to still enjoying a good aromatic black coffee and Petra asked for a Chai tea. She then amazed me by producing a prized Christmas tin full of dark chocolates and we all sat contentedly slurping away on our chosen brew and nibbled at dark, bitter but luscious chocolate.

Next with a zing in our step there was unpacking, We left the two baskets in a tub in Petra's work room, the tap trickling over them to wash some of the sand off. Ronan was shovelling the kelp into two large old baths to cure. Soon all three of us were raking up whale size portions of kelp, covered in the stink of fish. He placed the old dingy to one side to be broken down for something useful. The four big floats would be put at the gate before we went away, if they belong to someone or the community needs a float or two they would know where to come.

As they lugged stuff back and forth deciding where to put the things, I suggested we throw the floats onto the trailer and I would drive them down to the gates. 'Great idea,' Ronan said.

Once we had pushed and pulled them onto the trailer, I drove to the front gate, backed the trailer up and pushed them off onto the grass roadside. I did this in my own little world, happy as a pig in mud, as my dad used to say.

I pushed, heaved, grunted, fussed about and swore until they stood upright all in a row, happy with my work and a good day's solid exercise I drove back to the house. Parking the Pajero and trailer by the shed, I needed to shower. I stunk, my two friends nowhere in sight. Entering the house with a knock calling, 'Hello, anyone here?' I wandered towards the shower, the room didn't have a door, only a half-woven screen that you pulled across.

'Ronan and his half doors,' I muttered. I could hear the shower was on and stopped, recognising the sounds of a couple making love. I could see two slim, dark bodies entwined, totally engrossed in each other, his deep voice encouraging Petra, while she whispered her love for him.

I fled straight to my van, I felt like a voyeur. I also felt jealous, I still missed Russ. I still had feelings and memories of our years together when one of us was showering we encouraged the other to join in.

I remembered the laughing and giggles as we shared a warm sudsy shower or bath, held against his warm body, being told I was his beautiful woman, as his hands explored my body.

My earlier decision of going with Ronan and Petra on their journey now crashed round my head like broken glass as I sat in the Mermaid beet red and feeling sad, fearful, embarrassed.

I must have been in there all afternoon. I dozed, read my books and added photos to my laptop, then heard them both calling my name. I shut the Mermaid's door tight and when they knocked asking if I was alright I said, 'I had a headache and would not be in for dinner.'

I felt childish and silly making these excuses, but I could not face them. As the light faded they busied themselves with their dinner and the small treasures Petra and I had collected.

I rang Rae and Jess, their response one of joy. I was surprised when Jess implored me, 'Come home Nana, please! Mum's always sick now, she can't do stuff with me because she got pregnant.'

I found his attitude a little offensive and corrected him. 'It takes two to make a baby, Jess. Jono was involved as well.' I was not expecting the tirade of misery and unhappiness that suddenly poured out of my twelve-year old grandson. Then Rae was on the phone, 'Take no notice of him, Mum. He's angry because I can no longer afford private schooling or the holiday camps he went on.'

So that's what this was about, I thought, or did it go deeper? Jess was at the age where everything he did or said was full of drama, and why not? He was bought up to believe he was the best there was. Very articulate by the age three, Russ and I both instilled in him from day one that he was important to us and this world.

All I could hear from my grandson was whinging and whining about how unfair it was, to come home now and put me through college.

Rae's conversation went around and around; the pregnancy, her emotional gauge was off the screen and money was tight but the good news was she had enrolled in a home cooking advanced class at the local college. I listened to her plans for the future as a tutor for a social welfare scheme, it taught home skills to new mums and the unemployed. I applauded her enthusiasm over the phone. 'Good for you, sweetheart.'

I then rang Margi, who had just arrived home, and poured out to her all the things I couldn't tell anyone else, including walking in on Ronan and Petra in the shower. Margi gave me a lecture, 'Well it is their home. They can make love on the roof if they want to, Tara. Just because you're lonely and insecure doesn't mean the world has to bow down to you. I put you in their path because I know they are not only loving and generous, they are great healers as well and you sounded like you needed a spiritual cuddle. About time you gave that a thought instead of whining about how tough it is because you feel embarrassed. You're bloody lucky to have been welcomed by them as a friend. If the water is too hot then get out the bath.'

I was not expecting that and was shocked she would speak to me like that. It hurt, but I had to acknowledge she was telling me a few home truths; I sounded just like my grandson, needy and selfish. 'Thank you, Margi. I appreciate your honesty,' was met with a harrumph and, 'just remember they are my good friends.'

I then rang Jo. We chatted about her family going back to England within the next two weeks, how they loved my home and appreciated it. They wanted to talk to me about a house swap next year if I was amicable toward that idea. Was I? 'I hope you gave them my phone number,' I said and we both laughed at my eagerness to travel back to the UK. Jo also pointed out, 'Your home will now be empty. Why not let Rae and Jess live there until the baby is born? At least it will be lived in.'

'I don't want Jono living there if he turns up again.' That was my main concern. 'I feel like he would try to rip me off.'

'It's your home, Tara. Just a suggestion,' she replied.

I promised to send photos through email of where I had been. It was now midnight, the sea calm, the moon full and golden yellow.

Petra once again knocked on my door. 'Anyone home? I have fresh bran muffins,' she called.

As we sat inside the Mermaid, I made her a hot milo, buttered the muffins and told her about Gillie and Bridie. How it affected me deeply. Petra made a little moue with her mouth, one shoulder lifted in indifference and her next question shocked me. 'Did you want to return her flirtation, Tara?'

'No,' I replied, 'far from it.'

'Then what on earth are you beating yourself up for? You did what you wanted.' Petra was right, I was beating myself up inside, blaming myself for Gilly's attraction to women.

Petra encouraged me to tell all, so I started with Perth, my family let down, then the let-down of Gilly and Bridie, to now.

'And you can't see the point of this? That these are all experiences? Why not use your skills and write about how you handled their choices in life? Write about how it empowered you to be who you are. Tara, you need to learn all love comes easily when first you love and respect yourself. When that happens everything else that affects you is second place.'

When we looked out the door, it was daylight; we had talked half the night away. Sunday was fresh chocolate muffin day with hot frothy coffee at a café. We purchased the Sunday papers, one for each of us, then down to the beachfront for a read. I enjoyed the walk to the café and the eats and drinks and once we had settled ourselves in the sand, we chatted for a while about how the storm had changed the landscape.

Tall trees had come down leaving weird shaped spaces in a clean blue skyline. Ronan rubbed his hands together. 'All the more wood for me to carve,' he said. Petra snoozed on the sand, wriggling her body into a small hollow and finally, I did the same, the sea a soothing cradle to our dreams.

Chapter 49

Everyone up, was the order I was woken with. Ronan stood over us dripping seawater, Petra squealing as a fat salty drop exploded on her face. She jumped up ready for some fun, both of them long and lithe, full of energy as they bounded down to the sea, both laughing at each other trying to push the other into the water. Petra succeeded. Pushing Ronan in first, he came out yelling 'Woohoo,' grabbed her and ducked her under. They played for ages in the shallow water, then they spied me sitting there watching them with a silly grin on my face.

'Get her!' Petra yelled. Both of them charged up the beach, grabbed me between them, carrying me like a saggy bag of spuds into the water and gently placing me down. I sank. It was waist deep, so I wasn't in danger, only my pride and clothing soaked; it was freezing. I came up coughing, 'Hey, careful how you treat an old senior like me.'

'Oh, go on,' Ronan said, 'you're not as old as you look.'

'Pardon me.'

Then he burst out laughing, 'I meant you're only as young as you feel and I've told you to lighten up once before, have I not?'

'Yes, you have,' I grumbled. I made my way to the shore shivering, feeling the heaviness settling in with dripping wet jeans and my woolly jumper.

I knew my face was like a grey cloud. I felt grumpy and mean and cold, but I was having to walk home in salty wet jeans that were chafing the insides of my thighs, so I was not a happy chappy at all.

I sorted out some warm clothes and busied myself in the shed, quite happy after a warm shower and warmly dressed. I found the west coast winter a little daunting, it was cold all day and the wind could whip up in a frenzy with a snap of your fingers. The ground had become permanently soggy, like a lime green sponge. The only dry places were where I was working in the shed, in their work rooms and the house. I was quite content working to my own rhythm, in the background Petra was playing music and I could also faintly hear the comforting thunk of wood on wood as Ronan carved.

Petra and Ronan had started preparing for the journey; they packed and sorted, both very serious in their commitment to each other's wellbeing and safety. I looked on, the answer to their request–would I stay or go with them–was still rattling around in my chest. I hate being undecided. Decide Tara, my head demanded. I was torn in two, which way to go, as my heart wanted to go with them but logic said stay here. The inevitable happened at breakfast four days later. They both sat there and asked, 'Have you made a decision?' I had a choice: housekeeper or travel companion.

Everything here looked so nice and normal, except me. We ate, the two of them trying to include me in conversation; it must have been hard as I just nodded or shook my head.

I knew they were passing time, both eager to know my decision.

'I can't decide. I want to do all of it.' My sentence was bruised with pain. I really liked these two wonderful, simple-living people whose ethics and morals were pure. They glowed with happiness, they lived what they termed as truth, honesty and empathy. Others came to them from all over the country, locals and often tourists would appear for wisdom and knowledge of heart, mind and herbal lore.

'Yes.' I said. 'I have,' exploded out of my mouth, the weight lifted from my shoulders. They both leaned forward to hear my decision. 'I will accompany you until we get to Wellington then go it alone.'

'Good for you,' they said in unison. The relief of making this important decision made me feel lightheaded.

Petra offered me the job of cataloguing any fossils she found. I could be there as Petra's offsider, so to speak, handing out business cards, journaling her day for her but mainly recording the fetes, fairs, festivals and galleries she attended.

It sounded like a huge responsibility. This was normally Ronan's job, but he now had a time limit of construction and delivery for his work. They amazed me, both so into their holistic way of life but fabulous businesspeople, they crossed the t's and dotted the i's and used modern technology for their requirements.

Nothing left unturned, they Googled their way around the country. If a country fair application was rejected, they simply shrugged and said, 'Next,' as obviously it was not meant to be. Their home and farm were always cared for by a neighbour or friend, and if things had been changed while they were gone, their philosophy was, 'It's nothing we cannot change back to what we like.'

Tomorrow was going to be a huge day because of the things I had to do and the things they wanted me to do. It was more involved than I wanted to be but knew it would be okay. My mind simply wanted to rest, just to settle down for a night's sleep.

I had my morning water and lemon juice. The massive lemon tree in their backyard seemed to yell, 'Look at me.' The bright yellow fruit against the lime green background of trees and fields were a painter's delight but I had no time for that today, instead I took a photo.

Tapping out my daughter's phone number, it was time to tell her of my decision. How and what I said had to sound sincere, I didn't want them thinking I thought they were a charity case.

'Hi Mum,' a happy voice greeted me. 'I'm just having a cuppa,

Jess is out on his skateboard.' It sounded like they had both moved on from fear and despair.

'Hello darling, I have some news for you.'

There was a pause, her voice unsure of what I was about to say.

'I was hoping you and Jess could live in Durant until I get back, store your things in the garage and stay there until I'm home again.' There was silence from her end, so I continued, 'It would make me feel easier if the house was being lived in.' Still silence.

'You bloody beauty, when?' She yelled down the phone.

'Whenever you want Rae, Jo has the key; we can sort out the details later, just move in and be safe.'

'Mum, I'm due to have this little one in six months. What if I'm still there when I have the baby and you come home?'

I could hear the wheels of concern ticking over. 'Honey it's a four-bedroom house with two bathrooms. I'm sure we will sort something out.'

My next step was confirmed when Ronan and Petra arrived outside my door with a mug of hot tea and fresh scones with home-made lemon butter; my mouth watered up the smell was heaven. I could not say, 'Join me inside.' There is only room for one in the Mermaid, two at a squish.

They asked me to look at a proposal they had put together concerning our trip together, Petra had a clipboard sat under one arm, the newspaper under the other, both hands full of home produce. Ronan said, 'Let's celebrate our expedition together. I'm so glad you have chosen to come with us.'

I read what they had written on the clip board, there was a list of requirements to take. As I read it, I would be paying for myself except for camp fees which they would cover. I was wondering about the accommodation. Was I to camp with them in their tent? I knew my tent days were over, especially in the cold weather, I love my Mermaid, small it might be, but it was my comfy home for now.

All around me seemed to be satisfied with their role in life. Ronan's budgies tweeted and fought in the hazy sunlight, they seemed happy enough. At the bottom of the cage were spotted quails and in competition with the budgies were zebra finches, all doing what caged birds do.

The nanny goats were doing their munching thing and one billy goat chained up at the top paddock was complaining loudly that he was very ready and willing to make baby goats and would someone please untie me so I can do so. I wandered back inside the house, only to find Petra had her angel cards out. 'Choose one,' she said.

'Why?' I asked, 'what is it going to do?'

'Oh, come on, relax and join in with us to plan our trip with blessings and bounty.'

I chose one, and what popped out was amazing as it fitted my decision. The card was old and its once gold edges now frayed with use, 'What does it say?' Petra cried, 'come on tell us.'

I read them the card. The Angel Rachises says, *'We are all inventors, each one of us sailing out on a voyage of discovery, guided by a private charter of which there is no duplicate, this world is the gateway to other realms and possibilities.'* As I spoke, a light clicked on; it spoke the truth. I gave her back the card.

'Let me read your tarot for you,' Petra said. I balked at that, my experience with Venus still gave me the creeps. I declined and pointed to the charts on the table, I really was out of my depth with all this astrology stuff.

'So, when do we leave? And what do we leave in?'

Ronan bustled in his arms full of firewood. 'In two days, my friend,' his cheeks puffing as he stacked it by the fireplace. 'All ready and able to go?'

'I will be when I know what the accommodation will be like,' expressing my concern that the Mermaid suited one and one only. It was time to get serious, the how, why and wherefores were now clambering around inside my head. Petra produced a savoury goat's cheese and crackers with lovely herb butter she had recently made. I put the tea urn on and we all sat around the kitchen table, the old urn hissed and squeaked its steamy displeasure at being woken up. I loved the ancient old thing. I guess it was the oldest thing in the room next to me.

I gave us all a sheet of paper saying. 'Okay let's do this; let's work out what we expect from each other and how we are going to travel and who with. I am going first,' I announced, this was no time for emotions to be in the mix.

'If I am going to help and be involved as you have suggested, this is what I need for me to be comfortable and happy.' My voice now gathering strength. 'I want my own bed, preferably the Mermaid. I do not want to share a tent or be squashed up in a car for hours on end. Anything I buy or consider necessary to me is my own financial reasonability.' I looked at them both. 'They are my requirements.'

Ronan asked me to follow him. 'I hope this explains what we do when we are away on field or fossicking trips,' he said. I followed him to the big wooden shed way out the back of the property, Petra followed us outdoors.

He pushed at the door. 'Come on ladies give the old man a hand,' Ronan said, so we both helped him push the sliding door across, the dark musty shed now alive with dust motes that swirled around our heads, each one of us had a sunny halo. There to my surprise, was a big Jeep–the daddy of them all–and a massive caravan at least twenty-five foot in length. I just stood, amazed.

Petra said, 'Did you really think we were going in the little Pajero and the tent? That's for Ronan on his trip back, while we are touring this is what we call home,' Petra said, 'and you're going to help us drive this baby around the country.'

I was gobsmacked, no words could come out. I've never driven anything like this, I thought. Bugger, what have I committed myself to? They saw the look on my face. 'Come inside, Tara.' They ushered me towards the caravan door. It was home away from home; chrome benches, stove top, a double bed down one end, a large single bed up the other end, in the middle where there should have been table and chairs they had replaced it with a small office, with desk and shelves for a laptop and filing drawers, plus a tiny bathroom. 'It's all here, Tara. You only need your clothes and some spare cash, and we are off. We will lock up your Mermaid and jeep safely, so when you come back it will be here waiting for you.'

I felt silly. I had made such a fuss about who I was and what I wanted, how it was going to be, they must have thought what a bossy cow we have here.

'I'm sorry guys,' I spluttered. 'I'm embarrassed I made such a fuss.'

'It's okay Tara, we will all learn to understand each other very soon. We are to blame as well, we aren't used to having others with us on our trips, we didn't explain ourselves very well.'

Now it was exciting again! Two more sleeps and we are off, my blood tingled; I would be on the road again, great. The two days hurtled by. I packed my clothes in the drawer under the single bed and my favourite tea, honey and ginger was the first thing I popped into the cupboard. Petra packed the huge pantry. Ronan packed his tent and camping gear into the jeep. I helped them pack the caravan with their personal gear as well as the rest of my personal things.

I knew deep inside me I wanted to finish this trip very soon. I wanted to be there for Rae and my new grandchild when it was born. There were so many conflicting emotions doing a jig in my chest. I wanted to go but sad I was going, excited about my new adventure but sad I would not be a part of their lives once we had done this trip, and in a weird way relieved I would again be independent.

But living with these two, it was entirely up to me what I made of it. Family, partner, travel, life, it was *entirely up to me* what I did with the rest of my life. I am responsible for me and if I choose to share myself or not.

The day arrived and we were off on an adventure. Ronan had hired local men to farm-sit for the duration we were away, it was time to go. The shed door gave its shrill squeak as it was opened, the stutter of an engine being started over, then spluttering into life. Ronan drove out of the shed, our new home attached, dust swirled all around as the Jeep and caravan drove down beside the house, small branches and twigs cracking under its wheels, Magpies serenading us their goodbyes.

Ronan padlocked the shed which stored the Mermaid and handed me the key, standing to attention and saluting me saying, 'You're in charge, Tara.' He loved taking the micky out of me. There was a little more packing; the two farm-sitters wandering around Paradise making themselves known to all the livestock.

'Righto,' Ronan called. 'Time to go.'

My heart lurched–I was leaving my Mermaid behind. Petra saw the look on my face. 'She is here whenever you want to come back, nothing is written in stone, Tara.' I had to agree with her; no one was forcing me to do anything.

I jumped into the back of the Jeep clipping in my seat belt. They both laughed, Ronan said, 'No Tara, you sit in the front, you're driving.'

'What? Don't be silly,' I said. 'I can't drive this thing.'

'Well you had better learn fast because that's what you're doing today,' was his reply. We bunny hopped in the damn thing for maybe two minutes until I got the hang of the gears.

'Like this Tara, double clutch from now on, you're driving a real Jeep.'

Already Ronan was pissing me off with all the smart quips.

I followed instructions and off we drove, waving to the two new caretakers of Paradise, another adventure around the corner. Petra sat in the back, Ronan showing me how to drive this huge mother of a car. I could feel the weight of the caravan tugging on the back, it felt weird at first but then we settled down getting to know each other. Ronan patted my knee satisfied I was comfortable driving.

We had agreed I was prepared to take on part of the responsibility of driving and when I could no longer do so, I should just say so. In fact, it felt good to be behind the wheel once again, the road beneath us humming away. Destination, the country fair in Taihape, a small country town in the Waikato region. It felt right, it felt good.

Chapter 50

Who said country towns are Hicksville? Taihape bustled; it was a pretty, well set out township. Down one end was a small village and the modern part built all around, both blending well, honouring the past and present. We entered the caravan park, stopping to check in at the office, that's when I held up my hand and said to Ronan, 'Your turn now. I can't park this thing on my own.' He was happy to take over.

When we were booked in and paid for, it was dinner time. Petra offered to put something together in the van. If I thought I was to live a holistic lifestyle in paradise, I could think again. Petra produced a magnificent feast; four bean salad, hot home-made egg and feta pie, steamed pumpkin and broccolini, and hot lime and mint tea. I was starving, cleaning my plate completely and asking for another helping.

We sat outside the caravan all rugged up against the weather, all wearing the same coloured beanies and gloves but different patterns and styles, thanks to Petra's best mate, Sue, a very generous neighbour back at Opunake who bred black and white sheep. She carded, weaved, and knitted her creations and we were wearing the results of her hard work. As we talked about the day and what to do tomorrow, our breath came in big steamy puffs; this mid-country air was icy cold and damp.

Ronan phoned the two farm caretakers at Paradise. All was well.

An early night was called for as we had to be at the county fair and set up our stall by five am. I was not needed immediately; my job was to calculate sales, the GST and tax and update the catalogue. They offered me the chance to sleep in, one of them popping back to pick me up about ten am. 'Sounds good to me,' I said, stretching like a big cat.

I was quite surprised at myself; a very long time ago I would never have thrown my arms above my head stretching in public but living with these two had proved one thing–they were absolutely right when they claimed stretching your body is healthy. Crazy as it sounds, when I stretched my body, breathing in deeply, opening my mouth as wide as possible, it stretched the facial muscles. My tight jaw clicked in protest, but I found it was stopping the morning headaches or muscle cramps in the shoulders. Their way of living, their advice about the body and the way our thoughts react inside the body was priceless information.

Russ was now a little blurry around the edges. Once his memory was so sharp like an eagle's cry, now I had to concentrate to remember his red hair, his lovely, laughing eyes and the smell of his warm, clean male body. I wrapped my own arms around me. I missed his strong arms.

I knew exactly what he would be saying to me now. 'Let go, sweetheart. It's time for me to go. You're doing just great and you are where you're meant to be.' I knew it was true. I was ready to accept my life without him in it. I was ready, I was strong, I had learned to bend a little, I had a family and wonderful friends who had helped me as I had them.

I was just finishing my morning, putting on many layers of clothing, putting away my bathroom things when Petra arrived her face alight with excitement. 'Guess what?' she yelled. 'I've made a huge sale.'

'You have, at the fair already? What have you sold?' 'Well not exactly sold,' Petra replied. 'I've been asked to do a commission.'

We arrived at her stall, on the way there we passed a coffee vendor who also sold hot chocolate, scones and cream. With my very first frothy slurp, I felt my body relax, the aroma making Ronan and Petra both look up, their noses taking in the smell of hot chocolate and buttered scones. I could not help myself, 'No, you can't have sip. It's all mine.'

'Not for long, my friend,' Ronan said, striding past me hands in his pocket jingling the spare coins he had there. By the time he got back I was devouring my scone piled high with jam and cream. I knew I had cream and jam on my face, but I didn't care, I was enjoying myself. A male voice broke into my reverie. 'Excuse me, miss.' I turned to find myself looking into deep brown eyes that sparkled with humour.

'Hi there. How can I help?' I asked.

'Michael's my name and poetry's my game.' He handed me a flyer advertising a poet's night at the Blue Goose pub in town, and he was the poet, a one man show. He looked the part; faded tight jeans, a dark green wool jumper with a cream scarf, long graceful hands which reached for my hand, and on his left hand was a large silver ring with two small diamonds. Under the multi-coloured Rastafarian beanie was short black hair, his eyes lined with eyeliner, black eyelashes, tanned skin, white teeth flashed a smile at me. 'And your name is?'

'Tara,' I replied.

'Hello Tara, welcome to Taihape. I would love to see you at my show tonight.' As he said this, he clasped my hand in both of his.

Petra wandered over. 'And who do we have here?' she enquired.

'This is Michael.' I had no sooner said his name when he reached out for her hands, once again repeating his message. It sounded like a great night out. I was interested and so was Ronan, who introduced himself and was warmly greeted by Michael with the same spiel and given the same enclosed handshake. Petra shrugged, 'I'll see how I feel.' Petra was all business today.

Ronan had given her a lump of swamp kauri; it was a lovely deep gold and dark yellow mottled from thousands of years being buried under volcanic soil and peat and smelt of resin. Her interest was in slicing it into four or five pieces, if possible.

Ronan and I were interested in the poet's night, Petra saying, 'Then go. I'm busy with this.' We knew it would take a while, so we left her to it, the day passed quickly with clients and would be clients. When we closed down for the night, we asked Peta to join us and were met with silence, so just the two of us went to the pub for a night of poetry. Michael was there, his smile flashing welcome in the dim room. We were greeted with a cup of mulled apple cider which was really warming, leaving a ginger aftertaste.

As Michael read his work I was lulled into the pattern. Poetry reminded me of a musical score sliced and spliced, held together by words, a living book of rhyme now connecting the ear to the heart. He had produced a book for sale, it was beautifully put together, the artwork was stunning, every page imprinted with Michaels creativity. To be able to write in any form is a gift one should share. I purchased two copies, one for Petra and one for me. A poem that made me smile was called 'The Glass Ships', to be read once I was alone tucked up in bed.

I must admit poetry is one of my passions. I loved the words that would meld into a scene before your eyes. As I read that night, I realised not only was Michael's name printed here, but another poet's name as well–a woman whose poetry sang to me. She had written a poem called 'Ships and Sails', it was lilting and lovely. My eyelids closed for the night; sleep was a sweet surrender to verse.

I dreamed about the Paradise farm and it stayed in my mind, maybe it was the mist and constant rain that made me maudlin. I flicked the jug switch on, Petra and Ronan had already gone to their stall at the fair, I guessed they would be back for me about ten.

Breakfast was porridge with yoghurt, a hot cup of tea, shower and tidy up the van and then read until they got back. I was right into a book called the *Water Elephants* by Sarah Gruen. as I ate my breakfast her story unfolded. I was half-way through a chapter when the thought struck me, why don't I write a book about my travel's; where I've been, who I've met?

The thought turned into action and suddenly I had my own purpose: apart from travelling and helping Petra with her sales and marketing, I was going to keep a detailed diary, tracking everything I had done and places I've been. I could make it a touring book, or I could make it a novel or better yet, learn how to make a web page for myself and write like that, even design a blog page for myself. I had to stop and take a big breath as I had never contemplated this sort of communication before. I was making myself dizzy with the possibilities.

There was another epiphany as I sat there. I was really enjoying the bigger van; I did not have to go anywhere to shower, toilet, cook or write, it was all here for me to do inside and privately. Plenty of space to store things, I had room to move or spread my books. I sat on the double bed with my back against the wall and there was plenty of room. I looked at the other end of the van where the single bunk was. For some reason my eyes saw it all differently this morning, my heart was happy, I no longer ached with loneliness deep inside.

I had Petra and Ronan to thank for nurturing a part of me that hadn't grown. I felt deeply that the stunted emotional branch of Tara was no longer. I felt the change in my thinking. I was growing, and it was exciting; life was exciting. Also exciting was the thought of a new book, a novel of all the folk I had met and places I had been to, I had to start somewhere so why not today, right here and now.

Checking my watch, I had time to ring Rae and quickly email Jo. Jess answered the phone, he was home as it was Sunday. 'Nana,' he yelled, 'guess what? I'm in my old room at your house. I've got a fish tank with four goldfish and Mum said I can have a cat, once you say it's okay.' He sounded happy and full of optimism.

'Let me think on that Jess and I will talk to your mum about it.' He then asked his normal question. 'When are you coming home?'

'I knew I was part of a much bigger picture than I ever thought about. All the people you meet, love, despair with, agree and disagree with, including family, are all part of a huge mesh of crossroads in your life. It was a difficult road if you remained closed, so once you opened yourself to healing then it became easier. Did I hear a familiar deep chuckle?

Rae greeted me on the phone sounding puffed but like Jess. There was contentment there. 'Hi honey, how's it all going? All moved in and settled yet?'

'I'd like to say yes to that Mum but I'm so big and bloated most of the time I waddle. I can't wait until this one is born. What are you up to? Don't tell me, I know you're having fun, lucky you.' There was a smile to her voice; I didn't sense any sarcasm or jealousy.

'Yes, Rae, I am honey, but you will never guess what I've decided to do,' I said.

'Not more travel. When are you coming back, Mum?' Rae wailed.

'Rae honey relax. I've decided to write a book about my travels and who I've met. I'm keeping a record and once home I'll decide how to publish it, on the net, create my own blog, do a Vimeo and send it off to friends, or contact a publisher.'

I expected, 'Wow! Mum you have seen the light,' or, 'Hey, you're really cooking,' but all I got was a pause, then, 'Remember your last hassle with a publisher? Be careful this time.'

'I appreciate your concern Rae, but you have to trust someone. I do understand though and promise I won't do anything except think about it until I'm home. Okay?'

We parted with, 'Love you and can't wait to see you.'

Chapter 51

Ronan and Petra did not turn up until midday, both agreed, 'It's really slow at the markets and cold. You're better off here in the warmth.' Looking outside at the grey, drizzly day, I too agreed. I made them a hot cranberry juice each and thick buttery toast with my homemade jam. It bought back fond memories of Bridie.

Ronan saw the look on my face commenting, 'I see a story here. Come on... spill.'

So, as it rained and blew outside we three sat inside warm and comfy. I told them about my friend, Bridie, when I finished they were both very silent, no comments, no advice only, 'How very sad.' My two friends both decided to cuddle up in their small pup tent for the afternoon, it had been and still was the storage room for all our gear. I knew it wasn't about me, more about them and time out for them. I offered to cook our dinner that night.

Before I prepared the meal it was time to check on my lawyer's statements and my income from my assets. It all seemed to be good. I gave up a prayer of thanks that Russ insisted we both knew and were fully aware of what we could do with our money, including banks and lawyers, so I understood what the legal jargon was all about. To put it plainly, I was comfortably well off, my investments growing steadily thanks to some wise advice. A little voice whispered, 'You would give all of it away if it could turn the clock back.'

Now, time to make dinner. I felt very homey stirring a big pot of vegie soup, prepared before we left Paradise then stored in the tiny freezer in the van. I also made curry pikelets and soft cheese balls rolled in dried herbs instead of butter, plus some preserved figs with yogurt. I called out to Ronan and Petra to, 'Come and get it, it's on the table.'

They both looked like a couple of bear cubs rolling out of the tent, pink in the face, laughing at each other, trying to stand up, complaining of pins and needles in the feet. I heard Ronan say, 'I'm getting old, sweetie, I've got cramp in my foot.'

'Get inside and I'll stretch it for you,' Petra said. 'Hurry up I'm freezing,' the van door open allowing cold air to rush in. 'Get those awful boots off. Here, give me your foot.' Petra reached down to help him take his boots off, rubbed and stretched the calf muscles while Ronan groaned.

'Ahh, friggin foot.' It had almost curled up with the muscle and tendons tightening. The grimace on his face was enough for anyone to see he was in considerable pain and nothing was working.

I said, 'Here, let me try.' By then if anyone had suggested amputating his foot I'm sure he would have agreed. I put a small bean bag in the microwave. When the microwave beeped, Petra rolled up the leg of his pants, I took the heat pad and laid it along his calf muscle, my hands began deep long strokes, working on his hamstring. I asked Petra to warm some oil for me and to keep it warm as I massaged until his foot relaxed. His face relaxed as well. Finally, the last knot melted away and Ronan said, 'Ah Geez that feels so good, thanks Tara.'

The van looked like a war zone; blankets, oil bottles, basins of hot water, plus the meal was now cold, the steam that had been rising from the bowls of soup now gone, the warm pikelets cold.

'Not to worry,' I said, 'soon fixed,' and set to work tidying up the van while Petra cooed over Ronan making sure he was alright, tucking him up with blankets and the warmed-up bean bag. We were soon eating the hot soup and warmed up pikelets. 'Where did you learn to massage like that?' they both asked.

'Old dog, old tricks. My daughter was once a horrific colic sufferer, the only thing that worked on relaxing her little tummy was a hotty and a warm lavender oil massage. Guess I still got it,' I said waggling my fingers in the air.

'You sure do, that was magic,' Ronan slurred, sleep overtaking him.

Night-time arrived. They had both opted to bed down in the tent again and yes, I realised their young bodies craved each other but I saw Ronan look around the van as they left; it was warm and comfy. 'See you in the morning,' they said as they left, Petra adding, 'Sweet dreams Tara and thank you once again.'

There are times when I just like to sit in the dark on my own and think about the day feeling my chest rise and fall with my breath, my heart quieten. I hadn't done a lot of getting out and about so far, but it felt good just to sit still for a day. Tomorrow they were busy with the milled logs and something to do with contract emails. I found the tourist book I'd been given and had done most of the things advertised except for trout fishing, but it did not excite me at all.

I found the opportunity for spectacular photography was what I enjoyed the most. If you looked up from our camp site there was Mt Ruapehu capped with snow, totally magnificent in every way. This country was inspiring to say the least. I wondered just how many paintings and photos there were of this grand old dame, its snow crown wispy with smoke from the boiling Lake Ruapehu contained deep inside it.

The shower before bed was wonderful, hot water and soft home-made soap streamed over my body. I did notice I had become quite skinny and could feel my ribs. I was no longer a muffin top; I was as sleek as Petra. My hair uncut and curly had grown down to my shoulders, and I still had a slight summer tan. Hey, how about that– early sixties and going well. As I towelled myself dry, I thought, if my friends and family could see me now. I rummaged through my bag, finding a photo of me that Margi had taken on the Marai. Was that really me standing there? I looked frumpy and a little unsure, the difference between now and then was amazing.

That night as I lay in my bed. I gave up silent thanks for all I had received and where I was at this moment–safe, loved, great family and good mates. Tomorrow we're moving on to Wanganui, another riverside township. We had booked into the camp there for three weeks as all around there were little towns having fetes, fairs and the CWA (Country Women's association) had invited Petra to do a public talk. She needed me for this because from past history, this is where she made her biggest profit. I was looking forward to it so much, so when the alarm went on my phone I was up quickly and putting breakfast on the table. Petra and Ronan had both been up and used the camp facilities so they didn't wake me.

I served porridge with milk with the leftover figs as a side dish, it tasted great. While Ronan washed and dried dishes, Petra and I packed away what we thought necessary. Ronan yelled, 'Catch Tara,' throwing me the keys to the Jeep. 'If you bring it around, I will hitch up the van.'

It was all done within ten minutes, their tent and sleeping bags already stored in the Jeep's boot. 'Righto, everyone ready?' I called out. 'Off we go.' I let out the clutch, the van tugging on the car for a second or two, then it gave way and started to follow. I was busy looking in the rear vision mirrors, checking side mirrors, then very slowly started to gain speed.

Petra sat beside me in the passenger seat giving directions. This road proved to be like the rest, winding through mountainous scenery or on steep hill sides. My Aussie road skills were tested as I was used to long flat surfaces, so to see a small hummock was strange. Our landscape flat as can be, with very few winding roads, especially in the outback. I was still slightly bamboozled at all the gear changing with double clutching but learned fast as the miles unravelled.

Stopping off at a roadside park, we sat and munched on sandwiches I had made the previous night. The scenery was inspiring, so I snapped about ten photos, then back on the road again with my very first hill start with the caravan on the back. Ronan offered to take over for me, something stubborn said *you can do this*. My enthusiasm was my mistake as I just could not get it. I tried and tried until he screamed, 'Enough!' If you inch back again we will be over the cliff face and it was true, there just behind us was a huge drop.

I got out of the driver's seat, Ronan scrambling in to take over, and then it hit me just how close we were to going over the side through my stupid pride. Loose pebbles skittered and scattered down the side of the mountain, I had stopped just in time, the back of the van just about over the edge.

Petra's face was white with fear. Through my stubborn pride I had put us in a terrible predicament. Ronan revved the engine, let off the handbrake, the van shook as it inched forward a fraction, then slowly, ever so slowly he inched away from the danger I had put us into. My legs started to give way under me once I realised what I had done, they both had severe looks on their faces. I now sat in the back feeling like a scolded child, they both showed their displeasure at my actions. I could have yelled, 'Unfair! I'm not experienced enough. You forced me to drive' but the truth was I took no notice of his instructions or his warnings of danger. I had nearly caused a major accident and I was not proud of myself at all. Their anger about my behaviour, lasting until we arrived in Wanganui, was very obvious from where I sat.

Petra parked the car beside the van and erected a large canvas annex; this was to be her office while we travelled the countryside in the Jeep attending the fairs. I made dinner as it was five-thirty in the afternoon but still they did not stop and communicate. They chose to ignore my looks or any words I uttered, no conversation except between themselves. As I served up steamed rice and vegetables with goat's cheese sauce, I was thanked in their nightly prayer to the universe, then we ate in silence.

They were carrying it a bit too far I thought, time for me to speak up. 'I've apologised twice now, there is nothing else I can do, so are you going to keep me on the outer or are you going to be charitable?' Ronan looked at me, his dark eyes unreadable. 'Tara, Petra and I have discussed you and your obsession with following your own set of rules. It was a dangerous situation you had us in, completely ignoring my instructions. We are prepared to give you another chance with us, then if you do not do as we ask of you on this trip, you will be asked to leave.'

Wow! I did not see that coming, anger replaced my feeling of apology, I felt my face and eyes go hard.

'Who the hell do you think you're talking to? You and Petra begged me to come with you. I was going to be *SO* helpful, it was going to be *SO* wonderful and full of light and laughter. Well you're not such a bunch of roses either, mate, in fact you're bloody full of hot wind and hard work.'

There. I had spoken my mind, now they could deal with it. I got up, put on my anorak and went outside to cool off; walking does wonders for the soul. I was mad, yes, I had made a mistake and apologised for ever and a day. 'Bloody get over it and get on with it,' I muttered, but no matter the amount of excuses Petra made for him, I could not get my head around it; Ronan was a rude arrogant man and had become bit of a bully. I was not comfortable at all.

For three weeks I worked with Petra going to fetes, fairs and ladies' meetings of all sorts, clubs, societies, meetings of every description, anyone who needed a speaker, we put our hands up. We drove for miles attending all the meetings we knew about, meeting and greeting many people. I took copious notes, noted all sales, invoices, receipts orders, pending sales and filled her journal for the day to come; I had become her fulltime secretary. I enjoyed it, it did take up a lot of my time, but I was also seeing the New Zealand and its people like I wanted to. I was very aware I was here for a short time only. I kept reminding Petra, she seemed to ignore me, just kept giving me receipts and files to take care of.

We drove to so many places, all as pretty as each other; Bulls, Feilding, Woodville, Levin, Stratford, Eketahuna, Dannevirk, Waikane and last but not least Paihatua. Each little township had a speciality of some sort, whether it be collecting shells or painting toilet seats. There were quite a few of those in public toilets around the country. One had pretty fairies painted on its outside wall, one toilet had a collection of large paint tins with faces painted on them, the tins were squashed flat then framed with a Perspex cover. An amazing effect. How clever, I thought, the artwork on them was perfect. I had a close-up view of all sorts of art before it went on sale, and one that took my eye was a triangular canvas, a before and after of an old village painted on it. I loved it and took many photos to take back home. That's the trouble with being creative, your mind goes crazy with all the possibilities.

Chapter 52

In each place Petra was welcomed with open arms. At times she taught the basics in fossil, jade and Kauri amber jewellery, other times she taught bush medicine or making homemade soaps and lotions, and in some little townships she would just give a public talk displaying her crafts. Petra was a popular public speaker, everyone looked forward to hearing from her, a warm welcome was given, me included. Some days were long, especially her teaching days. Fortunately, accommodation was always provided, she would always ring Ronan and explain we were tired, it was now dark, and we had been invited to stay over. I particularly enjoyed those nights as frequently around the kitchen table we would listen to a widow's tale of her life here, how she came to be here, her family and about her life in New Zealand.

Most of them descendants of the English or Irish. They told how hard their lives had been then, until an eighty-year old exclaimed, 'But look what we got now. I love this modern age, don't you?' As she waved her mobile phone at us, then flicked the huge flat screen telly on for the news. She settled in her big comfy armchair like a chook settling on its nest, lots of clucking and humming, with a big sigh. On went the home-made woolly slippers and finally she popped a tobacco pipe into her mouth. My eyebrows shot up but her face showed peace and contentment, so why not.

If ever the talk got maudlin, as it did with some ladies, the township martyrs with an 'oh woe is me' attitude, Petra and I soon learned how to change the subject. Often loudly commenting on the amazing meals, the hospitality we had been shown. Never a day went by without someone bringing us a lunch and if it was dinner, it was usually a communal feast, everyone adding their special dish to the already groaning table. I found I was not fond of smoked eel pie, everything else we devoured, both of us ready with compliments for the hardworking, wonderful country folk. A kind word, the touch of another human hand, can work wonders. Stories of family now grown up and an empty nest or their husbands had passed on, so a hug and a well done meant the world to them.

The mantles over fireplaces that warmed us full of sepias and faded photographs, each one a story. One dear soul was Ruth, a women of eighty-four with a faint Scots burr, she had a fabulous photo of six young kiddies all sitting on a log, we expected to hear what they had done with their lives, both shocked to hear they had all passed over. A logging accident in Northland, taking four immediately, then the hubby and two remaining children dying of septicaemia. I asked about hospitals. 'What hospitals, dear? We had a bush dispensary and bush medicine with limited health care.' The remainder of her clan, as she called them, died within three weeks of each other. How crushed her heart must have felt. Mine was, listening to her memories of her little children, now an old sepia photo remained, faded as her memories were.

'I'm getting old and silly,' she announced. I stood and opened my arms to her; I wanted to warm this poor soul's heart with a hug.

'You may forget them Ruth, but they have not forgotten you. One day you will all be together again.' I hugged her tight.

There were some homes that were so old I wondered how safe they were. I will never forget one of them. Way out in the country, it was a wood shack with peeling paint, old scraggly plants, some dead, some struggling through weeds. Inside was such poverty; dirt floors, furniture made of fruit boxes, old sacking or faded gingham material covered doorways and cupboards, the toilet and bathroom were outside, a bucket sitting outside the porch with a fresh cake of soap and hand towel, the kitchen was a plastic basin on an old rickety bench and one cold water tap. Clean was not the word I would use for this ancient wrinkled crone and her home; it glowed, she glowed, everything was polished, scrubbed and swept.

When we hugged this tiny little lady for her generosity, she smelt of smoky lavender, her pure white hair pulled back into a bun was now thinning, the wrinkles on her work-worn face told of hardships. Not once did she complain, just the opposite. After a dinner of macaroni cheese cooked inside on the open fireplace, she played her ukulele, the old tunes rippling out, and I knew some of them. Memories of my mum came flooding back. I remembered how my dad had taught me to play the spoons. I asked her for two large spoons. I got two beautifully made, real silver dessert spoons and although I was very rusty, I played along with her as much as I could. All of us ending up with hoots of laughter, especially when I lost control, one of the spoons flying across the room. This was one lady I will never forget, Hinemoa, a true daughter of the Waikato country.

As we left to go to another's home to stay for the night, I asked was there anything we could do for her. She looked up at me and said, 'I have everything I need right here,' and she did.

Petra and I put on our coats, the night air was chilly, the river mist covering the ground, Hinemoa pushed the two silver spoons into my hand. 'Here take 'em and practise,' she cackled at her sense of humour. 'You will need 'em more than me.' She threw back her head and laughed, and at my great height next to her tiny body, all I could see was her baby pink toothless gums and her glottis waggling back and forth as she chuckled.

Petra and I looked at each other both dissolving into giggles as it did look funny. 'Goodnight, sweet dreams,' we wished her and left with my present safe in my pocket. I knew just how fortunate I was, as when I went home I would have my family waiting for me. Hinemoa had no-one. *No-one*… such a lonely sound. Yet she loved her life. I hope that when my day comes I'm as graceful and accepting as her.

It was time to help Petra to pack up her gear as tomorrow we would arrive in Wellington. 'That's if we ever do with Tara driving.'

Petra and I looked at each other, here we go again–Ronan's bloody smart cracks about my driving. Would someone tell me where the nice Ronan went? While we were at the meeting tonight he had been busy though, the caravan was neat and tidy.

Chapter 53

Along the way we had to visit Carterton, Masterton, Featherstone, Paraparaumu, Cape Palliser, Upper Hutt, Lower Hutt, Petone and Lake Ferry. We dropped off phone orders that had been taken around the country as we travelled down. 'This is going to take us more than a couple of days,' Petra said. 'I hope Ronan has remembered to book us into the Lower Hutt campgrounds for four nights.'

'So, we drive straight there, then, to sort the deliveries?' I asked, making sure the GPS was plugged in.

'Yup, that's the plan,' Petra said. I pulled over to tap Lower Hutt into the GPS.

I was told Lower Hutt took five hours or so but with so many stops to use the bathroom or, 'Gee, I'm hungry let's stop over there,' and not just from Petra—I was as bad, it took us seven hours to reach Lower Hutt. It was a mishmash of roads, turning circles, loops, plus new roads had been built since the GPS was programmed. Lower Hutt is one big bustling city, how we found the Lower Hutt camping grounds was a miracle in itself. We sorted ourselves out, who do we see first and what to drop off.

A small cupboard in the van was packed full of soaps, herbal remedies, jewellery and some of Ronan's carvings, which had all been ordered from their Perana website. I saw their site more than once and loved it; full of vibrant colour enticing you to peek at the goods for sale.

I read out the list of deliveries and Petra pulled them out and stacked them on the floor. Our first call was the Evans family in Masterton. Tomorrow it would start, tonight it was time for Petra to cook dinner as I was tired from all the driving. I needed to stretch my legs and torso, a brisk walk then some yoga stretches, which is exactly what I did. Walking back to the van the smell of cooking was heaven, at least, I hoped it was coming from our van. Yum, a huge platter of grilled fish with steamed veggies and mashed spuds; it tasted like heaven. I really don't remember the lights going off, I was asleep.

New Zealand bird life is not the raucous sound of the Aussie birdlife, but just as welcoming. These birds sing not squawk, they tweet not burst into laughter, the magpies the world over warble the same tune. But this morning was wet and windy, not a sound anywhere, damp, wet, miserable. I did not want to move a muscle. I wanted to stay all wrapped up in my bed but instead I heard a cheery, 'Good morning,' from the other side of the van. 'All ready for today?'

'Not really, Petra. I just want to lie here,' I admitted.

'Up you get, lazy bones,' my bed now being shaken by her movements inside. 'I'll put the jug on, and you can have an extra ten minutes,' Petra offered. I agreed by nodding and snuggling back down into my doona.

Petra sat on my bunk while we both munched on hot toast and Manuka Honey for our breakfast. 'Are you not well?' she asked, looking at me intently.

'I'm fine thanks, just really tired today.'

I knew I was her delivery driver and it was part of our agreement, but I wanted a day or two off. I wanted to tour and have a nana nap and a read, ring family and check on my emails, my personal life still needed to be lived.

Petra was very intuitive most times but when work focused she could be a workaholic, her staring at me made me feel uncomfortable. 'What?' I asked.

'Are you sure you want to carry on doing this? You do look tired.'

Once she had said it, it was like someone had pricked my balloon. I admitted I needed some time out on my own, but I also wanted to continue travelling with her as I had agreed.

'Tara, just say the word. I can ask Ronan to help me and you can go back to Paradise.'

Although I answered, 'I'm sure I just need a day or two off,' my heart cried a different story.

'Fair enough then, that's what you shall have. I will do the driving until we get to the South Island, you can navigate.'

'Okay,' I agreed, 'that's fine.'

A small voice said, *no!* I want to have some time away from it all, and the feeling of homesickness for the Mermaid overcame me. I shrugged it off as silly, mentally telling myself to get up and get on with it, my legs slow to obey.

I wanted to switch off the small talk in my brain. The hot shower didn't work as it normally did, starting the day did not help me switch on. Instead, I got constant chatter. 'You don't want to be here. It's cold, damp, windy, travelling nonstop, no touring or sightseeing. You don't want to do this. Tara you're in your sixties, woman, take some time out. Their business is not yours; you don't need to do this anymore.'

I wanted to shout *stop*, so much rattled around in my head as day by day we delivered to far corners, on the road bumping along, being told by a mechanical voice this way or that way. I disliked this journey I was on.

Perhaps I should go back and pack up. Just go home, my brain advised, then my heart would say, but there is so much more to see and do! My heart won out. I had to say something, though, so I asked for two days on my own. Petra could have the car, do whatever she wanted as all the deliveries were done. Petra willingly agreed to this and took off to meet and greet other clients. I stayed in the van, tucked up against the cold southerly wind that froze you once you stepped outside. The mist and damp I kept at bay by tucking up inside and reading, ringing my home, talking to my family and friends. I talked to Jo about going on or going back. Telling someone my own age how I felt, hearing sound advice from a much-loved friend, encouraged me to follow what I started and acknowledge the fact I was homesick for my home and family.

Fred, her husband, bellowed out, 'Come home Tara. We miss you.' Rae told me all about her baby shopping days with her Aunty Jo and Jess told me about his school activities. He was so happy to be runner-up in the sprint competitions and to receive an award he'd won as Aussie of the month in his school. He was fast becoming a basketball fanatic. It all sounded settled and happy. I confided in Margi how I was feeling, and she summed it up in a nutshell. 'Are you being paid for this work you're doing?'

'Well no, it's not about money. I was offered an opportunity to travel in safety, but I really miss travelling on my own.' Margi didn't have any sympathy. 'About time you made up your mind, Tara.' But I didn't feel that way.

All I wanted was some time out from being with another person non-stop. Petra was adorable in all ways and as a friend she was fabulous, as an entrepreneur, ruthless.

In my younger days I had been there, done that. I did the workday hard slog to be where I am today. I did not want to rush all over the place on a time schedule or as Ronan once put it, 'We are time poor, so need to be totally focused on the job.' The problem was I discovered soon enough I did not want a job, my time here was to relax and see New Zealand not dash off here, there and everywhere to make a sale or contact. I made the mistake of wanting to help, getting all excited about the places we were going and hadn't thought about responsibilities again. Was I being to touchy feely because I could not do things my way?

Well I had better make up my mind, I scolded myself, as today is Friday, and on Sunday we are due to board the boat to Littleton, South Island to start our journey there.

Chapter 54

The opportunity to make a definite decision came my way. I was busy sorting out the last of the deliveries for the North Island, cataloguing what Petra needed for the South Island, and had just finished making a grocery list. Petra barged into the caravan, she was white and shaking with tears streaming down her face. In dismay I asked, 'Petra, what on earth?'

I held out my arms. I hadn't seen her like this before, she looked like ten thousand demons where after her.

'It's Ronan,' she gasped. 'He has been badly hurt!' She broke down in my arms her sobs shaking us both. One cold flannel on her forehead and many tissues later, she had calmed down enough to tell me the shocking news.

Petra had been buying some goods and intended to buy lunch and bring it home when she got a phone call from the Wellington General hospital. Ronan had been transferred to the hospital by helicopter after his legs were crushed by a log falling off a trailer. After a hot cup of tea, her shaking almost stopped, the tears now intermittent, we talked about what we should do. The priority was to get her to the hospital.

'Is there anything else you need?' I asked while I started the car. Petra shook her head, a look of bewilderment on her white face. I put my hand on her knee, I felt empathy towards them both.

'It's going to be alright, he's in the right place to heal.' There was only a nod from Petra.

Turning into the hospital car park the GPS announced, 'You have reached your destination.' Petra bolted out the door, running for the hospital main doors. I parked and followed, the emergency department five minutes' walk away.

'Petra, wait up,' I called, but she was off. The trail of fear she left behind was palpable. I followed her in. Ronan was out to it; they had given him an injection to ease the pain. A huge sheet was draped over a cage covering both his legs. Pain flickered across his face as Petra kissed him, she held his face between her hands whispering her love for him. I turned and sat outside the curtain. There was nothing I could do for them, but I was there for them.

The surgeon arrived. He carefully examined Ronan's legs and kept saying, 'I see,' as he walked around the bed. 'There is much we can do to save muscle, there's a couple of bones with nasty breaks, but I'm concerned about the left knee–it's a bit of a mess. I would like to have him in theatre as soon as possible.'

I stayed with them all that day. Petra called it their Black Friday and to them it must have been. Nothing hurts more than an injured or sick loved one. I silently sent up a thank you for my health and my family's health. Petra just sat there like a stone, not moving in the visitor's waiting room, refusing any food or drink, I had to force water into her, telling her, 'He is going to need you well to look after him.' Five hours later the surgeon appeared, his work done, and he gave us the thumbs up sign.

'Looking great,' he said. 'Ronan is in recovery.' It would be wise for you to go back to the ward and wait for him to come down.' I asked, 'Can you advise us how long his stay here will be?'

He shrugged. 'As long as it takes, we want him stable.'

Petra opted to stay beside him. Not needed, I decided to leave. 'I'm going back to the van. Ring me when you want to come back.' I might as well have spoken gibberish, she just wanted to put all her energy into her man and who could blame her. I remembered how that felt when I was in Petra's shoes.

I gave her a hug. 'Call me if you need me.'

Driving back to the campground at dusk, with the wind and rain hammering to get inside, was a nightmare. The traffic was so bad I crawled along, just about the only thing visible were bright red taillights winking on and off. To make matters worse, the waters of Wellington Harbour pounded the shore not twenty metres away, the spray as well as the rain cascading over me, the window-wipers groaning under the onslaught. Visibility was so bad. I was expecting at any time to rear-end the car in front. Finally, I drove into the campgrounds, exhausted. A cup of tea and then bed, I was asleep before my head hit the pillow.

Woken by my mobile ringing, it was Rae and Jess. This was unusual as I always rang them. 'You okay, Mum? I keep getting weird vibes about you, are you in trouble?' I told her what had happened.

'Oh Mum, how awful for them. Does that mean you're coming home soon or are you going to stay and help them?' I knew what my answer was before I said it.

'I'm coming home, honey. Perth is where I've wanted to be for a while but before you get too excited, I have to drive back, sell the Mermaid and the car, then drive to Auckland and find my way back home. I also want to make sure Petra and Ronan are fine before I do this.'

'Great, can't wait Mum, we have missed you so much. We are going to be a family again.'

Finally, Petra was home. She gave me the news Ronan was going to be okay, with another operation on his knee required in the future, but for now he had to heal. She was cancelling the South Island trip and tomorrow she would be busy with the hospital, so I had a day to myself. I kept my news to myself. Maybe tomorrow when she had calmed down I would tell her of my plans.

When I woke she had gone to be by Ronan's side. I decided to see what Wellington had to offer. The weather had quietened down to a dull roar. The wind here was icy, artic cold, wrapping up and without a vehicle it was taxi time. I was a tad annoyed Petra would go without considering my circumstances but here I was in a coffee bar, relaxed and quite happy to explore on my own.

I ordered a large cappuccino and blueberry muffin and while I waited I flicked through a tourist brochure. Wellington seemed to have lot to do and see; I was interested in the cable car ride which went from Lambton Quay in the city to way up into the mountains, and once back down there was a mini tour bus around the city. Te Papa, the new museum sounded great, the zoo, the oldest in New Zealand had a guided tour that sounded like fun. Then I saw an advert that made my heart thump.

If everything was right and Petra's moon, stars and whatever else were in alignment with either Jupiter or Mars, I could get on a Princess Cruise ship travelling from Auckland to Fremantle. It sounded the perfect way to go home–a two-week cruise to Perth, Australia.

Once we both had dinner that night, I told her of my plans for going back to Paradise, selling up the Mermaid and the car, driving to Auckland and catching the boat home. 'Wow,' you don't do things by halves do you? When does all this take place?'

'Well, I'd like to see some of Wellington first, then drive back to Paradise, then head for Auckland with the cruise ship leaving in four weeks.'

'Go Tara, good for you. I was scared we had ruined your time away with us.'

'Good God no,' I spluttered. 'I've had a great time.'

Tomorrow I would go the travel agents and pay for my cruise. It's weird, once you're settled on a course it snowballs. I arranged to hire a blue two-seater Honda for my drive back to Paradise, mine for the following four weeks, and a much-needed GPS came with it. Soon I would be on my way.

But first to see some of the capital city of New Zealand. I'm on the cable car, the only running funicular railway in New Zealand, as excited as a two-year old. The cable car was old and a bit cranky, stopping occasionally to let folk on and off. We wound our way up to the top of the mountain, the scenery majestic. I wanted to yell, 'I'm the king of the castle.' I realised apart from planes or helicopters I had never stood this far up on solid ground. I was standing on top of the mountain with maybe a twenty-minute wait, perfect for photo time, after which I caught the cable car back down. Just in time to catch the bus for my guided tour around the city. This place was amazing, the old streets and original houses just added to it.

We stopped off at the James Smith's shop, famous in New Zealand, almost like Myers in Australia. A little shopping treat was part of the tour, two hours inside the famous shop. Our lunch was waiting for us all on the third floor. I had a delicious open steak sandwich with hot chocolate. I then shopped for baby clothes and for Rae and Jess, enjoying every spending moment of it, my credit card doing overtime.

Chapter 55

If I did have a moment of guilt I dismissed it thinking, I'm here once, make the most of it. I could see Charles, the tour bus driver, look twice at the two small trolleys of pretty wrapped gifts awaiting him as he pulled up. Then it was to my drop off spot, my hire car awaiting me. 'Just as well there is only one in the car,' Charles commented. He was a gentleman offering to help me carry the gifts to the car and helping me store them away. As we walked with the parcels piled high in our arms, he asked where I was from, his reaction one of surprise. My wife and I are planning a trip there in two months. I started telling him about places to go and see, and once my parcels were all safely packed inside the car, he invited me to his home for dinner.

'Are you sure?' I asked.

'Yes, we would love to hear about your home and city.' So I agreed. 'I would love to join you for dinner tonight. I'm staying with a friend, though. May I bring her as well?'

'Of course. I will ring my wife now and let her know.'

'She won't mind two female strangers turning up for tea?'

'Nah, she's a real peach my Fi.' He wrote down his address and phone number. 'See you at seven tonight,' he said.

I rang Petra and asked how Ronan was doing, asking would she care to join me tonight, that we had been invited out for dinner. She was hesitant, I heard her tell Ronan who encouraged her to join me as he just wanted to sleep.

Charles and his wife Fiona where delightful company. Their home full of memories, their four grandchildren rushed in and out of the dining room with either Charles or Fiona yelling at them to go and watch telly. 'We're entertaining here,' was a constant cry from Fi, as we were asked to call her. The cutest three-year old with blond curls, limpid brown eyes, stood there sucking his thumb, trying to talk, spit dripping down his chin, his nappy half off and a little pot belly hanging over the top. He reminded me of Jess when he was the same age. My heart melted even more when he put his hand out like an adult, shook my hand, spit and all. 'Hi,' he said, then toddled off to be with his siblings who by now were either laying or stretched over bean bags or the sofa. I could see the love in both Fi and Charles, they were very proud of their family, Fi apologising for the noise. 'No apologies needed,' Petra and I both said. 'Family first, always.'

We ate a wonderful lamb roast with all the trimmings; pumpkin, kumara, spuds, peas and brussels sprouts, and a pavlova for dessert. There was a mix of home-grown apples and feijoa fruit compote to eat with the pavlova. It was so nice to be eating a proper meal at a table, even Petra tucked in asking for a second helping of vegetables. A carafe of chilled white wine was placed on the table or Charles offered to open a red wine for us.

Their home was really a home; kiddies' drawings, handmade crafts, were dotted all over the place, knitted cushions, rugs made from material or hand knitted. Fi made rag rugs. I hadn't seen them for many years and hers were lovely, creative, colourful and big. My memory was of my paternal grandmother making small ones from old discarded dresses or sheets all ripped into strips, it tripped a memory, mainly me sneezing at the dust. My grandmother would sit for ages matching, winding, some colours so bright, some dull, a full dress would make a huge ball of strips. First they were washed and dried in the hot Queensland sun then wound around and around the back of a chair like wool and stitched through an old soft clean coal sack to make rag rugs for the kitchen, bathroom or laundry. I even had one beside my bed. Fi had taken it one step further her; rugs were a work of art and she sold them internationally and nationally, she was very humble about her achievements. Charles' chest was about to burst with pride as he added that one was accepted in a local museum for their wall display on New Zealand indigenous weaving. The one under the table where we sat was at least five by five square metres. She had encouraged her church group to help her, and it was made of many different blues, greens and mauves and swirled from large to small circles. It was purely abstract. I was amazed and said how it looked like the inside of the Paua shell. 'You got it in one,' Fi said, she was pleased an Aussie would recognise the pattern.

As the night wore on, we discussed what to do and see in Perth and surrounding districts. There was so much to talk about, warning them, 'Western Australia is a huge place. Make sure you have the time to see it all.' I advised them to Google what they wanted to see and do and gave them my card. They were most grateful. I really liked these two Kiwis and asked them to ring me once they were in Perth, I would love to catch up again. We all agreed it was a good idea. Funny, sometimes you make instant friends and other times you don't care if you never see then again. 'Ships in the night' as my Mum would say. These people offered their friendship and I was the lucky recipient.

As for Petra, she could see an opportunity here, and she asked if Fi would be interested in teaching her the art of rug making, offering her an hourly fee.

'Got to do something while Ronan is recovering. If you can teach me, I can spend some time at night doing this.' Fi thought it was a great idea and accepted. Petra and Fi now had their heads together making their plans. By the time we were leaving, Petra had her first instructions to source some clean sacking and draw her design on it, Charles suggesting, 'A silver fern, the Maori call it a Koru.'

Petra was delighted; I could see her head was buzzing with all the possibilities. As we said our goodnights I popped my head around the lounge door to say goodnight to the family. All you could hear were bowls being scraped out as they tucked into the remains of their nana's pavlova and fruit desert. Hopefully, it was a sight I would soon be seeing soon in my own home. I had driven to the dinner in the hire car, Petra wanted to go and see Ronan, so I dropped her off at the hospital entrance and she said she would get a taxi back to the caravan.

Once I was home and tucked up, the song 'I'm going home'–my lullaby, came to mind as I was falling asleep. If Petra came home, I didn't know when as I didn't hear anything. Her bed was slept in, but it was cold, so she obviously left early. My plans for the day were to pop in to see Ronan for a half-hour, a walk around the Wellington Botanical Gardens, and a visit to Te Papa the new Museum.

I was in luck. Ronan was wide awake and pleased to see me. 'Petra been in?' I asked.

'Not since late last night. She had wonderful time with you and your friends, thank you.'

'No worries, mate,' I said in a very drawn out Aussie accent, my humour lost on him. Ronan's eyes looked large and unfocused and I knew it was the pain killers; I had been there before with Russ. We hugged goodbye; this was my last visit to see how he was.

'Thanks for everything, Tara. You've been a godsend.'

I laughed at his comment. 'Yeah right, even the driving?' He had the grace to blush.

Excitement gripped my insides. You're going home, it whispered. 'Take good care of yourself, Ronan. Get well soon,' I called and off I went to see a little more of this city that was so damned freezing cold but so full of life.

Chapter 56

Botanical gardens are always great to visit. I had seen many on my trips around the world, and this too was a special place. For those folk living in Wellington who never visited it, they are missing an amazing experience. As I walked in the gardens the sun shone weakly, it's permanent battle with the rain clouds winning the fight for an hour or two. The roses were something special; vivid dots of bright colour from afar, the heady perfume lets you know before they come into clear vision what and where they are. Once beside them they were perfect, and so many varieties it was hard not to spend a whole day photographing each one.

An old Victorian glass house sheltered many different types of orchids, from tiny dainty Singapore flowers to massive Brazilian jungle ones clinging tenaciously to their tree trunk hosts or Punga logs. Ferns also grow here from tiny mist covered maiden hair to brutish stroppy ferns that grow in the African jungles. I spotted an Australian pig fern here standing triumphant amongst its peers from around the world. Butterflies were everywhere, the humidity in the glass house a perfect home for them. I saw a café halfway through my walk, the smell of baking enticing me. It was also a tourist shop with many knick-knacks to buy; they burst out from the shop onto the veranda, a vast assortment of 1950's kitsch, from miniature plastic fish magnets to enormous mosaiced garden hangings six foot tall, all very colourful.

My buying started with a toy stuffed Kiwi for Jess and a little stuffed toy sheep for my new grandchild. Jo and Fred both got a Paua encrusted pen set, and for Rae I found a really pretty Paua earring and necklace set with a solid silver setting. For me, I found some Paua drop earrings. After I had filled my bag with all the goodies I ordered my lunch: cheese, chicken and asparagus pie with a hot cup of tea. As I ate a hailstorm hit the grounds, it came down hard and fast. I could see the roses taking a beating, they were now tattered and torn, what a pity. Only an hour ago I took the most fabulous photo of a tangerine rose called a Peace Rose, its smell was a heavy scent. I flicked through my shots on the camera and there it was, a memory of Wellington. I could almost smell the rose again.

Time to move, this lovely food was weighing heavy in my stomach, so off the comfy café chair and into that biting cold wind. No wonder the Eskimos were tubby in photos I'd seen; they ate to gain weight to keep that awful cold wind out and we are not too far from the Scott base in Antarctica, I believe. God its cold.

I headed for the Te Papa Tongarewa, Wellington's National Museum. I'm not one for museums normally, I get bored unless they have an art department or something to do with the arts on display. The ancient story of a Moa bird, its huge skeleton in a glass case caught my interest, the Maori killed it for food. All I can say is they must have had to feed a huge number of people.

I followed the tracks of the Maori people and the insects, bird life, animal life that was once a large part of New Zealand bush life, Moas's now extinct. But why? In Australia we still had emus, they were not an introduced bird and had been in Australia for thousands of years. It became clearer as I read about human urbanisation and the human need to kill and master or covet the land. I had recently listened to a talk back show with Germaine Greer on eco-feminism, her outlook was bleak, her message. 'If we do not stop cutting, chopping, killing, ignoring this planet, our home, it was going to end up a disaster.' It was up to all of us to say 'no' to this sort of mind-bending destruction in the mineral and oil mining industry, replant the mine sites and let nature back in to help.

Germaine talked about Mt Whaleback in the north of Western Australia. How the mining magnates are the ones to prosper, the rest of us are working bees, destroying the planets natural resources. Her statement that we start growth from the ground up made a light go on for me as I agree wholeheartedly; if we destroy our planet where does our human family go? Space?

How awful to never see a tree grow or a frog leap into a pool or an insect or a butterfly in all its natural wonder. Was my grandson's future really in a bubble? Only able to breathe stale oxygen regurgitated one zillion times before he and his family could breathe it? Was this really our future? Why not act now and turn the tables on those profit pirates that are only getting richer by polluting our world. Start by shouting aloud, 'No!' Germaine was on fire and she was right, eco-feminism is not about females ruling the world, it's about nurturing our planet so we can live here on our home called Earth. I had caught myself yelling out, 'Yes!' and punching the air, my beliefs in a nutshell.

Up above me hung massive skeletons of blue whales, grey whales and Orcas, this place was amazing. I took my time walking through many displays, then I was in the art department. One wall was covered in Maori weaving, the ancient cloaks of beauty behind glass were absolutely gorgeous; tiny Kiwi feathers with Paua shell, bell bird feathers that had a gunmetal blue to them, what exquisite weaving. Then I saw it, right at the end, an exhibition of weaving and wall hangings from the late 1900s to modern day. Her name on a small plaque *Modern day Abstract Rag Rug, by Fiona Hutchinson.*

To say this was better than the one I had stood on the previous night would be an understatement. It had fire from volcanoes, the edges were pure white depicting the snow on the mountains, then a blue-green of the Pacific, green shades for the trees, yellow for the sun, then an explosion of reds, orange, crimson scarlet to the centre of the rug where one small dot was black. Many people, including me, were taking photos. Once I had dragged my eyes away, I rang Fi to say, 'It's gorgeous. Why didn't you tell Petra and me how exotic your museum piece was?'

Fi was very humble when she said, 'I knew you were going there; I knew you would see it.' Well she was right. I and two hundred people had seen it today. I said I was so darn proud of her. 'When you come over, Fi, bring some of your work or photos so I can introduce you to some art groups.'

Now it was time to go back to the van and pack up my gear as tomorrow was the start of my journey back to Perth.

What a place New Zealand is, I thought. Full of surprises at every corner, that's when you could see around the corner as, apart from Italy, I had never come across such winding roads. I was packing my bags rather haphazardly; I was quite tired having fought my way back here in the heavy rain and howling wind. I was really pleased to be getting out of this frigid weather, we were now the only ones in the caravan park. The other folk were permanents, small heaters or fires glowed through small windows, laughing off the biting wind and freezing rain.

Petra charged in, the wind doing its best to pull her back out again, her beanie had come off, her hair like blond whips snapping. I pulled her inside, tugging the door shut after me. 'I'll be glad to see the back of this awful weather,' I said. Petra was quiet. I looked up and she had that haunted look again.

'What's wrong, Ronan not well?'

'No, you're leaving us at first light tomorrow. I'm finding it hard to say goodbye, Tara. It scares me a little.'

Putting my arm around her, I told her what I would have said to my own daughter. 'I'm only a phone call away. I can come back if you need me, but I really do need to go home.'

Inside me, I couldn't wait to pick up my Mermaid and car, I just wish I could take them home with me. 'I understand,' she said, 'I do, but I'm finding it hard to let go, that's all.'

It was a different story for me. *I'm going home* was my lullaby, it went around and around my head and heart all day today. I was glad to be going home as well, no regrets, no sorrow. I had met some wonderful people, had some weird and wonderful experiences and been a guest in an almighty land. There was nothing small about pristine, beautiful New Zealand.

I was up and packed already to go, wrapped up tightly against the cold. I made enough noise to wake the camp up but still Petra slept on. Finally, I was impatient to start off, the car chuffing out small puffs of white exhaust fumes into the rain. 'Petra wake up, it's time for me to go,' I said as I gave her a light shake. Her voice muffled in the pillow and thick quilts, 'Tara just go, I can't say goodbye.'

I understood completely. I too just wanted to drive off, we both hated the last goodbye.

Dropping a kiss on top of her blond head, I left clicking the van door shut, gave it a light wrap with my knuckles, got in the car and drove off. I stopped for one more look at the caravan, and there was Petra's face up against the window, her eyes followed me out of the park. I gave one last toot to say goodbye, put my hand out the window and waved, then merged into the frantic traffic of a Wellington workday. Monday morning six thirty am, where did all these people come from?

The drive was uneventful. It rained and blew, the little Honda shaking sideways when the wind gave it one big extra push. Driving in a storm is a scary thing, even in Perth, but this weather was not a storm, this was normal for this end of the country. The Levin road sign said twenty kilometres to go. *Hurray, I'm buggered.* A slight headache was coming on behind the eyes, time for me to stop driving and have a cup of tea and lie down. I found a motel, got my room key, parked in front of my room, went in and lay down. I took two painkillers, then I burst into tears. How confusing is the heart? I was chomping to get going yet I missed my two friends incredibly; it felt like I had left a shoe behind.

Chapter 57

Stop this right now, I ordered myself. You're tired and hungry, with a really sore head. A big thanks to whoever cleaned this room, as tucked in between the packets of sugar were packets of plain biscuits, lovely. Drink, eat, shower and fill up my hot water bottle, wrap a towel around it and ahh… relax, rest my head. I slept. It took three hours of a restful sleep for the headache to leave but once it did, my energy came back and I was up, starving for some dinner. They had a menu in the room, a local restaurant delivered to your room, great. I rang and ordered a hot roast meal with all the veggies offered and gravy. Within the half hour it was delivered, and I almost devoured it on the spot. I had not eaten all day. A chocolate bar when I filled the car with gas, and water for myself was the only intake for me that day. No wonder I had a headache.

I put all the pillows I could find on the bed, which was against a wall. Time to ring people and let them know I was safe.

I rang Rae and Jess. 'I'm on my way home today,' I said when they answered the phone, a squeal of excitement from them both. Jess yelled, 'What tomorrow?' Rae explained it wasn't tomorrow I was arriving; it would be in about months' time. 'Bugger,' I heard him exclaim. I left early the next morning.

Next stop Palmerston North. I had not called in here before, so breakfast at a roadside café, check that all was good with the car, oil, water, top up with gas, tyres checked, all good. While I sat with a cup of tea at the café I rang Petra again. 'How's it all going?' I asked. She sounded great, full of pep. Friends had arrived to see them and stay with her for a week. They had decided to move to a rental house in case Ronan could come home for a weekend occasionally while doing therapy, the large caravan towed back to Paradise once she had found a place. The caretakers of Paradise had offered to stay on there to help her with Ronan's needs, lifting and carrying and therapy etc. It all sounded like she had what she wanted and needed for now. 'Good for you, Petra,' I said, 'getting it all sorted out it sounds great. I'll ring you tomorrow.'

I knew once the shock had gone, they would sort it and felt I was better off out of the way. This was about getting Ronan better, not about me.

'Love you, miss you Tara,' was the end of our phone call. I miss you too, I thought, my heart gave a slight tug of sadness, but I knew I was doing the right thing.

Palmerston North or 'Palmy' as they call it, is quite a big township. I love the way the Kiwis enclose all old and new, it was seamless, as the older streets gave way to new homes and streets. It was very easy to drive around or was it because that bloody awful rain had stopped at long last? Whatever it was I was happy to be here. Stopping off at a nearby fruit and veggie shop, I asked the lady serving if they had a phone book so I could ring a motel. I asked twice and she ignored me, so I asked again. Suddenly, 'Two doors down, lady' was almost screamed at me.

I was shocked. 'You want to buy anything?' Uttered with another scream. Looking at her closely I could see she had two hearing aids, huge looking bolts sticking out of each ear. I shook my head, mouthed, 'Thank you,' at her and wandered two doors down. Sure enough there was a shingle out advertising vacancies. I rang the bell, and to my amusement the same old lady huffed and puffed her way through from the back gate to the desk. 'Yes,' she screamed at me. I spoke really loudly, 'I want to get a room for the night.'

'A what?' she screamed.

'A room for the night please,' I screamed back.

'Why didn't you say so?' She yelled, 'keep your hair on, no need to yell at me.'

I felt my fingers clench at my sides. This was going to be wonderful I could just see it. She gave me a key to a room down a great long corridor, screaming into my face, 'Number 51.' I couldn't wait to get there, scribbled my name down and paid her with a credit card.

'Don't take Amex,' she screamed.

'It's not Amex,' I screamed back, 'it's Visa.'

'Oh, alright then,' she grumbled loudly. She got out an old zip-zap machine, blew the dust off, wiping off any residue left with her fruit stained apron. She just stood there and stared at the machine. I stood there and stared at it as well. What she expected to happen I did not know. 'Hope this bleeding machine works,' she screamed and put my card in upside down and backwards.

I knew this was going to take forever, so I screamed, 'Let me show you how it's done.'

I put my card in the right way, zapped the cover across, pulled out the receipt, signed it, took my copy and gave her the one she should put in the till. Instead, she binned it. 'Don't need the receipt,' she screamed at me. By now one hour had ticked by and I was about to burst out laughing at us two ladies in a room screaming at each other. Should I scream and explain she needs this receipt to put in the till? 'It tells the bank to pay you the forty-five dollars I paid you for the room.'

Her rheumy old eyes looked up at me in such surprise. 'It does?'

I nodded.

'Well bugger me,' she said.

Then I did laugh, and she did too, her face one big pink wrinkled mess, her cackle would have woken the dead. She slapped her knees then clapped her hands, wiped her eyes on her apron. 'Guess I need to pay more attention.'

I could not wait to tell Petra about this experience. I wondered how many times the lady had done this and received no payment at all.

My room was pretty, an old cottage-feel to it and spotless. A large white fluffy towel and face cloth rested on the bed, a cane table and chair against a window all done out in pink chintz material, the bedspread and light shade all made of the same material. Four large puffy pillows rested against the bedhead, a worn grey carpet with a rose-coloured mat beside the bed; everything said welcome and relax.

I was about to ring Margi for a catch up when there was a sharp rapping on the door. Opening it, there stood the little old lady with a huge tray. It had tea, toast, marmalade, butter and milk, plus two boiled eggs that sat there with little bright red, woolly knitted caps on them. She screamed at me, 'Here's your breakfast.' I took the tray mouthing, 'Thank you.'

I had not ordered any breakfast, nor did I have the energy to scream back at her. I went to shut the door, but her hand stopped me. 'I'm Dotty,' she said.

'I know,' I yelled back, if only she knew I was being sarcastic. I was peckish anyway, *what the heck*. As I ate, I read up on what to see in Palmerston North. Not a lot but there were two or three interesting spots I could have a quick look at, as tomorrow I was on the road again to reach Wanganui.

What this town had to offer was what I had done before but I did venture out and go to the movies, nice, warm and cosy. A strawberry and chocolate ice-cream made my day while I watched a movie I had missed in Perth, 'Hildago', a movie about an American cowboy brought up by a Red Indian with an amazing horse. They travelled to Egypt in a race across the desert, against Sheiks and thieves and of course, two beautiful women were involved.

I enjoyed every swashbuckling minute of it and of course, the hero got the most beautiful lady. It was late afternoon when it finished, and the rain had returned. I made my way back to my room; the tray I had left outside had been removed and there was a note from Dotty tucked into my door inviting me to watch TV in the private lounge. No, I thought. Nice of her to invite me but I could not stand a night of yelling at each other, and from here I could hear her TV, it was on so loud, so no thanks, I'm off to bed. The shower was communal but like the bedroom spotless and looked like there was no one else staying here. I had it all to myself. I just stood there and let the water spray every nook and cranny. I hummed away to myself as I washed my hair, shaved my legs and loved the feeling of being clean, then into the pink fluffy bathrobe provided by the motel and wandered back to my room.

Dotty was banging at my door.

'Everything alright Mrs?' she screamed. Heavens! This is exhausting, I thought. I just smiled and nodded my answer. Dotty wandered off muttering to herself and I went into my room. I suddenly felt alone, everyone had someone, even Dotty had her dog who I noticed winced whenever she conversed at screaming level. Okay Tara, you've been here before, it's alright to be alone, this you already know. Sleep took a long while to arrive that night. Two days drive to Opunake and Paradise and the Mermaid waiting for me.

Early morning arrived bleak and cold, again the sharp knocking on the door. 'It's Dotty,' she called, 'I've got your breakfast here, Tara.'

I must look half-starved, I thought. I padded over to the door, opened it and she charged in like miniature bull in a china shop. Her wrinkled eyes missing nothing, slamming down the tray and screaming at me, 'Breakfast dear.' It was a repeat of yesterday, but it would sustain me. I dressed feeling the damp in my clothing; I was looking forward to getting to Paradise. I packed my bag and left calling out goodbye to Dotty. The blue car welcomed me, looking like a happy blue bubble in the rain, waiting just for me. 'I am now even closer to my home,' I said out loud, yelling out a huge whoopee. I sounded like Dotty on steroids.

As I drove, I wandered how far it was to Opunake. Maybe I didn't have to stay another night in a motel in Wanganui. I pulled over into a small curve in the road, a shop was not too far away, and I could just make out its lights. It was still extremely wet and muddy, so I didn't pull over too far, then tapped Opunake in the GPS. It blinked a couple of times as if to say, 'Hang on please I'm waking up.' It gave me the directions but not the time. I rang Petra to ask her opinion, the reception was very poor, winding down the car window, 'Hello Tara,' was all I heard as a massive truck whooshed past my little car, a wave as big as the car itself launched itself from under the truck and rushed straight through the car window all over me.

'Shit!' I burbled spitting out rank muddy water. 'I'm soaked.' Water dripped from my face and my hair streamed down; the car was now one huge puddle. I went from shock to rage in two seconds. 'What the?' I yelled. 'How dare he,' I spluttered spitting out more dirty water. I was coughing and gagging, it was a wonder my heated fury did not dry me out in an instant.

The taillights of the offender stopped just ahead, winking at me encouraging me to get out and give the driver a mouthful of abuse, so I did as they instructed. Getting out the wind caught my door, wrenching out from my hand, my temper now exploded. I slammed the door shut and stalked toward this cattle truck and trailer, the cattle mooing and grumbling their distaste at being in the rain, the driver was in the shop only twelve long anger-filled strides down the road.

'Hey you!' I hollered, 'look what you did.' I stood there in the doorway, my now long hair blowing up and around my head in the wet and wild weather, my wet woolly jumper and jeans stuck to me. I stunk of cow shit and drain water.

'You stupid idiot,' I yelled. 'You literally drowned me and my car. Didn't you see there was a car parked? You're so bloody up yourself driving a big truck.'

I was shaking with anger and didn't focus on what I was saying and doing and took one step into the shop and up and over I went. Both feet slipped out from under me, crash, my body hit the shop floor. The shopkeeper said, 'Jesus lady, careful! Are you okay?'

Not even the fall and my bruised bum could mask my indignation and anger at the moron who had just dumped a ton of water into my car. A fuse had been lit and was now on fire; he copped it from me with both barrels. By now I was almost screaming at him as he tried to help me.

'Don't you touch me.'

He held up both hands in front of him. 'Hey, hey, stop, I'm sorry, stop,' the driver pleaded as I tried to get up. The shopkeeper and driver both tried to help me up. I felt like a drunken sailor. The mud on the floor caused a mud wrestling match between the three of us. Finally we stood up hanging on to each other, then all three of us suddenly took off in a macabre dance, our arms and legs shooting out all over the place on their own free will as they both tried to help me stand up and I tried to push them off.

Finally, with much pushing and grunting from me, the driver and shopkeeper making similar noises, we all stood upright, hanging on to each other but again our feet started sliding away from us. I saw the funny side, so did the driver, and the shopkeeper joined us in the maniacal laughter. My sides hurt, my back hurt, my eyes streamed tears, I laughed so much I was in danger of wetting myself. The older man held my elbow leading me to a chair, 'Brandon's my name and driving's my game.'

'Then you're not very good at it, Brandon,' Mrs Grumpy had returned.

His eyes were full of laughter as he said, 'Well I could say the same for you and your standing skills.'

Touché.

The shopkeeper's family stood in the doorway their mouths open like four little goldfish in animation, his wife placed newspapers over the mess I had made with my dripping wet clothes. I couldn't apologise more sincerely, offering to help mop it up before her day got busy, her broken English making it hard for us to comprehend what each other wanted. Brandon gave me the best advice. 'Leave it alone and come with me.' The shopkeeper agreed, opening the door for me. I held tightly to Brandon's offered arm as we made our way out.

'I am so embarrassed,' I told him. 'I don't normally lose it.'

Brandon shrugged his shoulders. 'Well by the looks of your car and you, I should be the one apologising. I honestly didn't give it a single thought as I passed you.' His admitting he was in the wrong mollified me somewhat, but it did not take care of the mess the car was in, or me come to that. Everything was soaked; clothes, blankets, basket of food, handbag, presents once so prettily wrapped now flat and ugly. The seats dripped and the car leaked in two long dribbles under the mudguards, a muddy tide mark was now appearing inside the car.

When Brandon opened the driver's side I heard him say, 'Well that's fucked,' which for some reason really tickled my funny bone. I leaned over hooting with laughter.

'I think you're in shock,' he said. I could not agree more.

My phone was playing up; it was wet so I could not ring out. We looked at each other. I could read his mind. Brandon could leave and be on time for wherever he was heading, leaving me to struggle or he could help. Thank God he chose to help.

'Look lady,' he looked at me, 'here is an idea: get into the sleeper of my truck, strip off and put on some of my clothes there in the backpack.' I did as he suggested, the little bunk at the back held Brandon's personal gear all neatly folded. The cab of his truck was warm and cosy, and he waited outside in the rain, his heavy oilskin protecting him from getting too wet. I stripped off down to undies and bra, thought about it for a nano-second, they both came off as well, grabbing an old hand towel out of his backpack, I dried myself thoroughly and dressed in Brandon's work gear; long black singlet then a pair of dark blue overalls all clean and patched. I did not care about the look, they were warm, hallelujah. I could feel the warmth start to creep back into my body, adding thick warm woolly socks, ah bliss, I was warm once more.

Brandon banged on the side of the truck. I banged back to let him know I was dressed and he could come in. The aroma of hot coffee from his thermos drifted through the cab. 'Sorry, no milk or sugar,' he said.

Brandon asked, 'What do you think we should do?' I had no idea and must have looked every part of a dizzy female. He patted my knee. 'Here's a thought, have you got the phone number for the hire depot?' I nodded my head.

'Well, now you're warm and dry, you stay in the cab. I will put all your gear into storage under the truck. While I do that why don't you ring the enquiry number, tell them what has happened and ask what we should do.' He handed me his phone.

I agreed, so while it thundered and rained its worst, Brandon went backwards and forwards transferring all my soggy things to the trunk on his truck, but first he kindly bought me my handbag with my cruise travel documents and passport, all soaked, as I sat sipping hot coffee and rang the car hire firm.

They were most upset for me and my situation and would send a tow truck from Wellington to pick the car up, so I was to lock it up and leave the keys with the shopkeeper. I made sure they knew where it was, giving the name of the small shop close by and the road I was on.

That was not the end of it. They requested a written confirmation, forms to fill out etc from the driver of the offending vehicle, which was Brandon. But on the good side, I was safe and warm, with no actual harm done to me, my pride dented a little but that was all.

Chapter 58

Once that was all done, Brandon sat beside me in his truck I poured him a hot coffee and handed him the towel I had used so he could wipe his face and hands. 'I'm not too bad,' he said looking at his soaked jeans. 'Now what am I going to do with you?'

'Find a motel and drop me off, please. I have to be in Opunake tomorrow then Auckland city in nine days.'

Brandon had a drawl when he spoke, his smile lopsided and twinkling hazel eyes, a good-looking man who had shown me nothing but consideration. I was not scared of my situation, why should I be? So far he had been a complete gentleman. He looked at me. 'Opunake, huh?'

I nodded, 'I have friends expecting me there.'

'Well Ma'am, I'm headed in that direction, why not ride with me then you will be safe? I will get you there on time, I promise.' It sounded like a wonderful idea to me and I agreed to ride with him. I borrowed his phone again and rang Petra to tell her but it was engaged so I left a voice message for her to ring me. All I wanted to do was grab my gear and rush up to Auckland to catch the boat home and the universe was putting a big roadblock in the way. First Ronan now this. What was going on? I thought. It took five hours of slow travelling, light conversation and a little snoozing on my part, to reach Opunake and there it was… Paradise.

Brandon turned into the driveway, the truck crunching on the gravel as we turned and stopped. The rain continued to pelt down, the wind blew brown sea foam across the road and onto the truck window. Brandon said to me, 'This is it, Tara.' My instincts were to cower inside my warm comfy bubble of the truck's cab. Brandon rummaged around in the cab and found an old dusty umbrella. 'I can offer you this,' he said. He shrugged into his still damp oilskin raincoat, got out of the truck, walked to my side, opened the door and helped me out.

The trusty umbrella blew immediately inside out, now totally useless, the wind merciless as it screamed, pushed and blew with a mighty force. We stood there with rain running down our faces. Brandon opened his coat, pulling me inside, trying to shelter me and himself, the trees we stood under not that much help either, the poor man did not know what to do.

I gave him a quick hug. 'Brandon, thank you. I'm going to walk up there. You go and deliver your cows, and once you're free would you come back and bring my things back to me?' With my handbag over my shoulder I took off into the screaming wind. In two minutes, I was soaked through once again, my knuckles knocking on the door of Paradise were frozen.

Kingsley, one of the farm sitters, answered the door staring in amazement, David, his partner, reaching past him to pull me inside. They led me to the warm fire in the lounge, offered me a hot shower and hot food, then a warm bed–the couch in front of the fire, bliss. I accepted all of it in that order, waking up the next day to the sound of knocking on the front door. David shook me fully awake, softly saying, 'Tara, Brandon is here with your gear.'

Sitting up groggily, I opened my eyes to all three men standing in the lounge with their backs to the warm fireplace and three pair of eyes looking at me struggle about in my large cocoon of blankets. It was no use; I had completely wound myself up tight. I tried to sit up and flopped down again, Brandon now laughing, 'You don't seem to be able to stand up again, Tara.'

I was not going to be embarrassed again, so I forced myself to stand up straight, but the room went around twice and I fell again, Brandon the first to catch me and put me back on to the couch.

'Methinks you need to rest up, you feel very hot.' He was right, I was boiling. I don't remember much after that until a day later I came around and croaked, 'What happened?'

David was the only one in the lounge with me, my eyes all gummed up and blurry.

'Welcome back, Tara. It looks like you have a bad cold.'

No kidding, I thought. I felt like crap. 'Take it easy, Tara, you've not been well, bit of a nasty cold and tired we think.' Now the 'we think' made my brain start, who is the 'we' he was talking about? All the thoughts in my head tumbled around. I had to be in Auckland to catch the ship home but where was all my stuff? How come I was still on the couch? Why did I feel like I had swallowed razor blades? My body just lay there, my mind so full of everything, all the if's and why's. I tried to move but it was difficult, I felt so tired. Kingsley wandered into the house giving David a hug, then noticed I was awake. 'Hey, the wanderer returns.' Both men stood beside me looking down at me. I felt really uncomfortable under scrutiny but too tired to object.

Spoon fed by Kingsley, my hands and face washed by David, and although I appreciated it I was not ten years old. They finally left the room, going to do the daily duties around Paradise. I snoozed until I felt a hand on my head, it was Brandon and an older woman.

'How ya doin mate?' Brandon asked, the woman looking concerned. He turned to the woman beside him, 'Tara, this is my mum, Titch.'

From that moment and the look in her eye I knew I was going to get better; I was not going to be sick, or miss the boat, not on her shift. This was one lady who knew exactly what to do and she did it.

Brandon did as she requested, quietly and efficiently, and by that afternoon I was ensconced in their cabin in a place called Ahititi, an hour from Opunake.

Titch stood for no nonsense and no back chat, if she gave an order, it was obeyed immediately, if not you were asked to leave her presence. I stayed on the couch in the day and in the spare room at night. Her eyes followed where I went and what I did, the bathroom was my main visit. If Brandon and I were anywhere together she suddenly appeared, her hand on my arm. 'Come on Tara, time to rest.'

Brandon looked like her; large, hooded hazel eyes, strong jawline and lean, long body, with greying curly hair. I learned from their conversations he had inherited his dad's cattle trucking business after he passed over two years ago. Patches of conversation flowed over and around me. I wasn't included but I was looked after.

Warm nourishing food, a warm bed and my temperature taken every two hours, home remedies administered regularly in a no-nonsense manner with my stash of painkillers for headaches; it all helped immensely. Brandon had dried out my paperwork, my clothing, and all the gifts had been unwrapped and dried off and left on a side table for me to rewrap before I went. Somehow, even my phone still worked. All I had to do was get better and move on, which I was fine with as all I wanted to do was get to Auckland and sail away.

Four days of being looked after was enough. I was feeling eighty percent better, time to get some energy flowing into my bones. I was now too skinny; my ribs and cheek bones very pronounced, my hair looked oily and scraggy, the neat plait I had adopted now more like a rat's tail. I asked if I could use their shower, an abrupt nod of her head and given a rough towel was her answer. Titch did not believe in wasting words with a stranger. I felt warmed in and out by the boiling water, while drying myself Titch knocked on the door. As I opened it her hand shot around the door, in it my fresh dry laundry with a, 'Here,' was all I got.

I knew it had nothing to do with me. This was Titch, I had been her guest for nearly four days and her behaviour towards me had not changed. She was not rude or nasty, she was in total control of her life and her son, or so she thought. Things were about to change considerably, and I unintentionally was the instigator.

Funny how life works out. If Brandon had not drowned me that night or I had not stopped to ring Petra, or Ronan had not been injured none of what was about to unfold would have happened. I had experienced first-hand how the universe works and was about to learn more.

My stay here was nearly over, time to get moving. I rang Petra first and told her what I had done, seen and where I'd been, her catch cry for me the whole time I stayed with them was, 'You really don't do things in halves do you.' She chortled, Ronan calling out in the background, 'Tara we miss you, come back.' He sounded much better.

Both wanted to know about Paradise, asking so many questions they were tripping over each other's sentences. I smiled as they sounded happy and together, that was the main thing. I had to admit there was no way I was going anywhere until I could get to my car and the Mermaid. The storm had done major damage to seaside roads, which was the problem I now faced. I rang Rae then Jo, both concerned they hadn't heard anything, no emails or texts. I told them why, and both were glad to hear I was now up and about and trying to get to Auckland, and both green with envy about my cruise from Auckland to Fremantle.

'Way to go Mum,' Rae said. 'Keep safe and Mum, keep me informed. Once you're on the ship I will be counting down the days until we see each other again.' It had been many months since I left. Rae was due to have the baby in three weeks.

Jo calling me a, 'Lucky cow. How did you score that cruise? See you soon, Darl, can't wait.' Finally, I got to Margi, who was really concerned about me. I kept saying, 'I'm fine, really.'

She offered to pop down and pick me up. 'Margi, thanks love but I'm okay and I will pop in and see you very soon and will stay a night with you. Okay?'

'You know that's fine,' she replied, 'can't wait to see you again.'

That same afternoon the hire car firm rang wanting details and a written confirmation of what had happened from Brandon. They had never had this happen before and the car was written off as the water damage was considerable.

'Tell me about it,' I said. 'I was the recipient of the water.' The lady on the phone chuckled, 'What a thing to happen. That's a story for the grandchildren.'

It felt great to say it certainly will be. Grandchildren, how that word made my heart sing and soon I would be holding another baby that had some of my blood in its veins. Now I had to find a ride back to Paradise to pick up my vehicle and the most beautiful Mermaid in the world. I got excited thinking about it. Time for action. Titch watched me from the kitchen window, I could feel her eyes on my back as I sought Brandon out and didn't have to go far, following his big muddy footsteps to the shed in their back yard. I could smell the freshly chopped wood stacked up beside it. I started to turn away as I suddenly realised it was Brandon's private quarters. There were net curtains at the windows, the fire lit inside adding a soft mellow light. Healthy geraniums were in three big terracotta pots on the outside leading onto a small porch, a stained-glass window in the door; all said private property. I decided my needs were a tad more important than Brandon's privacy. I knocked and my world as I knew it turned once again.

Brandon called out, 'Come in Mum.'

'It's not Mum. It's me, Tara.'

The door opened and there stood the saddest man you have ever seen. The eyes said it all, so different from the humorous twinkle I had first seen on the road, there was now empty sadness. It was so tangible, and it hit me in the chest. I put my hand on his arm.

'What on earth is wrong? Are you unwell?' I might as well have offered to stop the Huka falls with one finger, the misery was so deep. I led him to the seat beside the fireplace. 'Brandon what is it? Can I help?'

He croaked, 'No one can. I'm stuck here forever.'

I put my hand over his, kneeling beside him. 'What's up?' I asked again. The emotions on his face now naked in the glow of flames, they showed his age and sorrow. I saw naked loneliness and a hurt so deep it was gut wrenching.

It took all afternoon for him to get his story out, buried deep in fear of hurting his mum and, 'Letting the old girl down,' as he said. After two cups of tea he was exhausted and looked sleepy, his story ringing in my head and his prayer for help had astonished me. I was exhausted listening to him. I went back to the main house for my regular afternoon nana nap, much later pondering his dilemma. Titch had made scones and left one on a saucer spread with butter and peach jam, the cup and tea bag sat beside it for me to help myself. Titch sat with her back to me in front of the fire, her knitting needles working furiously, her shoulders stiff and unyielding. I wanted to put my hand on her shoulder but her body language said, 'Go away.'

What Brandon had confided in me was how unhappy he was. He wanted something different in his life, now stuck with cattle delivery which he'd loathed from childhood, stuck with his dad's business. He hated the painful mooing of trapped animals, hated the smell and the terror in their eyes when delivered to the meat works, hated the killing, hated the smell of blood. What he wanted wasn't considered at all, he was simply there to look after Titch until she died. Unpaid servitude as he put it, no love was shown, he was an investment paying off a debt or that's how he felt, and to be honest that's how it looked to me. Not once had I seen any love between these two as I had seen with other mums and sons.

I had said very little, letting Brandon spill his thoughts, getting it all out. I offered nothing but an ear and once he had started I sat beside him quietly listening, then busied myself putting wood on the fire and making the tea. He wanted an escape, he wanted to work on his passion, I could see it all around me, Brandon loved to weave. A small loom sat in one corner, his work hung on the wall and was on the floor, he loved to spin the fresh wool, card it, dyeing it in different colours, then spinning it and knitting it into creations he designed. He sold his work many times, even offered commissions overseas, which meant travel, his father ignoring his creative talent. Titch too scared of being alone to encourage her creative son, both telling him from any early age it was a sissy occupation, leave it to the women. How sad, to let the fear of being alone rule your life.

At the end of Brandon's emotional spill was a plea. 'Tara, I don't know what to do.' I had no answers. What could I do? I was here because he and his mum felt responsible for my dilemma. There was no-one I could even ring and talk to as this was none of my business, yet it was in a way. When another confides in you and asks for help, do you ignore it and hope it might go away or do you think, conjure, intend, whatever, just find a way to help?

I did not have any answers. I did however ask before I walked back to the main house if Brandon could give me a ride back to Opunake. He agreed to tomorrow, four days to go, countdown.

The morning dawned and I was feeling almost one hundred percent better. Titch was making breakfast and I could hear her and Brandon talking in the little kitchen.

'Good morning to you both,' I chirped. 'What a lovely day,' as I walked into the kitchen. There was a silence then, 'I see you're feeling better,' was her greeting.

'Very much so,' I said. 'Thank you for your care.'

Her next statement stopped me. 'Your things are packed and in my car. I'm driving you to Opunake in fifteen minutes. Your breakfast is on the table and so is the bill.' I heard breakfast then the word bill exploded in my head.

'What bill?' I queried.

'For the room, medicine plus food. I have not charged for petrol to get you here, or the nursing you have received.'

I was speechless and stuttered, 'But you... Brandon... but they...'

Titch put down the wooden spoon she was stirring some jam with. 'You expected those two young queers to nurse you? What a laugh, they don't want you there ruining their sick fun and games.'

I must have looked surprised as she continued, 'Oh yes we know all about them and that sort. I bought you here to make sure you got well and my Brandon was not held responsible for your mistakes.'

I started to boil. 'That's called kidnapping, Titch, plus extortion.' Titch blanched.

'Don't talk rot. I was helping you.'

'No Titch, you bought me here with the thought of charging me in mind. I don't have a problem with coming here, I was too sick to argue. I do however have a problem with this,' waving the handwritten bill of two hundred and fifty dollars under her nose.

Brandon grabbed the note, 'Mum enough!' He screwed it up and threw it in the fire; I thought Brandon was going to cry. I grabbed my bag noting I had all the documents and passport inside. 'Let's go, now please, you make me feel sick.' Titch grabbed her car keys as I stopped by the back door.

'Actually Titch, I would prefer Brandon to drive me. If I'm being charged for services, then I will choose my driver.' Brandon was almost smug as he took the keys out of his mum's hand.

'See you tonight, Mum.'

I walked out into a bright blue day; the wind still cold, its fingers looking for any corner it could creep into. We drove off in their old car, Opunake and my Mermaid here I come. Our first stop an ATM machine, I withdrew three hundred dollars, giving it to Brandon. 'Here,' shoving the cash at him. 'Hide this. Tell her I refused to pay. Go and have beer with your mates or be a sucker, give her the money, I don't care.'

I was really upset at the whole situation so talking was out of the question for me. We had a silent trip for the hour's drive back to Opunake.

Kingsley and David were very enthusiastic at my return to Paradise; tea was made, we talked about where I was off to and who I wanted to see, what I was going to do and when. Brandon looked amazed at me wanting to travel on my own all the way back to Perth and on a cruise ship, when Kingsley asked him, 'Have you ever travelled, Brandon?'

Even I was surprised when he answered, 'Oh yes, Auckland and back regularly with the cattle.'

'Is that it?' I asked, 'a day's trip from here and back? But you're in your forties surely?'

The two young men both cleared their throats and busied themselves cleaning the table. Oh no, Tara has her foot in her mouth again; I had made a blue again. It's not politically correct to be so tactless. Who cares, I thought, this man is suffering. I wasn't surprised after our talk, I dug deeper. 'Brandon have you ever been married?'

'No,' he shook his head.

'Have you ever had a serious girlfriend?' He again shook his head, 'Mum won't allow it.'

'Then it's about time you did your own thing, my friend, and made some friends. Let's start with these two young men.' Brandon looked embarrassed.

'Tara they are... you know.'

'No, I don't know Brandon. They have treated me with respect, what more can I ask for? And what's more you're talking about their sexuality, what makes you think they would fancy an old man like you? Why not try to understand a little?'

My inner voice now yelling, come on girl shut up, you've said enough.

Chapter 59

It was getting late and it was a full day to Auckland. I had to make a move or I would not make the boat that left in three days, both young men asking me to stay on for the night to be safe, Brandon repeating their request to stay and leave at first light to be safe. It made sense as it was looking very dark and stormy again. I agreed to stay on but in my Mermaid. I walked out the door to go to the barn where she was kept. Brandon hurried behind me, 'Mind if I have a look, before I go back to Mum?'

'No, not at all, you're welcome to,' I said, and I meant it; my heart kept saying, poor Brandon, so down trodden, and although he complained and had a meltdown in front of me I felt like he was as much to blame as Titch. Then again, I had learned very early on in life that blaming keeps us helpless. I taught this to Rae and Jess, to take responsibility for yourself and be proud of who you are.

What could I possibly teach this man in the next ten minutes that we had together? The answer was not a lot. Maybe I was not the teacher he needed but the antagonist he needed to make him live the life he wanted, not the life his mum planned for him. Only time would tell.

I hauled open the barn door and there they both were, my car and the Mermaid, waiting patiently for me. If I could have had a home coming party with all the bells and whistles right there and then, I would have.

I could almost feel them smiling in welcome. Silly I know, but that is how I felt until I heard a gasp from behind me. Brandon then walked around me, running his hands over the Mermaid's body. I actually felt protective about her.

When Brandon looked at me I could see had fallen in love, his face was a picture. 'Is this the Mermaid?' How come logic, the head, and emotion, the heart, can argue with each other? I wanted to fling my arms around her and cry, 'Don't you touch her!' On the other hand, I had her up for sale in the newspapers. Confusion took over. Taking a big breath, I steadied myself and calmly said, 'Yes Brandon, meet the Mermaid.'

'She's a little beauty,' he said tapping her rear end, 'and you say she's for sale? How much?' I named the price I had put in the paper. Brandon looked stunned. 'How much?' His look told me it was out of the question but I also knew I must sell before I go back but so far not one phone call for the car or the Mermaid.

I wished Brandon a good night, unlocked my door, stepped in and I was home; all my trinkets and photos around me. I made the bed, opened windows and the skylight to get rid of the closed-up smell. I undressed and wrapped up in my own doona for the night, setting the phone alarm for three am. Closing my eyes, I settled down to sleep in my bed in my home for the first time in six weeks. Tomorrow was my last day here; I was definitely on the road to Auckland. What I would do, then? I had no idea. Sleep claimed me for the night, the wind outside the barn doing its best to get in and give the Mermaid a good shake, and as another storm raged outside I slept safe and sound inside.

The alarm rapped its tune of a woodpecker and I was up and out, showering in the house while Kingsley and David made me a hot breakfast and helped me hitch up, David backing the car out with the Mermaid hitched on, driving out the barn then around facing the driveway. My time here had come to an end. These two had made me a picnic hamper and a thermos of tea and I was about to hug them both goodbye when Petra rang. 'Everything alright?' she asked.

'Yes, all is good. I was about to take off when you rang.'

'Take care, Tara, we love you. Come back soon and say hello to us all please.' My heart was a heavy lump as I agreed but I knew it would be many years before I was back here in Paradise.

'Give your man a hug for me,' I said, 'and take care of yourself. I will ring you once I'm on the ship.' I clicked the off button.

Kingsley and David did their fussing bit, hugs all round, I then revved up my jeep and drove away the headlights pointed north. 'I'm ready to go home now,' my heart sang.

Through Stratford onto the highway to Taupo, through the desert road, every mile I seemed to know well. As I drove past landmarks, I mentally crossed them off my list. I had read and marked the road map, entering my route on the GPS. Reminding myself I had to stop at the last petrol pump before the desert road. Another three hours went past. The sea long gone with its angry waves and black cloud burdened sky, I was now in the middle of the North Island amongst mountains, volcanic rocks, paddocks or bush, not a wave in sight. Time to stop and have a cup of tea and a sandwich. There wasn't a sound as I got out to have a stretch, my legs felt a little wobbly, not used to driving for so long. The silence was profound, enjoyable. I watched the sun come up, a pink dawn lighting up the edge of huge long white puffy clouds. How pretty, I thought. Pouring a cup of tea, I walked to the front of the car and leaned against the hood of the vehicle that had seen me through thick and thin and not missed a beat. The lamb sandwich from the picnic basket tasted like heaven, I was really hungry.

The feeling of relaxation crept upon me; I knew this was the last I would be seeing of the North Island national park. I felt like I was saying goodbye to a friend, the tears hot and salty on my cheeks. What a silly woman I am, I thought, but the feeling persisted so I let it go and let the tears fall as Petra and a dozen others had advised me to do. I blew my nose on an old tissue, which reminded me I needed a new packet and soon, dried my eyes and put away the picnic hamper. Back inside the jeep out of the southerly wind that still had a cruel bite to it, and off I went once more.

'On the road again,' I hummed to myself, quite happy to be on my own, when I heard a faint blaring of a horn. Looking into my rear vision mirror, I could see a whole lot of lights coming up behind at a fast rate of knots, the blaring getting louder. I panicked and put my foot down.

I was tearing along at a hundred and twenty, the mermaid having difficulty in keeping up and starting to sway. Huge brilliant headlights now so close, glaring angrily at me, the horn blasting away, but there was nowhere I could slip into, drive over to the side, or park until this angry monster passed me by as this was a long and narrow road.

I was really scared and did not know what to do. I could not push the car any more than what I was doing now. The truck drew closer, its horn now screaming for me to get out of the way. The Mermaid now swaying badly, my heart was in my mouth as the truck overtook me, the airhorn and lights blinding and deafening me. My one thought was this maniac is going to kill us both. Tears spilled down my face as the threat of death took over, as I'm sure that's what it was trying to do as it roared past me, immediately swerving right in front of me. *What the?*

I was speechless as he slowed down to a crawl, then stopped, fear and adrenaline taking over. I was burbling out loud, 'What's with this manic idiot redneck! He nearly killed me.' I sat behind the wheel shaking and crying at the same time. The driver got out of the truck and slowly walked to my Jeep. His shadow menacing, I was now expecting a bullet or an axe through the window, my head beaten in, robbed, raped, all these dreadful thoughts rushing through my terrified brain. His features not recognisable under the cowboy hat he wore, the sun was behind him, making it hard to identify him.

A big hairy fist banged on the car window. I sat there, my eyes sticking out like dog's balls, my breathing so hard I felt I was on the verge of passing out.

'Tara,' the shadow said, 'it's me, Brandon.' His words ringing like bells in my ears, I wound down my window and gaped at him.

'Brandon! What do you think you're doing?' Then all the fear and terror rushed out, 'maniac, idiot, fool, redneck, pervert, stupid, unholy nutter, twit, bastard,' until I wound down.

On the next intake of oxygen, he copped it again. I screamed directly into his face, 'You stupid bloody fool, you nearly killed me! What on God's good earth do you want?' I sat there panting out of breath and trying to gain some sort of equilibrium.

When we were face-to-face I raged. 'You could have killed us both; you have no road sense.'

Brandon's sad eyes now twinkled with mirth. 'Tara, you would not stop or answer your phone. I had to chase you, but anyone would think a Taniwha was after you. You can drive, though, I will give you that.'

'Brandon, what do you want?' I was in no mood to play games with this mum's boy. 'I'm on my way to Auckland, so just piss off.'

His answer surprised me. 'First, I'm sorry I scared you, second I want to buy the Mermaid.'

'You what, buy my Mermaid? What? You can't, can you?' popped out.

Brandon took my hand, the one that was itching to slap him sideways. 'Tara, follow me to the gas station please, I want to ask you something very special.'

'Something special' bounced around inside my head as we sat facing each other in the early morning. Small white puffs of air escaping our mouths as Brandon spoke, 'I'm going away. I'm going to travel New Zealand. I want to see what you have seen, be where you have been.'

My heart went out to him. 'Brandon, you have listened to my experiences, but you will have different ones.' I wanted to say, 'What about Titch?' It's none of your business, rang through my head. We both sat there, sipping coffee.

'I still want to buy your van,' Brandon said, followed by an awkward silence then a voice in my head saying, 'It's time to say goodbye, Tara. Time to let the Mermaid go.' It was a tough choice. Was I big enough or was I petty and small minded? Was this a test of my faith, of all I had learned on my journey?

'Okay Brandon, I don't have the time to argue with you, I'm leaving New Zealand tomorrow night.' It seemed this morning was going to be full of surprises. He reached into his faded blue overalls, pulled out a tatty pile of grubby money held together by an old worn hair band and placed it on the table.

'I'm a grand short of the asking price, Tara, but it's all I have. Will you sell her to me?'

'Brandon?' I looked at him, then the money. 'Are you sure?'

We shook hands. 'I'm sure.'

How Brandon got this money I had no idea and it was none of my business.

'I can see you're having a hard time. Don't stress, Tara, I haven't hit the old bag on the head and robbed her, nor have I robbed anyone else of their life savings. This is from my weaving and knitting. I saved it wishing for a rainy day, and today is my rainy day. I want to buy the Mermaid and take her with me on my journey. I want to travel down to the south and visit the folk who have hired me to weave. I want to pick up new ideas from them. I want to expand.'

Wow, that was a huge sentence for this quiet man. How does one refuse? I could not crush this man who now had a dream, especially since I had been part of it, so why refuse him when what he was doing was helping me as well? 'Let me get the paperwork for her, we can do this now.'

All the questions were building up. It was hard but I bit my lip. If the universe had planned this, who was I to say no.

I put the money into my handbag and passed over the keys. You can have it all Brandon, its ready to move into. All I want is the photos of my kids and a few personal items. We got up and walked to the van together, Brandon again patted her rear. 'Hello my Mermaid,' he said. I felt so much better knowing she would be loved and cared for. Collecting my gear, I stowed it in the car, Brandon now owned a fully functioning caravan. He held out his arms to me and I stepped into the circle knowing I was safe with this man. He kissed my cheek, nothing but friendship in our eyes.

I asked one thing from him, 'Brandon, be who *you* want to be, do what makes *you* happy, the answer is not in the dollar, it's in your heart, then the search for happiness is over.' It was time for me to leave. What or how he was going to get the Mermaid home was no business of mine; he looked like a boy who had just discovered Christmas. Keep safe, Brandon. I wish you well.

As I drove off I took one last look at the Mermaid, Brandon stood beside her waving to me as I moved forward. *Auckland here I come, I have twenty-four hours to sell my jeep, pop in and see Margi and family, then board the cruise ship home.*

It all seemed to be flowing, the money now locked away in the glove box, the radio pumping out the music of a New Zealand artist Bic Runga, her voice was beautiful singing about this country and the beauty of it all. Taupo was my time for another break. I walked into good old McDonalds for a cheap meal and hot drink. Now to find a bank to put all the cash into. I felt relief as I handed the money over to the teller, her huge smile telling me it was safe with her.

I was on the road again, the miles zipping by. Next was Hamilton four hours away. I was hoping to be in Auckland by late tonight.

The Hamilton turn off sign zipped past, vacancies available blinked on and off, reminding me of when I had passed through on my way south and was searching for accommodation. I decided to keep going; I wanted to get to Auckland, which was not too far away. Another stop at a gas station for more fuel and a check on the oil and water, all perfect.

Auckland and Margi I'm on my way. Once at the junction to Auckland, so many signs called out to pop over and visit me; Morinsville, Ngaruwahia, Huntley, Raglan, all with stories to tell, people to meet. I knew I would not be back this way again; the journey home had already begun for me.

I knew where I belonged, but travel was a huge part of my life and I did not want to stop, ever. My time here had taught me this, *'Journeys also take place in the heart not always on the road.'*

I could remember Russ with love and not feel the hurt. I would remember my time here in New Zealand without needing to revisit. I loved who I had become. I had journeyed in my heart and my life, with many friends showing me the way, and I considered myself blessed. Now it was time for Rae, Jess and baby and my home in Perth.

The thought of warm sunny days was so inviting. I was over the damp and rain. Ringing my friend, I told her, 'I'm on the roundabout now Margi, about half an hour away,' her voice music to my ears. 'Welcome back, Tara.' I found her road, the GPS said, 'Turn left, turn right and you have reached your destination.'

There was Margi and her family standing there smiling, welcoming, kids giggling, chasing each other. Turning the key off and opening the door, I was enveloped in so many arms and legs and faces; what a wonderful welcome. Margi giving instructions of, 'Stand back, clear off you lot, get out of my way, coming through,' flicking them away with that ever present tea towel over her shoulder, she huffed her way towards me, 'Tara, Kia Ora, welcome back.'

I felt like I had been to the moon and back, the amazing adventurer was back on terra firma. Once inside the questions started, the first one was 'Aunty, where is the Mermaid?' They all leaned forward waiting for my explanation.

'I sold her because I'm going home to Australia tomorrow.'

'How can you sell a Mermaid?' One child I had not seen before asked, Margi explaining it was the name of my caravan. Then I rummaged through the car for the rounds of cheese I had bought Margi and Tom, I also bought Tom a large salami. Another pot of tea was made, Tom cut thin slivers of sausage, Margi sliced the cheese, and I busied myself buttering some bread slices for us. The kids were sent into the lounge to watch TV under the strict surveillance of the older kids. 'And no blinkin noise,' Margi warned. 'Us adults are talking.'

I told them about the operation Ronan was about to have, if not already. 'The poor man,' Tom sighed. Margi was more proactive, 'Poor man nothing! Worse things have probably happened, there is a lesson in it for them.' Maybe she was right.

I told them about Dotty and her screaming. We all giggled as I remembered the kind lady. I told them about Hinemoa way out in the country, her dirt floors and sacking for doorways, outside dunny and her lovely heart. I then told them between yawns about Brandon and Titch, Margi exclaiming, 'She did what?' They were in hysterics when I told them about Brandon chasing me with his truck, tears falling down Margi's cheeks. 'Tara you have had such a time of it.'

'Yes, I have,' I admitted. Tom stood up scratching his pot belly, 'I'm off to bed and you have to work tomorrow, Ma.' His name for Margi.

'In a minute, you go on.' She put her index finger to her lips and peeked in on the kids in the lounge, most had fallen asleep on the two huge couches. Margi sat down next to me and held my hands, 'And you my friend, how are you now? From where I sit you certainly have grown from the little wimp I first met, look at you,' her fat rolly arms gave me a hug.

Margi was not one to spare her words. She was right, I had grown in leaps and bounds, my heart and head willing to learn and pass on my lessons whenever possible. I went to sleep on the camp stretcher tucked up in their home that night, so happy with my trip and my life. Russ was my last thought as I drifted into my dreams. The morning arrived and in Margi's house it was chaos, an Asian market would have been proud, the noise deafening with kids and Margi yelling directions and orders, and Tom moaning about his breakfast. I stayed in bed until I heard the kids rush out the door for school.

Margi yelled at me, 'I'm on roster until three pm but I'm driving you to the ship okay?'

'Okay,' I yelled back. 'See you soon.' When I heard the front door slam shut, the excitement grabbed me, and leaping off the little bed I sang, 'Tonight, tonight I'm sailing back to Perth.' What to do first? I made a list of what to do and what to pack, who to ring and who to see.

My main concern was selling the car or finding a seller on my behalf. I rang the car salespeople where I had bought the car in Silverdale. He was delighted to hear from me but sorry, he did not want to buy a second-hand jeep. He wanted to know how it all went and if there were any problems? I was honest. 'She's a dream.' The best they could offer me was to put it on their sales list and contact me if they got any enquiries. I left it with them, not happy but not much I could do. The newspaper adverts had not worked, nor had the for sale sign I had handwritten in Opunake and stuck on the back window. It was now mid-afternoon and I was feeling jittery, my clothes now in two piles: one for the rubbish and the clean pile folded for my suitcase. I needed another bag for the gifts and rummaged through what I was throwing out and a bright plastic holdall emerged.

Finally, I was sorted. Time to put my boat ticket, passport and papers into my shoulder bag, and with a huge sigh I was ready to go.

Now what to do about my little jeep? I had put the ownership papers aside and had toyed with the idea of asking Margi and Tom to sell it for me but did not want to be pushy. It was too late to find a dealer and get a reasonable price for it, Margi and Tom were my only choice.

My mobile phone winked into life. I had missed three call's: Petra, Rae and Brandon. I had an hour to wait before Margi came home, so finding a comfy seat I dialled Rae.

'Mum, how are you going, excited yet?'

'You don't know the half of it,' I replied. 'I'm beside myself.' We chatted for ten minutes. 'Send Jess my love, see you very soon.'

As I clicked off Petra rang me, her voice had tears in it as we said our final goodbyes and Ronan got on the phone telling me, 'I was part of their family now and always welcome at Paradise.' Now the tears fell down my cheeks. I invited them to Perth anytime. 'I can't simulate Paradise but will do my best,' I promised.

I phoned Brandon and he was happy. Titch had a huge melt down when he arrived home. I was definitely not on her Christmas card list and she had chucked him out. He was now in Palmerston North staying with a friend, 'A new friend,' he said.

Okay Brandon I'll bite. 'What's her name?'

'Lynda, and Tara, she's so nice.'

I was pleased he finally made that step to see some of this world. I was sad to hear Titch had lost it, it would not be nice to be in her shoes. I was tempted to ring and have a chat with her, but common sense prevailed; I knew the reception I would get. Blaming keeps you helpless, again came to mind. From what I saw, Titch blamed the world, the cows, the very air she breathed and possibly me for her problems in life. I was glad to hear Brandon had met a woman, he was touring in the Mermaid and he was not changing her name.

'She's magic.' We said our final goodbyes, both happy with our decisions.

Margi arrived home, and right behind her the family off the school bus, Tom a few minutes later. One big bustling yelling, scrambling family that oozed love, support and care for each other, the older ones helping the smaller ones change into play clothes or offering help to Margi and Tom.

'Well Tara, you better pack the cab up, you have to be there by five pm today. It's an hour's ride from here, but first a cuppa for Mum,' Margi announced. 'I'm as dry as a wooden Tiki.'

That gave me the opportunity to ask if they would they sell the car on my behalf.

'Leave it here, Tara, Tom can do all that. I will send you any money we receive.' Okay, that was the best I could do, time had run out for me.

I will never forget New Zealand, its soft green forests that were so lush, the bountiful ocean, the Mermaid and most of all the welcoming people I had met.

Chapter 60

We arrived at the cruise ship depot and the ship was enormous, totally different to what I had expected. Tom, picking up on my apprehension said, 'What's up Tara?'

I said, 'Look at it–the ship is huge.'

Tom laughed, 'What did you expect? One of our wakas and a paddle?'

I checked into a long line at customs where machines buzzed and clicked, then finally it was time to move through to the queue of folks behind a glass partition waiting to board.

It was time to leave my dear friends. A lump formed in my throat that felt like a brick as I looked at these two, dear people who had been such a driving force in my travelling New Zealand. Their faith in me had never wavered, always a welcome and a hug via the phone or advice of what to go and see or who to meet. I owed them a lot.

'Tara, one more thing before we say goodbye…' Margi, Tom and their family sang *Pokarekare Ana,* a song I loved since they had sung it at the Marai up North in Awanui. Now I did cry. I felt my face pucker up, my eyes sting and a huge sob left my gut. Their voices surrounding me, beautiful and harmonious, it was ancient, from the beautiful land I was now leaving, and it tattooed a Moko on my heart forever.

Margi walked me to the doors which whooshed open. Gently she hugged me and said, 'Harerai, Tara. God speed.'

'Harerai, Margi.' She offered me a Hongi and we touched noses,

'Love you always and thank you.'

As I walked through the doors that ended my New Zealand adventure, they kept singing. I could hear them so clearly other passengers stopped and stared, some asked each other questions. As I looked back, I saw just Margi standing there, our eyes locked and we waved the once. My Maori sister in New Zealand, we had made a spiritual connection that was forever.

The Sun Princess, the original Love Boat on the TV series, towered above us as we lined up to embark on our journey. The excitement lurched around in my stomach. We were greeted by a charming young lady and other crew who beeped us all on board. Blue cards were issued to us, it was our cruise card and worked like a credit card on board the ship. I was shown my cabin on Dolphin deck number 223. It was ironic. I was on another Metal Mermaid, this one taking me home.

I raced up on to the deck to wave my goodbyes to my friends on the wharf, trying to find them amongst hundreds, then my eyesight focused. There they were a small tight group of people standing by Margi's taxi. I waved my yellow scarf in the air, they saw and waved back. *Goodbye my dear friends. One day we will meet again.*

The ships horn let out one shrieking blast, the ship shuddered her response as we cast off. I stayed up top, the pilot now taking us out to sea. The other passengers walked away from the rail but still I stayed wishing my friends Petra and Ronan as much love as I could feel, imagining a golden bubble around them, one of healing and safety.

My journey home had begun.

The music started and one hell of a party began. The person who led the band, dancers and singers was the cruise director, a super ball of energy throughout the cruise. His humour was very English; dry, sarcastic and very funny. He made you feel like an old and loved friend who he had not seen for a while. His second-in-charge was

Simon, also charming, welcoming and funny, his humour a younger version of his boss. Music blared from the ships speakers as we sailed out of the harbour, Sydney our first stop, three days away. The party atmosphere commenced and from go to whoa, I loved it. The excitement of waking every day to another adventure either on shore or onboard was amazing and it seemed you only had to cough and there would be someone with a tissue for you.

From the time you entered the Horizon breakfast bar, which groaned with every available food you could imagine, to planning your day was a true pleasure. There were daily classes on board ranging from cards or a knitting circle to belly dancing, guided tour talks about our next port of call, movies, cards, massage and pedicures. It was all there, and if you went on a tour it was all managed seamlessly for you. Sydney loomed in the misty morning, the excitement I felt being back in my own country gurgled around in my tummy seeing the famous 'coat hanger bridge' and Sydney Opera House. Tours were suggested, so I chose the Opera House. What an amazing story it has to tell and what an amazing number of steps you have to climb to get to the main foyer.

Some days I would opt for the afternoon movie, or the two kilometre walk around the deck. Brisbane was warm and sunny, so I chose to go on a boutique brewery tour. It was interesting enough, but not being a big drinker I was a little disappointed in what the massive brewery expected from a small bus load of sixty-plus seniors. I could have stayed on board and done many of the classes advertised in the 'Princess Patter', a newsletter produced every night for your convenience, full of classes, talks, movies and night-time entertainment. It was all entertaining. Cabaret dine and dance, comedians, Dolly Parton and Rod Stewart impersonators, Mike Harris, the comedian, was so funny I was in pain with laughter every time I went to one of his shows. It was there I met so many women who travelled alone or with another female, as apparently, it was cheaper to purchase a cabin for two.

Airlie beach was fun. We arrived in time for the afternoon markets and they had it all from massage and tarot readings to veggies and mango drinks made for you on the spot, jewellery from Indonesia and pretty batik clothing. Once on board at four pm, a quick shower. As always, the attendant had been in and my cabin was spotless, fresh towels, clean bathroom, bed made. When I first came on board I was assigned a dinner time and place at a table at one of the two silver service restaurants. The meals were superb, and the atmosphere was wonderful. At my table were four other people, both married couples, we all got on famously discussing the day's events.

One night I sat on my own on the deck, next to me tucked up on the stern was a bronze statue of two seniors staring out into the ocean, the sea air caused a Verdigris green patina on them. They were my companions for the hour watching the dark sky, its zillion stars and the full moon. I pondered about life and where to next, the soft wind playing with my hair and around my face. It was time to go inside, wandering downstairs to the deck below. There was a movie showing on one huge mother of a screen, deckchairs were set out, tartan blankets were put on them, a few people were watching the movie 'Winston Churchill' and had blankets all snuggled around them as the wind was chilly, so I joined them. When I went to bed that night it was midnight, and on the bed was a little dog moulded from the bath towels. The cabin crew are so clever.

The next day at sea, I went up for breakfast and while I had fresh pancakes and crispy British bacon on a sun-drenched deck, I marked out what I wanted to do for the day. First was a towel folding demonstration. Wow, what these guys could do with a hand towel was eye popping. From a plain bath towel emerged an octopus, a turtle, a dove, parrots, monkeys, dolphins, it went on and on the grand finale was the parrot that sat on a wooden hanger just like a real bird. The crowd went mad, cries for more ringing around the Atrium. I then chose to pamper myself, submerging in a dreamy pedicure labelled the Fire and Ice treatment. It was divine and I floated out of the spa, headed off to my cabin and slept for an hour.

That night was a choice of going to my restaurant or the famous pizza place, I opted for a pizza and a light beer. Relaxation was the key word on this cruise or as the cruise director would yell from the intercom frequently, 'Enjoy yourselves, you're on holiday.'

Port Douglas was our next port of call. I had arranged a tour with a man called Grubs who owned a motor trike tour company. He was very informative, fun and a little crazy, just what the doctor ordered to whip away any blues that remained. We zipped through bush and waterfalls and met country people; he knew them all. We rushed through cool mountain air to the tip of the ranges, then back down to the heat of Port Douglas. In two hours, I had covered so much of this charming little place I was mentally winded, but it was exhilarating and wonderful, another unforgettable tour.

Another day at sea before we berthed at Darwin. I went on a discovery talk about the immigration of Darwin. Back onboard and a salad for lunch, then a walk around the deck, one mile in total. I managed half of it and stopped for a chocolate snow cone, yummy. Movies inside this time at the Princess Theatre. They had the new black and white movie 'The Artist' showing and after that I opted to walk back to my cabin that was four decks down and a lot of stairs; good for toning the butt, I thought. As I approached the main atrium of the ship, a jazz band was playing, they were fabulous, really swinging, and if you thought you could belt out a tune, a little like karaoke. It was such a happy relaxed atmosphere. I watched, clapped and cheered on the singers with the other onlookers. In bed that night, the thought I was to be at home very soon stirred that little excited worm in my gut.

Life on board had something new and exciting happening every day. I met so many people from all walks of life, all willing to tell me about themselves, never suspecting their story may be the next novel I may write one day. They told of heartbreak, being lovesick, seasick, there were widows, widowers, loving couples and couples that toured. They told me about places I had never seen and would probably never see. I loved it. Every morning, you could sit with someone different and had so many different things to do, or you could opt out and sit in the sun and relax.

Finally, Western Australia. We sailed along the Kimberley coastline, the land of red, gold and bronze that stole Russ's heart; the desert land glowed in the sun then the sunset became a deep scarlet and bronze. Everything the magazines and newspapers write about the region is true, magnificent in every way. Photographers snapped frantically away until the light had gone and it was night and even that was amazing. The Southern Cross shone as bright as ever in the clean night air.

We reached Broome. I booked a tour to the Willy Creek Pearl Farm. Boarding the coach was simple as it was all well organised. The coach ride to the pearl farm was horrendous; we bucked and jolted over disgusting unkept roads. My back ached and the woman sitting behind me was in agony. It made me look closely at what more touring might entail, this was not comfortable at all.

Chapter 61

I knew my days aboard were coming to an end. I tried to keep the excitement at bay, trying to savour every remaining day. Another day passed at sea and I chose to go to the small café in the casino where you could quietly watch people with many different expressions on their faces.

That night, a comedian was telling jokes in the Wheelhouse Bar, and I was sitting with a group of people, enjoying their comments as well as the comedian's very quick repartee. Suddenly, one woman took serious offense to his sarcasm. She was quite drunk and what was supposed to be a fun time turned into a slanging match from her to the comedian, who said very quietly, 'Dear God, why did your mother have you?'

The problem was he forgot he had the microphone in his hand. The place erupted, a screech of dismay from her and laughter from the audience as that silly soul sashayed out of the room. The huge sigh of relief that went up from all of us was unanimous. We all settled in to have some laughs before supper and bedtime, his reward was loud applause as he gracefully apologised for the commotion.

At supper, there she was again, picking up on other people's conversations, then being insulted at their angry reactions, I guess there is one on every cruise. Geraldton was our next port. I did not want to go ashore and did what a lot of others did and stayed on board.

The cruise director was on and off the ship's intercom egging us on to this or that, join in and have some fun, repeating his mantra, 'You're on holiday.' You could see people smile as he spoke. I rang

Rae. 'I'm twenty-four hours away, honey!' She was as excited as me. My cell phone cut out as they can do on board a ship.

I walked down to the library and internet room, checked my banking then logged on to email Jo and Fred that I was arriving in twenty-four hours and giving my arrival time. I noticed I had twelve emails waiting, so I answered them. Six were, 'Do ya wanna buy… ' and six from New Zealand. All my friends there had wished me the very best for my travels and asked that I please keep in touch.

The last one was a photo of the Mermaid. My heart lurched as I enlarged the photo on the screen. On her doorstep sat Brandon, holding a beer in one hand and a meat pie in the other, a cardboard sign saying 'Home sweet Home' hung around his neck. He had the biggest, silliest grin on his face. I also noticed the road sign next to the van announcing you have entered Kaikoura South Island. So, he had done it, made the break and was travelling his dream.

'Go Brandon,' I wrote back, 'live your life and enjoy.'

During the next twenty-four hours I felt like I was wired to an electrical socket, I was so excited. After nearly a whole year away, I would be home at last. I knew I was a different person, I certainly looked different. I also knew I ached to see and hold my daughter and my grandson. I wanted to be back at the home Russ and I had shared. I slept very lightly that night, woken the next day by the rattling of chains; we had arrived in Fremantle.

Excitement is not the word I would describe to say how I was feeling. I jumped up, showered, dressed in jeans and T shirt, my hair up in a ponytail, then went for breakfast and to say goodbye to my new acquaintances. Some were carrying on with the cruise which from here continued on to sail around the world. I saw the marvellous deal only eight days into the cruise when out came the tempting beautiful brochures enticing you to spend. For me, I was ready and only too willing to go home to my family.

As I packed the last of my clothing, I put on a tiny bit of makeup and packed away all the stuff you buy and take on a holiday; my heart knew I was doing the right thing for me. Finally, I was out of my cabin, my cases taken on shore and there was only customs to clear and I was free.

I was over the line and at last standing in Fremantle once again.

I heard Jess, before I saw any of them.

'There's my nana!' A tall young man rushed up to wind his arms around me, my arms naturally opened to enfold him, hugging him back. We stood there for a second, my face buried in his hair, tears stung my eyes as my grandson said, 'You're home, Nana.'

Yes, I was, but now I had a taste for travel. Was this the end? Or will the call of adventure be too much for me to resist.

'Always be a first-rate version of yourself, instead of a second-rate version of somebody else'

– Judy Garland

Translation of Maori words used in Metal Mermaid.

Powhiri = Welcome ceremony.

Whare = House

Marai = Meeting house / land.

Moko = Tattoo on face or chin.

Waka = Boat.

Tiki = Maori God.

Paua = shellfish

Wahine = Female.

Warrior = Male.

Kia Ora = Welcome / Hello

Haeremai = Greeting.

Harerai = Goodbye.

Hongi = nose to nose

Kai = Food.

Puku = Tummy.

Mukupuna = Grandchild.

Whanau = Family

Taniwha = Mythical shape shifter Spirit

Acknowledgments

The name Mermaid is affiliated with a freedom of spirit, a questioning spirit and a life sworn to adventure, all the traits a true caravaner needs to experience. From the richness of adventure, my novel Metal Mermaid was born.

To my family and extended family in Australia, thank you for all the inspiration.

To my friends and my family in London, thank you for the encouragement, kind words and the willingness to read through my novels, always with positive advice.

To my husband Lou, where would I be without that crazy sense of humour you possess, thank you for believing in me.

All of you add a spicy richness to my life. I consider myself blessed to be part of your lives whether it be from blood or a deep lasting friendship.

Thank you, I wish you all enough.

Thank you also to my parents Dick and Hilda Wickham now long gone. I want to honour them both by thanking them for the childhood I had, coming from an Irish, English, and perhaps Jewish background they enriched it in ways they could never know. I am also part of a large family from the *Tūhoe* iwi or tribe (Children of the Mist) from the Te Urewera in the North Island.

I hope you enjoy reading this as much as I enjoyed writing it, I also hope it will encourage you, the reader, to travel in whatever Metal Mermaid you choose.

Kez

www.ingramcontent.com/pod-product-compliance
Lightning Source LLC
Chambersburg PA
CBHW031402290426
44110CB00011B/240